Ignore the Hype

Ignore the Hype

Financial Strategies Beyond the Media-Driven Mayhem

Brian Perry

WILEY

Published by John Wiley & Sons, Inc., Hoboken, New Jersey.
Published simultaneously in Canada.

Library of Congress Cataloging-in-Publication Data:

Names: Perry, Brian, 1974- author.
Title: Ignore the hype : financial strategies beyond the media-driven mayhem / Brian Keith Perry.
Description: Hoboken, New Jersey : Wiley, [2020] | Includes index.
Identifiers: LCCN 2020021874 (print) | LCCN 2020021875 (ebook) | ISBN 9781119691228 (hardback) | ISBN 9781119691303 (adobe pdf) | ISBN 9781119691273 (epub)
Subjects: LCSH: Finance, Personal. | Investments.
Classification: LCC HG179 .P366727 2020 (print) | LCC HG179 (ebook) | DDC 332.024—dc23
LC record available at https://lccn.loc.gov/2020021874
LC ebook record available at https://lccn.loc.gov/2020021875

COVER DESIGN: PAUL MCCARTHY
COVER IMAGE: © ISTOCK / ERHUI1979

Printed in the United States of America

SKY10022872_112720

Contents

Acknowledgments xi
About the Author xiii
Preface xv
Introduction 1

PART I: YES, THE GAME IS RIGGED, BUT YOU DON'T HAVE TO PLAY 7

Chapter 1: The Times They Are a-Changin' 9
- There Is a World of Difference Between Speculation and Investing 10
- So, Why Is It So Damn Hard to Ignore the Hype?! 12
- To Play, or Not to Play, That Is the Question 14
- Life at the Speed of Light 15
- Lower Transaction Costs 17
- Self-Directed Investing 20
- High-Frequency Trading 23
- The 24-Hour News Cycle 24

Globalization 29
The Rise of the Institutional Investor 31
The Bottom Line 33

Chapter 2: Don't Play a Game That's Rigged 35
The Upward Path of Markets 36
Asset Class Returns 38
A Twist in the Plot 40
Time *in* the Market versus *Timing* the Market 41
Why Are Las Vegas Casinos So Nice? 43
The True Cost of Sitting on the Sidelines 45
Does Crisis Equal Opportunity? 48

Chapter 3: Guess What? A Forecast Is Just a Guess 51
But Forecasting Is Fun 52
Economists 54
Wall Street Analysts 55
Media Pundits 57
The Federal Reserve (the Fed) 58
So, What's the Problem? 59
The All-Star Team 60
What Should You Do with Forecasts? 62

PART II: IF YOU DON'T KNOW WHERE YOU'RE GOING, YOU PROBABLY WON'T GET THERE 65

Chapter 4: You Must Know What Drives Investment Returns 67
You Can Beat the Dealer, But Can You Beat the Market? 69
It's Hard to Stand Above the Crowd in a Room Full of Tall People 70
So, What's the Solution? 71
Indexed Products 72
A Rules-Based Approach 75
Fundamental Factors for Success 78
Stock Market Factors 79
Growth Stocks 80
Value Stocks 81
Bond Market Factors 87
The Bottom Line on Factor Premiums 93

Chapter 5: You Must Have a Specific Financial Goal 95
Step One: Determine Your Vision of Retirement 96
Step Two: Determine How Much You Spend Today 98
Step Three: Determine When You Want to Retire 99
Step Four: Determine How Much Income You'll Need in Year One of Retirement 99
Step Five: Determine Your Sources of Retirement Income 103
Step Six: Determine How Much You'll Need from Your Savings and Investments 103
Step Seven: Determine a Sustainable Distribution Rate 104
Step Eight: Determine How Much Money You Need to Retire 105
Step Nine: Determine Your Plan to Accumulate the Money You Need to Retire 105
Putting It All Together with a Step-by-Step Example 107
Already Retired? 111
The Bottom Line 111

Chapter 6: You Must Invest to Meet Your Goal 113
How Much Money Do You *Want* to Make? 114
How Much Money Do You *Need* to Make? 115
How Much Risk *Should* You Take? 116
Sleeping on a Bed of Money 120
Adding Some Stocks to the Mix 121
Portfolio A 123
Portfolio B 123
What Portfolio Do You Want? 124
Still Not Convinced? 125
Enjoy Your Retirement! 127

Chapter 7: You Must Practice Smart Diversification 129
What Is Smart Diversification? 130
You Don't Want to Be a Pig! 130
Owning What You Know May Not Be Best 132
It's a Big World 137
Sometimes You're Trapped by Your Own Success 140
Dealing with Concentrated Positions 143
Smart Diversification Enhances Your Odds of Success 145
Winning the Lost Decade 147

Chapter 8: You Must Learn How You'll Be Taxed 151
But First, *the Hype* 153
And Now, *the Truth* 154
Income Taxes: A Quick Primer 154
Are Taxes Going Higher? 157
Tax Diversification 158
Do You Know Who Your Partner Is? 159
As If That's Not Enough ... 162
What's Certain in Life? 163

PART III: JUST BECAUSE YOU'RE PARANOID DOESN'T MEAN THEY AREN'T OUT TO GET YOU 169

Chapter 9: How to Avoid the Taxman Without Going to Jail 171
Building Your Tax-Free Pool of Money 172
Accelerating the Flow of Funds to Your Tax-free Pool 176
Building Your Taxable Pool of Money 177
Do You Want to Keep More of What You Make? 181

Chapter 10: Sorry, But You're Probably Your Own Worst Enemy 185
Tales Your Parents Told You 187
Anchoring 189
Confirmation Bias 190
Overconfidence Bias 192
Herd Behavior 194
Framing Bias 196
Hindsight Bias 198
Self-attribution Bias 200
Myopic Loss Aversion 201

Chapter 11: FYI, the Media Doesn't Care If You Make Money 205
But Then There's the Media ... 206
Did Black Monday Spell Doom for Investors? 211
What Side of the Aisle Are You On? 214
Would You Hitch Your Family's Future to the Circus? 217

Chapter 12: Avoid the Wolf in Sheep's Clothing 223
Does It Pass the Sniff Test? 224
Who's Got Your Back? 224
Focus on Minimizing Unnecessary Fees 229
Is What You're Buying Even an Investment? 232
Drowning in a Sea of Complexity 234
Do You Even Know What You're Buying? 236
But My "Regular" Bonds Are Free from Commissions, Right? 237
What Are You Using Derivatives For? 241
Market Voodoo (AKA Technical Analysis) 243
Let Me "Sell" You an Annuity ... 244
Now, Let Me "Explain" an Annuity ... 245
The Bottom Line 247

Chapter 13: How to Survive a Bear Attack 249
Prepare for the Bear 250
Risk Capacity versus Risk Tolerance 252
Rebalance to Stay on Course 254
Buy-and-Hold Investing 257
Buy-and-Forget Investing 258
So, What Do You Do When Market Valuations Are Extreme? 259
Does What Gets Measured Get Improved? 260
Ready for Some Good News? 262
A Better Life 263

Conclusion 267
Index 271

Acknowledgments

This book wouldn't have been possible without the generous assistance and support of numerous individuals. So, to all my colleagues past and present, thank you. The knowledge, experience, and expertise you've shared with me can be found throughout this book.

I'm blessed to work for what I believe is the best company in the financial industry and to share my days with an incredible mix of smart and talented coworkers. Every day their combined efforts help thousands of people *Ignore the Hype* and move toward the life of their dreams. Thank you all for choosing to use your gifts and talents to help people. It's not an exaggeration to say that the world is a better place because of the work you do. I hope this book helps us reach more people, because I truly believe that together we are saving lives. And thank you, Alyssa, for your help with graphics, as well as for getting the manuscript in the right hands.

I'm incredibly grateful for the team at Wiley – it takes a village to produce a book, and this one would be far worse without your efforts. And a special shout-out to Kevin Harreld for believing in this book – I hope your faith in it and in me have been rewarded by the finished product.

Finally, even as a writer I don't have the words to properly say thank you to Kristi, William, and Dylan. This book wouldn't exist without your love and support. I also couldn't have done this without your willingness to sacrifice nights and weekends together while I sat in front of my keyboard. Any success it, or I, has is as much yours as mine.

About the Author

Brian Perry is executive vice president at Pure Financial Advisors. In that role, he uses his extensive background and experience to promote financial education and help individuals meet their financial goals. In his quest to help people live the life they deserve, Brian has published widely, appeared on TV and radio, and spoken at countless seminars, workshops, conferences, and classes. Having spent more than two decades in the financial arena, Brian previously worked as an institutional portfolio manager and as a bond trader for several investment banks. He has an MBA in international business as well as a master's degree in international affairs. He also holds the designation of Chartered Financial Analyst and is a Certified Financial Planner™ professional. Brian's previous book, *From Piggybank to Portfolio: A Financial Roadmap for New Investors*, was published in 2009. He also recently wrote an eBook, *Retirement Revamp: Financial Planning in Times of Crisis* to help people better understand and navigate the financial implications of the COVID-19 pandemic.

Preface

It's true – the media does promote fake news.

This litany of misleading reports, flashing news headlines, sound bites that fail to capture a speaker's true sentiments, bombastic personalities, half-truths, and outright lies is damaging the very fabric of our society. And I'm not talking about politics. I'm referring, instead, to the financial realm, and the media-driven lack of clarity, coherence, and patience that is ruining the futures of tens of millions of people just like you.

Fortunately, there is a solution. Education provided in a clear-cut and easy-to-understand manner can help you cut through the noise. This education needs to be based on facts, not fiction, and must be based upon evidence, rather than guesswork. This education needs to work for the long haul; theories and concepts that come and go like the seasons' newest fashions are of little use to the average person seeking a path to financial independence. This is particularly true in the information age, where a constant flow of news headlines too often prompts emotional reactions. And it is these emotions, in the end, that effective education needs to account for and overcome, lest individuals succumb to the fear and greed that have always typified peoples' responses to market cycles.

Ignore the Hype: Financial Strategies Beyond the Media-Driven Mayhem is part of the solution. By examining the historical record in order to separate fact from fiction, readers will get a clear sense of what has and has not worked in the past. This book relays the lessons investors can glean from the successful experiences of others, including:

- *Accept that the game is rigged, but know that you don't have to play*, which suggests an alternative to the hedge fund and media-driven mayhem that overwhelms so many individual investors.
- *Realize that forecasting is just a fancy term for guessing*, which examines the abysmal track record of market pundits and proposes a superior solution.
- *Accept that failing to plan is planning to fail*, which provides a method to determine how much money you need to meet your financial goals.
- *Understand the drivers of investment returns*, which identifies the common traits of securities that have produced superior results across time.
- *Know how you'll be taxed*, which discusses steps you can take today to pay less taxes tomorrow.
- *Avoid the wolf in sheep's clothing*, which tells you how to identify a trusted professional and avoid Wall Street's lousy products.

Ultimately, this book is designed to drill home the key point that, by following time-tested principles founded on investor experience and academic research, people just like you can achieve financial success in a manner that doesn't place them on a collision course with hedge fund managers, sovereign wealth funds, and high-frequency traders. Instead, a disciplined investment approach, designed to protect you from your emotions, can produce attractive investment returns without engaging in a competition you cannot win. When combined with comprehensive financial planning and cutting-edge tax minimization strategies, such an approach can give virtually anyone the tools required to achieve financial freedom.

– Brian Perry, CFP®, CFA

Introduction

The philosopher George Santayana once said, "Those who cannot remember the past are condemned to repeat it."

The century of financial history we have to work with has provided you with a treasure trove of lessons. These lessons tell you what works and, just as importantly, what doesn't work. Both lessons are equally valuable.

In investing, little things make a big difference. And as you'll learn from this book, financial success for most people isn't about that once-in-a-lifetime coup. Instead, the key to financial freedom is to find a disciplined, repeatable process, based upon empirical research and the historical record. Then, you must have the intestinal fortitude to stick with that process through good times and bad.

And therein lies the Great Challenge. In a world of constant change, how do you stay the course? How do you ignore the hype about the next great investment? When times get tough, how do you know if you should hold steady to the path you're on or change and adapt your approach?

The reality is that in attempting to navigate your way toward financial freedom, there are two things you must get right.

First, you must identify and implement an approach that will work for you. Ideally that approach will be based upon empirical research and the experience of others. Most importantly, that approach must fit well with your personal goals, constraints, time horizon, and risk tolerance.

Once you've identified your approach, the second thing you must do is ignore all the insanity going on around you and stick to that approach. You must also continue to evaluate what you're doing and tweak it as necessary. Notice that I used the word "tweak" as opposed to "abandon." By the way, the dictionary definition of "tweak" is "improve (a mechanism or system) by making fine adjustments to it."

This is an important distinction because, once you've identified your approach to your finances, one of the biggest risks you face is abandoning that approach. Of course, this presupposes that the process you plan to use is a sound and logical one.

The good news is that history provides clues about the best way to find just such a process. So, rather than fumbling through the darkness like some ancient explorer in search of El Dorado, you can instead learn from and assimilate the lessons of the past and let those lessons guide you to the Golden City.

Therefore, the first goal of this book is to teach you an approach that will give you a high probability of attaining financial freedom. Importantly, this approach will be free from hyperbole or speculation and will be based on sound financial research.

If you consistently follow the approach laid out in this book, and you do so over a sufficiently long period of time, you are virtually certain to attain a degree of financial success greater than the majority of the general population.

Of course, you'll need to keep in mind that financial success is a relative term and expectations should be realistic. What might be attainable for someone earning a million dollars a year may be unattainable for someone making $50,000. The goal is to attain a significant level of financial success relative to your means. For many folks, this means they are able to live a lifestyle in retirement comparable to that which they enjoyed while working.

Always remember that with the power of compound interest, which Albert Einstein reputedly described as "The most powerful force in the universe," time is the ally of the patient investor.

Ultimately, identifying and implementing a process designed to produce financial success really isn't that difficult. Even relatively novice readers of this book, should, upon its conclusion, be able to design and build a system that will allow them to embark upon the course to financial freedom.

And that, dear reader, brings us to the second goal of this book. And that is where the trouble often begins. Staying the course and sticking with the approach you've identified can be incredibly difficult, especially in a world of information overload and political, economic, and financial turmoil.

On the surface, this shouldn't be the case. After all, the approach you're implementing is based on sound fundamental research, has logic on its side, and has worked for millions of people just like you.

"But wait," I hear you saying. "Weren't things different way back when? So maybe this approach worked 10, 20, 30, or 40 years ago, but things are different now."

And you're right, things are different these days and those who suggest otherwise are either deceiving you or themselves.

For example, we now have the threat of war in the Middle East or with North Korea or maybe even someday with China. And this certainly is different, because in the 1960s we had war with Vietnam and in the 1940s war with Germany and Japan. And yet this approach worked during those time frames.

But now, we have the risk of weapons of mass destruction in the hands of terrorists and surely this makes things different. And you're right, it does. Because for most of the twentieth century we were worried about Russia's WMDs, rather than terrorists' WMDs. And yet this approach worked during those time frames.

Surely, though, the political uncertainty we face is unprecedented and we need to change our approach because of that. I mean, presidents even get impeached these days. And you're right, the political uncertainty we face is different than that which we faced in the past. For instance, I'm virtually certain Richard Nixon will not resign the presidency in the next several years. Nor do I think that adults of any gender, race, or creed will have to once again fight for the right to vote, as they did for so much of the twentieth century. And yet this approach worked during those time frames.

But, who knows what will happen with the economy? Maybe inflation will accelerate. It might, yet I tend to think we are unlikely to see the double-digit inflation that we saw in the 1970s. And yet, even if 1970s hyperinflation comes to pass, remember that this approach worked during that time period.

These days, markets are more volatile and prices swing much more quickly. So maybe this approach worked during times of relative calm, but it can't work now. Maybe, maybe not, but it worked in 1987 when the *stock market fell by nearly 25% in a single day*. And it worked in the early 2000s when the stock market got cut in half. And it worked again in the late 2000s when the stock market again got cut in half.

And of course, now we have the COVID-19 pandemic, and shelter-in-place, and we've never had anything like that before. And its true; we've never had COVID-19 before. But we did have the Spanish Flu in 1918, which infected roughly 1/3 of all the people on earth, and is estimated to have killed more than 50 million people. And yet, this approach worked back then.

Let me be clear: I have enough experience that I can speculate about what the future might hold, and sound intelligent doing so. But I absolutely cannot claim to know with reasonable certainty what is actually going to happen next week or next year or next decade. The world will change. Politicians will come and go. The economy will experience periods of growth and times of recession. Sadly, we likely haven't seen the end of war in our lifetime. And we will definitely see both bull and bear markets. Of all this and more I am certain.

There is one more thing of which I am also certain. And that is the following: an intelligent and well-researched financial approach, such as the one laid out in this book, will continue to provide a high likelihood of success, provided the user has the intestinal fortitude to stick with it.

The bad news, as you'll soon discover, is that financial success takes both time and discipline. Few people get rich quickly or by accident. And of those that do, few stay rich.

Discipline will prove especially important, because there is a wide assortment of distractions intended to divert you from your steady approach. These developments urge you to do something, rather than just patiently following the disciplined path you are on.

Let's face it, slow and steady isn't always a lot of fun. After all, the tortoise might have beaten the hare in *Aesop's Fables*, but that turtle didn't exactly run an exciting race. Remember, however, that done correctly, the goal of investing isn't supposed to be excitement. The goal of investing is supposed to be success. And then, once you've attained your financial goal, you can use your newfound freedom to generate excitement in the other areas of your life.

Broadly speaking there are two main approaches to navigating the financial markets. In Aesop's time they were the tortoise and the hare, but today they are known as *trading* and *investing*.

Trading is exciting and promises great riches quickly. This is the world of hype, media speculation, and background noise. However, as you'll read in this book, the odds of trading your way to success are quite slim, and you'll be competing against other players more skilled and better equipped than you.

On the other hand, investing can be dull and promises moderate riches slowly. But the odds of success are quite high, and you won't need to compete with and defeat the best players in the world in order to achieve success. Best of all, the long-run growth of the economy will act as a wind at your sails on your voyage toward financial freedom.

This book will examine the lessons offered from a century of financial experience in an effort to accomplish three goals:

1. Articulate the differences between short-term trading and long-term investing, and more importantly, convince you that an investment-oriented approach offers the best odds of success.
2. Explore and explain a variety of tools and techniques to help patient, long-term investors set and meet their financial goals.
3. Provide strategies you *must* utilize to avoid roadblocks on your path to financial success.

You'll notice that on that last point I used the word "must" as opposed to "should," because ignoring the noise and following a patient approach to your finances isn't something you "should" do. The steps laid out in this book aren't optional, unless you consider financial freedom optional. However, I personally believe that financial freedom is something each and every one of us *must* achieve in order to lead fulfilling lives. And, I believe that the lessons in this book are things that you *must* do in order to achieve financial freedom. Ergo, as my old college logic professor would conclude, you *must do the things in this book in order to lead your most fulfilling life.*

The steps I've laid out have never been easy. And the continued evolution of the financial markets, media, and technology has only served to exacerbate the eternal challenge individuals have faced in resisting the temptation to make changes to their portfolio. When you, too, face such a challenge, as you often will, try to remember the words of Jack Bogle, the founder of Vanguard and inventor of the index mutual fund, who famously said:

> Don't do something, just stand there!

This book is intended to make following that advice easier, and to make sure that, while you're doing so, your portfolio is invested in such a way that your chances of a successful outcome are as high as possible.

In investing, as in life, there are no certainties, but you can increase the probability that you'll meet your financial goals by incorporating the experiences of investors just like you. And just to reiterate, while there are no guarantees, given enough time, the techniques and strategies laid out in this book will enhance your odds of success to the point where financial freedom is nearly guaranteed.

If that promise sounds like something you'd be interested in, read on, and discover the things you must do to achieve financial freedom.

Part I

Yes, the Game Is Rigged, But You Don't Have to Play

Chapter 1
The Times They Are a-Changin'

In order to be financially successful, you must learn to ignore the hype and drown out the noise. That is not negotiable. If you cannot ignore the mayhem that surrounds you, you have virtually no chance of achieving financial success.

Yes, this can be difficult. In fact, entire industries exist for no other reason than to bombard you with a constant barrage of hype and noise. Sometimes it's the media, and flashing headlines warning that you risk financial destruction if you don't do something right now. Sometimes, it's brokerage research reports touting the latest hot stock tip.

Almost as dangerous are the legions of nonprofessionals eagerly lining up to give you advice on a subject they themselves know little about. Here I'm referring to well-meaning, but misguided efforts by friends and family to tell you how to make financial decisions.

Obviously, the people in your life aren't intentionally leading you astray. And sometimes their advice may be sound. But there are two problems with following their advice.

The first problem is that the advice itself may be not be very good. Think about it this way. If you go to the gym and get a personal trainer to help you get in shape, you're probably going to look for somebody fitter than you, somebody who obviously knows their way around the gym. The same should hold true for your finances. Before taking financial advice from somebody, you should have a pretty good idea of what their personal financial situation is.

Does that person have similar goals, constraints, and resources as you? And have they done a good job within those confines of navigating the path to the financial future that you desire? If so, maybe it does make sense to listen to what they have to say. But if not, it's best to politely thank them and then move on.

The second challenge is that, even if the information itself is valid, it may not fit within the context of your overall plan. Remember, you're not trying to build a collection of investment ideas or financial concepts, but, rather, a coherent and holistic collection of strategies designed to help you meet your unique financial goals. *That is why the first step on the road to financial freedom is always a financial plan.*

The constant barrage of hype and noise will be a recurring theme throughout this book. The best, and perhaps only way to ignore all this is to find your True North, otherwise known as the financial plan and strategies most likely to help you achieve your financial goals. In identifying this plan, you must come to a level of conviction that allows you to avoid the temptation to stray from the path you've identified. If you can do this, your odds of financial success are high. Failure to achieve this conviction level often comes at great cost.

When it comes to your finances there are two main approaches. They are speculation and investing and they are as different as night and day.

There Is a World of Difference Between Speculation and Investing

Investors let markets work for them over time. Investors are bloodied, but not knocked out, by market crashes. Investors let the long-run-upward progress of the economy and corporate profits work in their favor, comfortable in the knowledge that time is their best friend, and compound interest their staunchest ally.

Speculators, on the other hand, depend on the greater fool theory, because inherent in every speculation is the belief that you know better than others what something is truly worth.

Speculation, *otherwise known as short-term trading,* is an exceptionally difficult endeavor, which is why successful traders are so well paid.

Furthermore, an already difficult task becomes nearly impossible when done without the benefits that come from a full-time, professional focus upon the financial markets. The vast majority of individuals should therefore avoid trying to trade as if they were a hedge fund manager or investment banker.

For one thing, the risk-and-reward scenarios for hedge fund managers are extremely skewed. If a hedge fund manager is successful, he or she is richly rewarded. If on the other hand managers lose their investors' money, the worst thing that can happen is that they have to close their funds. Importantly, the managers do not have to reimburse the investors' losses. This means that hedge fund managers have a strong incentive to invest aggressively in hopes of generating sky-high returns.

Compare this situation to your own. You benefit from higher investment returns through a larger portfolio and eventually perhaps an enhanced standard of living. In this way, your *upside incentive* is similar to that of a hedge fund manager. However, it is on the *downside* that you bear little relation to the hedge fund manager, because, while hedge fund managers can simply walk away if they lose their investors' money, you don't have that luxury. Any losses you suffer may prevent you from achieving your financial goals. This means that not only must you focus upon growing your portfolio, but you must also focus on preserving your principal and sustaining any previous gains you have enjoyed.

With that in mind, you would do well to take a long-term approach to investing, one that allows the power of compound interest to work in your favor over time.

Investing is a process in which you do the following:

- Identify precisely what your financial goal is.
- Calculate what rate of return you require in order to meet your financial goal.
- Determine, based on the best available information, which portfolio mixes are most likely to help you achieve the return you require.
- Select from the available portfolios the one with the least amount of risk.
- Monitor and adjust your portfolio as necessary.
- Let time and the power of compound interest work for you in meeting your goal.

Compare that approach with short-term speculation.

Here is the dictionary definition of speculation:

Speculation: *The forming of a theory or conjecture without firm evidence*

I'll leave it for you to decide whether you want to trust your family's future to that. If not, then it's time to shift your attention to speculation's evidence-based cousin, investing.

Critically though, investing will require you to form mental and emotional defenses that will allow you to ignore the hype.

So, Why Is It So Damn Hard to Ignore the Hype?!

This is a piece of cake. All that you need to do is identify a logical approach to your finances, implement it, and then stay the course. Do this and one day you'll be financially free and able to live the life of your dreams.

So why is it so damn hard to do that?

After all, that process sounds pretty straightforward and, although it's not simple, a book such as this one will lay out in sufficient detail what you need to do in order to achieve that life of your dreams. And let's face it, you already know without my telling you that you should stay the course and ignore the hype.

So again, why is it so damn hard?

Well, imagine an ancient ancestor of yours. This ancestor is out for a leisurely walk when suddenly he sees someone running toward him at a rapid pace. As the newcomer speeds by he shouts, "Look out! There's a saber-toothed tiger coming." Your ancient ancestor immediately turns around and follows the other guy as they both run away as fast as possible. The saber-toothed tiger doesn't get them and they both live to tell the story around that evening's campfire.

Word rapidly spreads among the local tribes that there's a saber-toothed tiger around and it might not make sense to visit the part of the forest where it was last seen. Everyone wisely follows that advice. Knowledge such as this has been vital to humanity's development for 200,000 years. Even if a rumor couldn't actually be confirmed, it still made sense to listen to it because no one actually knew what was out in the dark forest and the consequences of stumbling upon that angry saber-toothed tiger were too terrible to imagine.

Well, the last saber-toothed tiger died off somewhere around 11,000 years ago, and the world has changed in a lot of other ways since then. What hasn't changed is our propensity to listen to what our neighbors say as we try to learn from the collective wisdom. This system works in a lot of ways, but it also has some drawbacks. That's because your neighbors are prone to fear and greed. And guess what? So are you. That's why it's so hard for you to ignore what the crowd is doing and stick with your chosen course.

There then lies the solution to your financial troubles. All you need to do is rid yourself of fear and greed and you'll be good to go.

My work here is done and that's the end of the book.

Good luck!

What's that? You're still reading and I'm still writing?

Oh, yeah, that's right. You're all human after all so there is literally no way to rid yourselves of fear and greed. Darn!

Well, then? This book will have to be somewhat longer, because since you're unable to rid yourself of fear and greed you'll have to resort to Plan B. Plan B involves learning tools, strategies, and techniques designed to make it easier to avoid giving in to those emotions you're unable to get rid of.

It won't be easy. But it is possible. First, you'll need some education around a logical approach to your finances, an approach you can believe in. Following that, you need to be aware of some of the more nefarious influences you'll come across on your journey toward financial freedom. To be fair, mere awareness is unlikely to solve your problem, but it is a starting point toward formulating solutions for avoiding the temptation to give in to fear and greed.

To Play, or Not to Play, That Is the Question

Change is constant in this world, but the evolution of financial markets has not been a steady, uniform process. Instead, the pace of innovation has accelerated like a snowball cascading down a hill.

Consider, if you will, the impact that social media has had on the dissemination of financial news, or the increasing sophistication and competitiveness of today's institutional investors, or the rise of high-frequency trading and the manner in which it magnifies market movements.

All these developments and more have not only introduced new complexities for individual investors to consider, but have also accelerated the impact of prior evolutions. As such, the skill level required to successfully navigate the markets has increased exponentially. Phrased differently, the game has indeed become rigged in favor of those investors able to bring massive quantities of resources to their efforts.

With that in mind, the individual has only two choices. The first is to try to compete with better equipped players in a game that is clearly rigged against them. **The second – the preferable – choice is to choose not to play the game at all.**

Just so there is no confusion, let me state again, here at the outset of this book, that the game is inarguably rigged against the individual investor and that there are certain disadvantages that you are unlikely to ever overcome.

There – I've said it, and I'm not sorry. Consider yourself warned. Because the truth of the matter is that, given how markets have developed over the past several decades, the average person has little hope of competing with the big boys. To even attempt to do so often constitutes a fool's errand, and is likely to result in frustration, poor performance, and ultimately failure to meet one's financial goals.

That, in a nutshell, is the bad news.

The good news is that *ordinary people just like you can still successfully and profitably invest in the financial markets.*

Furthermore, in some ways you actually have important advantages institutions lack. The key to your financial success is to maximize the inherent advantages you possess while avoiding the temptation to mimic the behavior of the institutional investor.

Although you can still profit in the financial markets, doing so will likely involve adopting strategies and tools different from those you've used in the past. Success requires mental and emotional fortitude, a willingness to stand apart from your peers, and formulating a disciplined and repeatable approach to investing. On the plus side, while markets and economies have grown more complicated, your approach need not be overly sophisticated. In fact, you might even say that successful investing is simple.

Of course, just because something is simple doesn't mean that it is easy.

Life at the Speed of Light

All around us, people seem busier these days. No one wants to wait for anything. Heck, between online shopping and delivery drones, we can get almost anything we want within 24 hours. For those unwilling to wait this long, 3D printing technology may soon allow instant home fabrication of a variety of goods.

And let me ask you a question about smartphones. The last time you waited in line for a movie, concert, Disneyland ride, or grocery store checkout, how many people in that line weren't multitasking on their phone, whether with social media, online shopping, or texting? My guess is not many. For better or for worse, our society has evolved to the point where patience is a very rare quality indeed.

This mentality extends into the financial arena: no one wants to invest their money and patiently wait for it to grow over the course of years or decades. No. We all want to trade, Baby, so let's light this candle and make a bundle fast.

How could we not, when the headlines are full of stories about Wall Street whiz kids who make millions a year and teenage tech entrepreneurs who make billions from their parent's garage? Never mind the bad old days, when wealth was generated over the course of decades through a combination of hard work, saving, and investing.

Since 1960, the average holding period for a stock has declined from eight years to eight months. Let me state unequivocally: an *eight-year* holding period constitutes an investment, whereas an *eight-month* time frame is a trade. And as I'll emphasize again and again throughout this book, there are fundamental differences between *trading* and *investing*.

The rapid pace at which many people turn over their portfolios is the antithesis of ignoring the hype and sticking with a long-term plan. But admittedly, the evolution of the financial markets has made it harder and harder to stick to a long-term approach, as evidenced by the decline in average holding period for a stock purchase.

Figure 1.1 shows some of the changes that have occurred in the economy, the financial markets, and the world. Many of these changes are net positives for you as an individual investor. But, as with many things in life, these changes represent a double-edged sword because the same developments that provide benefits also exacerbate the urge to give in to instinct and emotion and *to do something*.

Figure 1.1 How the World Has Changed for Individual Investors
SOURCE: Analysis by Brian Perry.

Lower Transaction Costs

The Change: From the time of its inception in 1792, the New York Stock Exchange set fixed commission levels. The result was that it was very expensive to trade stocks, particularly for individual investors. This was because the fixed commission represented a greater percentage of the total transaction proceeds on smaller trades. This meant that buying or selling stocks was expensive, which was bad. On the other hand, this expense caused people to carefully consider what they were doing prior to buying or selling, which was good.

However, on May 1, 1975, commissions were deregulated, and brokers were freed up to charge whatever fee they wanted.

This event became known as May Day, and represented the start of a long-term downward spiral in transaction costs.

Discount brokerage firms, such as Charles Schwab, came into existence and began offering reduced transaction costs for trades. This meant that the commission an investor had to pay to buy or sell a stock began to decline. This trend toward shrinking transaction costs accelerated during the 1990s when the bid and ask prices on stocks began to be quoted in smaller and smaller increments. Previously, stock prices were quoted in increments of one-eighth of a point, whereas today they are quoted in pennies. This means that the bid/ask spread on stocks has shrunk dramatically, further reducing transaction costs.

Around the same time, the development of the Internet and the advent of online trading gave more and more investors the ability to execute their own trades, as opposed to calling a broker. Facilitating an online trade is more cost effective for brokerage firms; some of the cost savings are passed along to individual investors in the form of even lower commissions.

In 2019, this downward trend literally reached absolute zero. Major brokerage firms, such as Charles Schwab, TD Ameritrade, and Fidelity now offer clients the ability to buy and sell securities commission free.

A logical question, of course, is how companies stay in business without charging commissions. Generally speaking, the firms make money from the actual execution of the trade or they hope to entice investors to move money over to their firm. Then, while commissions remain zero, the firms hope to sell more lucrative products and services such as money management or cash management platforms. Thus, while the race to zero does negatively impact the profitability of these brokerage firms, it does not decimate their business models.

The Impact: In and of itself, the sharp decline in the cost of transacting in the financial markets is a good thing. Indeed, among the main beneficiaries are individual investors, who, as noted earlier, used to pay a disproportionately high commission when measured as a percentage of their transaction proceeds.

However, one of the unintended consequences of lower transaction costs is that it reduces one of the main impediments to rapid-fire trading. Previously, even if you were inclined to make a trade, you had to evaluate it in the context of the high commission you would pay. In the absence of this barrier, it's now easier to succumb to the desire to rapidly turn over the holdings in your portfolio.

Are you ready to have your mind blown? Fidelity Investments has literally millions of clients, so when they analyze client returns, they have a lot of data with which to work. In an effort to better understand investor behavior, Fidelity segmented their client base into various cohorts to determine what types of investors do best over time.

What Fidelity discovered is truly eye-opening, though perhaps not surprising. It turns out that the second-best-performing cohort were *those investors who forgot that they have an account. Yes, people that didn't know they had an account outperformed those that knew they had an account.*

Can you guess what the number-one-performing cohort of investors was?

Dead clients.

That's right, it turns out that one of the benefits of dying is that it becomes impossible to churn your account.

So, there you have it: if you want to increase your odds of achieving financial success, all you have to do is pass away.

Alternatively, if you want to achieve financial success without the adverse consequences of being dead, you can continue to read this book and follow the advice it gives.

Again, the more often you make changes to your portfolio, the less likely you are to meet your financial goals. So, while the explicit cost (the commission) to trade may have declined, the implicit cost (not meeting your financial goals) remains as high as ever.

Self-Directed Investing

The Change: One of the most important changes individuals have experienced over the past three decades has been the shift from defined benefit to defined contribution plans.

A defined benefit plan is commonly known as a pension. The way these operate is that you work for an employer for a number of years and hopefully they pay you for your work. They also promise you that, if you work for a sufficient period of time and leave in good standing, they will provide you with a future pension benefit. In other words, the employer pays you while you are working, and then they continue to pay you once you stop working.

From your standpoint this is great. Having that future guaranteed income helps with your retirement planning. It's different from the employer's perspective, though. They've made a contractual promise to pay you a specific amount each and every year in the future. As such, they need to set aside and invest money today so that they have the resources to pay your pension in the future.

Because of that, defined benefit plans place the emphasis for saving, investing, and distributing funds on the employer. As an employee, you don't necessarily care what the markets are doing. As long as the retirement plan and employer remain solvent, you'll get your guaranteed income in retirement. As such, when most individuals were covered by a defined benefit plan, market fluctuations were less front-and-center in the public consciousness.

However, since around 1980, defined benefit plans have become increasingly scarce outside the public sector. Instead, defined contribution plans have become far more common. These defined contribution plans are relatively recent creations. The Individual Retirement Account (IRA) was only created in 1974, and the 401(k) account was only legislated into existence in 1978. Employers, tired of being on the hook for employees' retirement distributions, were quick to latch onto these new tools, and rapidly shifted away from defined benefit and toward defined contribution plans.

With a defined contribution plan such as a 401(k), the onus for the successful accumulation, investment, and distribution of funds shifts from employer to employee. When you are responsible for accumulating enough money to fund your future lifestyle, the daily gyrations of financial markets become much more real.

Today, most people work for organizations that offer defined contribution retirement plans such as a 401(k) or 403(b). Individuals without access to one of these plans might utilize an Individual Retirement Account (IRA) to save for retirement. This means that many more people are now directly participating in the financial markets.

The Impact: As is generally the case, there are both pros and cons to the transition from defined benefit to defined contribution plans. The main benefit is that people have more control over their financial well-being, and more flexibility when it comes to choosing whether to remain with their current employer. However, the downside to this flexibility and control is that individuals with little or no training in financial matters must now in effect become professional investors, at least in regard to their own retirement funds.

Defined benefit plans generally have pension boards overseeing them. The members of these boards have what is known as a fiduciary duty to make sure the funds are properly safeguarded and invested. The fund then hires actuaries to run calculations that determine how much they need to put aside today and what rate of return their investments must generate in order to fund future retirees' cash flow. Sophisticated, professional investors then control the investments.

Contrast that with the challenge facing you as a person whose background, schooling, and expertise lie outside the realm of actuarial projections, fiduciary standards, and investment theories. Despite these shortcomings, you still need to determine how much you need to save, how to invest those savings, and then how much you can distribute each year in retirement. And if you fall short on any of those tasks, the result is a future of financial ruin.

No wonder people say finances are one of the main sources of stress in their life!

This scenario is exacerbated by the phenomenon of *other people's money*, which refers to the fact that it is easier to stay calm when the money in question isn't your own. So, for example, a defined benefit plan manager can act in a more rational manner because it's not her money she's investing. But an individual managing his or her own 401(k) account is subject to greater emotional volatility, since he or she is dealing with his or her own money.

This becomes especially important during times when markets aren't doing well. For instance, the U.S. stock market posted poor returns throughout most of the 1970s, especially when inflation is taken into account. However, employees who were covered by defined benefit plans had no real need to concern themselves with the stock market's stagnation. To be clear, their employers may have been having difficulties meeting the actuarial assumptions built into the pension plan, but this issue probably wasn't front-and-center for the employee.

Contrast that situation with the first decade of the new millennium. From 2001 to 2010, the S&P 500 suffered two brutal bear markets, ultimately ending the decade lower than where it had begun. And this time, many individuals were responsible for investing their own retirement accounts, which made this feel more real than what occurred in the 1970s.

When individuals who are responsible for their own financial well-being see news headlines about declining stock prices and view their portfolio statements on a more or less real-time basis, the constant barrage of negative headlines and declining portfolio values creates an almost unconquerable urge to *do something* to improve portfolio performance.

Unfortunately, this urge to *do something* often results in taking action at precisely the wrong time and in precisely the wrong manner. Whereas a professional investor would (hopefully) hold on to stocks during the worst of a market decline, individuals often panic at the sight of their rapidly deteriorating net worth and sell just as the market bottoms. This results in locking in portfolio losses, and often leaves the person emotionally frozen and unable to reinvest in stocks even once they resume an upward trend.

Readers that experienced the nearly 50% stock market sell-off and equally sharp market rebound of 2008–2009 or the extreme volatility prompted by the COVID-19 pandemic can no doubt relate to the emotional challenges investors face when navigating volatile markets.

High-Frequency Trading

The Change: Recent years have witnessed the rise of machines in the financial markets. High-frequency trading firms utilize algorithms to facilitate buy and sell orders. These algorithms then seek out the best pricing, often leaping ahead of orders entered by or for individual investors. Time is of the essence for high-frequency traders, to such a degree that many firms have installed their own fiber optic cables and located their offices in geographic proximity to major exchanges in the hope of shaving nanoseconds off of their trade execution times.

The consequence of this is that high-frequency traders now dominate trading activity in many markets while their use of technology allows them to profit nearly instantaneously from incremental price changes.

While exact numbers are difficult to determine, some researchers estimate that more than half of all trading in U.S. stock and futures markets is originated by high frequency trading firms and other algorithmic traders.

This rapid turnover has been blamed for an increase in market volatility, though studies have proven inconclusive, in large part because high-frequency trading firms are reluctant to share the data behind their trading. Nonetheless, it does seem reasonable that a significant increase in turnover from firms interested in profiting from tiny price differentials in various securities (as opposed to the fundamental value of a good business) could lead to larger price fluctuations.

The impact of high-frequency traders inserting themselves in the middle of trades executed by other investors has also been viewed as an additional expense investors pay when executing their orders. To a degree, this can offset some of the price advantages individuals have received from the lower transaction costs previously discussed.

The Impact: Raise your hand if you measure your trade execution times in nanoseconds.

Me neither.

Simply put, just as in the *Terminator* movies, there is no way for the average individual to compete with the rise of the machines. And unlike many of the other evolutions described in this chapter, there is no positive impact I can find from this development. High-frequency trading is, at least in my opinion, unequivocally bad for anyone not engaged in the practice. After all, high-frequency trading firms exist to make money for themselves, and their profits come directly from the pockets of other investors. As such, high-frequency traders are the financial market equivalent of toll collectors.

So, what's an individual to do? My advice is to not even try to compete. Investing and trading are inherently different activities. Traders are at risk of losing out, with a share of their profits being sucked away by the high-frequency firms.

Investors, with their longer-term time horizons, should find their holding period returns relatively unaffected by the high-frequency traders exacting their pound of flesh from each and every transaction, which is yet another argument in favor of adopting an investing, as opposed to a trading, approach.

The 24-Hour News Cycle

The Change: Now, I'd like you to remember back to a different time. I'm talking here about ancient times, long, long ago. Someday, people may refer to this as the last, great Dark Age.

It was a time of hopelessness and despair.

A lonely time.

A boring time.

I'm referring of course to the 1980s.

You remember the 1980s (and if you don't, just try to imagine a world where you can't check Facebook every 90 seconds!). That distant decade, which my six-year-old son refers to, as "You know, the 1980s, when really old people were alive."

Well, the 1980s certainly were a transition point, because that decade represented both the first decade with 24-hour cable news channels focused upon the financial markets, as well as the last decade before the widespread adoption of the Internet. To be fair, the Internet was actually invented in the early 1980s, but its current user-friendly form that we all know as the World Wide Web only came into existence in 1990, and widespread usage really only began in the second half of that decade.

Why does that matter in the context of a finance book? Because, prior to the 1980s, the nonprofessional investor only knew what was going on in the stock market when they looked up stock prices in the *Wall Street Journal* or similar, specialized publications. And even these relatively well-informed individuals were analyzing market movements with a significant time delay. Less committed investors might only notice the gyrations of the financial markets when they were sufficiently notable to merit front-page coverage in mainstream newspapers.

Then, the 1980s ushered in the era of the 24-hour news cycle on cable TV and dedicated financial news networks. These outlets allowed committed market watchers to track the gyrations of individual securities and the broader market indexes on a more or less real-time basis. The individual, sitting at home, could now access market updates nearly as quickly as a professional sitting in a brokerage office.

The rise of cable news channels in general and financial news channels in particular changed forever the way people consume information. During the newspaper era people received their news via the morning or evening paper, or perhaps from the broadcast network's evening news. The advent of cable news ushered in an era of around-the-clock coverage. As outlets have proliferated, the fight to attract eyeballs has intensified, leading many to resort to increasingly breathless reporting with an eye toward the sensational.

Financial news channels such as CNBC further exacerbated this trend for investors, and individuals who previously might have had no idea what markets were doing on a daily basis were now bombarded with breathless headlines from TVs hanging in restaurants, barber shops, and bars, not to mention their local brokerage firm. Importantly, many of the "expert" reporters telling you when to buy and sell have relatively lean or even nonexistent financial backgrounds. Rather, many of these individuals were chosen for their journalism backgrounds, on-air personality, or looks. There's nothing wrong with that, this is TV journalism after all. But it pays in finance, as in life, to consider the source you're taking information from.

During the TV era, people's information flow was subject to the editorial decisions of the cable news provider. If, for instance, you wanted to track IBM stock but the news outlet wasn't covering or discussing IBM that day, you may still have been left in the dark.

This shortcoming was rectified when the 1980s transitioned into the 1990s and the World Wide Web gradually became ubiquitous. At that point, the cost of producing and disseminating content on the financial markets declined sharply, resulting in a significant increase in the number of information outlets providing real-time updates, news, and analysis on the financial markets and individual securities. Furthermore, individuals then effectively became their own editor, able to find information on nearly any security or investment idea that tickled their fancy.

The Internet exacerbated the movement toward nonstop news coverage, and greatly expanded the number of media outlets that need stories to draw eyeballs. Furthermore, there are lower barriers to entry online than over the airwaves, bringing into further question the journalistic and financial credibility of many outlets.

And, particularly in the realm of blogs and online chat rooms, the motivation of commentators is an open question. Though it is illegal to promote false news in an effort to manipulate financial markets or stock prices, it does occur.

Social media has provided the final push in the battle for around-the-clock news, providing consumers with a never-ending bombardment of opinions and news stories. Many people check their social media feeds first thing in the morning and repeatedly throughout the day, providing them with not only important updates on what their best friend from the sixth grade had for lunch that day but also breaking news events and their social network's take on those events. Additionally, we live in an era where you need to filter information flow in order to determine if you are viewing "real" or "fake" news. This can be difficult to do in the financial realm, particularly if you don't have extensive expertise.

The bottom line is that whereas three or four decades ago the average person may not have been aware of market movements until they opened their annual brokerage statement, in today's day and age, notable and even inconsequential news headlines are conveyed almost instantaneously to investors big and small.

The Impact: As with lower transaction costs, the more democratic distribution of information is an inherently good thing. Used properly, instantaneous access to information can improve decision-making. And wider dispersion of information helps prevent pricing abuses that could be present if information was concentrated in the hands of a select few. At the end of the day, any business in which information is tightly guarded lends itself to potentially abusive behavior, and the dispersion of information shifts the balance of power to the consumer (in this case the individual investor).

However, as with lower transaction costs, there are downsides to the more widespread availability of information that we now enjoy. First of all, as the number of information sources has multiplied exponentially, the veracity of some of those sources has declined. As such, not only do you need to decide how to incorporate new information into your investment thesis, but you also need to determine whether the information you are considering is accurate and unbiased.

Furthermore, whereas there was a time when you might not know for days, weeks, or even a year that the market had fallen, you can now access that information more or less immediately. Sometimes you get that information even when you're not looking for it. Heck, the elevators in my building even have scrolling news updates and stock tickers!

Want a vision of hell on earth? Just imagine being on that broken-down elevator when stocks are crashing. Then you can spend a couple hours in a small metal box, watching your net worth plummet while hoping the elevator doesn't emulate the market's collapse!

The bottom line is that, depending on your mentality, instantaneous information updates can cause you to do things that aren't in your best interest. At the most basic level, it's a lot easier to panic and sell during a market crash when you know there's a market crash.

So this information availability, which again is a net positive, also exacerbates those basic human emotions of fear and greed and makes it a lot harder to stay on track toward financial success.

Ultimately, the impact of the financial news media is insidious enough that an entire chapter of this book is devoted to the topic. But for now, let me be very clear on this – the purpose of most of the financial media is **entertainment** and **information**, *in that order*.

There is nothing wrong with information consumption. An awareness of what is happening in the economy and the financial markets can make you a better investor. The challenge is that the constant bombardment of sensationalist headlines exacerbates the other trends outlined in this chapter, all of which contribute to *an urge to do something*, even when the most successful course of action might be to *do nothing at all*.

Accept the news media for what it is, and utilize its output appropriately, and you'll be well on your way toward meeting your financial goals.

But if you struggle to do this, or if you find yourself susceptible to fear when the going gets tough or the urge to make more money when things seem to be good, then I'll give you arguably the single most important piece of advice in this entire book:

> *If you are the kind of person who is going to change your well-researched, long-term financial approach due to what you see or hear in the media, then you must do everything in your power to avoid reading or watching financial news coverage. Practice self-discipline, or cancel your cable or newspaper subscription, or don't read financial blogs, or take whatever other steps you need to take. You must do this, or your odds of financial success will plummet.*

Globalization

The Change: Globalization has also played a role in shortening our attention spans and investment time horizons. Round-the-clock trading of all types of financial instruments means that the markets never close. And when you couple that with the enhanced interconnectivity of the global economy, it's easy to succumb to the urge to closely track not only domestic but also international economic and financial developments. For a professional investor, this may be necessary. But for an individual, the value of constantly monitoring global developments or trading Asian currencies in the dead of the night is limited at best. Plus, it takes time away from other activities, and money is, ultimately, just a tool. Remember, the goal of investing is to generate financial freedom, not to become a slave to your money.

The Impact: Thirty years ago, most U.S.-based investors probably kept the majority (if not all) of their investment portfolios in the United States. But today, many investors have a sizable allocation to international securities. *This is a good thing and there are tremendous benefits to global diversification.* In fact, this is another topic that is important enough to warrant a great deal of additional discussion later in this book.

But it is important to remember that global investing multiplies the information flow an investor would otherwise receive. This in turn can make it harder to stay the course and resist the temptation to react to market movements. Remember, the key to financial success is to *act* according to your plan, and not to *react* to external conditions.

Think back to the last time you watched a financial news channel or visited a financial website. In addition to all the other headlines flashing across your screen, you were also bombarded with the latest stock market results from Germany (the DAX), France (the CAC 40), the UK (the FTSE), Japan (the Nikkei 225), Hong Kong (the Hang Seng), and countless other international markets. In addition, key international currency exchange rates flickered across the screen in a constant rotation with other "important" financial indicators.

With so much data and information coming at you, it can be exceptionally difficult to fight the temptation to constantly shift your portfolio from the United States to the United Kingdom and from the United Kingdom to Japan, and then back again to the United States. Again, economic cycles and market movements do vary greatly across international markets, making a strategy of diversifying among international markets a potentially profitable one. But most investors will find that a disciplined and rules-based approach to global diversification makes the most sense.

To be fair, some hedge funds and sophisticated institutional investors have made fortunes through macro trading, which involves rapidly moving money around the globe based on economic developments and shifting currency values. But successful macro trading requires a particular skill set. For starters, a solid background in international economics is required. Additionally, an understanding of a wide range of financial markets, from stocks to bonds to currencies and commodities, is generally necessary to successfully invest in a macro style. Finally, a constant flow of information needs to be monitored and analyzed so that decisions on where to allocate resources can be made. Think for a moment of the sheer volume of information that is released on a monthly basis in the United States alone. Now multiply that a dozen times and you begin to get an idea of the scope of the logistical nightmare macrofund managers face.

For these reasons, most successful macrotraders employ large teams of expert professionals with experience monitoring and analyzing the economies and financial markets of countries around the globe. As an individual, alone and possessing only a finite amount of time with which to track your portfolio, the task of analyzing the vast quantity of information required to be a macrotrader becomes virtually impossible.

Importantly, I want to reiterate that just because average investors should not spend their time shifting assets around the globe in rapid-fire fashion doesn't mean that they can't benefit from international diversification. There is a vast gulf between trying to time global financial movements and setting a reasonable portfolio allocation among global markets and then periodically reviewing and rebalancing that allocation. The first approach is best left to professionals and world-class experts. The second approach is a sensible, long-term portfolio solution for average investors.

The Rise of the Institutional Investor

The Change: Headlines often tout the massive short-term gains achieved by hedge funds and Wall Street traders. But you are not a hedge fund and probably aren't going to achieve such returns. And to be fair, even most hedge funds don't achieve massive success; after all, if huge returns were common, they wouldn't be newsworthy, and you wouldn't be hearing about it in the press.

In fact, each year a large number of smart, experienced, and talented hedge fund managers are forced to close their doors because they are unable to provide superior performance. As an example, Figure 1.2 shows the number of hedge funds that shut down over one recent four-year period.

These statistics obviously prompt the question: If hedge funds, with all their resources, struggle to succeed, what does it mean for the average Joe?

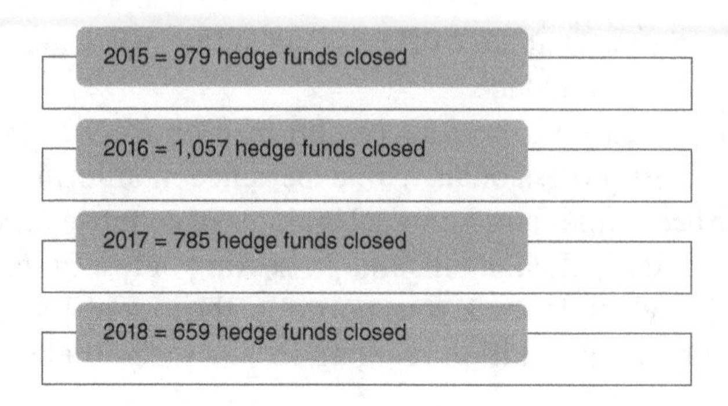

Figure 1.2 Hedge Fund Closures by Year
SOURCE: Analysis by Brian Perry. Information courtesy of Zero Hedge.

The answer of course, is that the struggles of the so-called smartest investors in the world provide further proof that "beating the market" is an incredibly difficult endeavor. Professionals, as well as amateurs, should carefully consider what inherent advantage they hold over their competition, and why it is that they are likely to succeed when so many others fail.

The Impact: Consider the resources available to a hedge fund, pension fund, sovereign wealth fund, or mutual fund while remembering that even with the plethora of tools at their disposal they still face a difficult path to success. Remember, too, that trading is a zero-sum game, and that for every winner there needs to be a loser. Now think of the resources you have available for trading – a home computer and access to the Internet, maybe conversations with your broker, or access to the market analysis tools on the online trading platform you use.

In a zero-sum game, where the competition is a trillion-dollar sovereign wealth fund or a trader at Goldman Sachs, is it realistic to expect consistently repeatable "victories"?

Success is possible of course. After all, David did slay Goliath, and the U.S. hockey team did beat Russia in the 1980 Olympics. But remember that the nickname for that epic victory is the Miracle on Ice, which should tell you pretty much everything you need to know about the long odds the U.S. team faced. To each his own, but I'd personally rather not have to rely on divine fate in my quest for financial independence.

Even if you are inclined to await Divine Providence, ask yourself this: If those two hockey teams had played 10 times, 20 times, or 100, how many matches would the United States have won? I don't know the precise answer to that question, but I do know that if the Americans were likely to win more often than not, the victory in Lake Placid wouldn't have been so memorable.

This is important because with very few exceptions the road to financial success requires repeated victories, as opposed to one shining moment. Because of that, whatever investment approach you choose needs to be *repeatable*, so that success can be replicated again and again over the course of years and decades.

And so, I repeat, what inherent advantage do you hold over Goldman Sachs or a large hedge fund, and is this inherent advantage something likely to lead to repeated victories?

You need to answer that question for yourself, but the key is to answer it as honestly as possible.

Personally, I'd rather avoid competing with the big guys and instead focus on strategies for success that don't rely on playing a zero-sum game. Better still, I want to utilize strategies that can be consistently applied in order to produce sustained success across years and decades.

Those strategies do exist. And if you have the discipline to stick with winning strategies and avoid the mistakes that doom many investors, you'll be well on your way to financial independence.

The Bottom Line

The continued acceleration of the flow of information and cost reductions for trading securities have provided you with ever greater ability to take control of your finances. However, these benefits come with a warning signal. Because the very tools that allow you to take a proactive approach toward building your financial future also exacerbate those basic human instincts toward fear and greed.

With that in mind, one of the most important things you can do if you hope to achieve financial freedom is to find an approach you can stick with regardless of the stresses society or your peers put on you to change your approach midstream or to take action at what potentially might be just the wrong time.

Chapter 2
Don't Play a Game That's Rigged

So, if attempting to mimic the behavior of institutional investors by analyzing and reacting to the day-to-day gyrations of financial markets is unlikely to produce the outcomes you desire, what should you do?

The answer is fairly simple and one that you've undoubtedly heard before. You should start with a financial plan that clarifies and specifies your financial goals. Then, you should find an investment approach that works for you and stick with it for the long haul. And of course you should do all of this in a tax-efficient manner, since a dollar saved is a dollar earned.

Of course, that's "boring" financial advice and also easier to say than to do. Therefore, the remainder of this chapter will attempt to provide you with a better understanding of why financial advisors often give this advice. This chapter will also demonstrate the downside of deviating from your long-term approach.

The Upward Path of Markets

The Grand Canyon is one of the world's most iconic sights. I've known many people who have visited, and none have ever come back disappointed. The sheer immensity of the crevice gouged from the earth boggles the mind. Standing on the cliffs and looking at the floor of the canyon 6,000 feet below, you see the Colorado River. At that height the river looks small, which makes it even more amazing when you stop to consider that it's that river that created the canyon.

The river is heavy with sediment and over the course of some five or six million years, it has gradually ground away at the surrounding rocks. The result is an ever-deepening ravine. The present view, the one that draws millions of visitors from around the world to stare in awestruck wonder, is the result of that river.

Of course, six million years is a long time. If we were able to step into a time machine and flashback to the point at which the Colorado River first began its work, the resultant view might not be very impressive. Sometimes, great doings take a while.

Such is the case with compound interest. Just as the silt in the river eventually carves a magnificent canyon, so, too, does

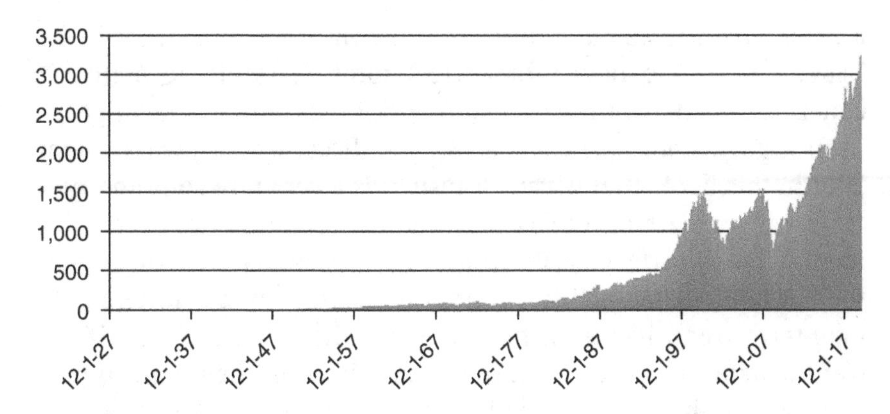

Figure 2.1 S&P 500 (1927–2019)
SOURCE: Data courtesy of MacroTrends Data Download.

compound interest turn small sums into large fortunes. Unfortunately, though, the urge to shift in and out of markets often prevents people from enjoying the true benefit of this magnificent power.

Let's take a look at what compound interest can do across long periods of time. We have data going back to the 1920s, and we can use this information to measure progress and performance. Of course the world was very different back in the 1920s, but it's helpful to take a look at a long data series because it incorporates many different political, economic, and financial environments.

The message that data gives us is quite clear: over very long periods of time, investors who resist both the urge to speculate and the urge to panic do very well, indeed (see Figure 2.1).

What's really interesting about the chart is that it doesn't look like anything happens until about 1980. This is an illusion, given the scaling of the chart, but the visual also demonstrates a deeper lesson. Just as the Colorado River did its work for countless millennia before creating one of the most impressive sights on earth, compound interest does much of its work in the background. For years, its effect might not be apparent. But when its impact does burst forth, the effect can be magnificent.

The chart also shows that there have been bad times over the past nine decades. Undoubtedly, there have been many periods during which it was tempting to abandon the market until it was "safer." With the power of perfect foresight and the ability to consistently time your way in and out of the market, this might've been a good approach. But as will be discussed in greater detail later in this book, that perfect foresight is a very rare commodity.

So, if we work off the assumption that you don't have the ability to see with perfect clarity what the future holds, it becomes clear that, despite the many fluctuations the market has encountered, the long-term trend has been higher. What that means is that if you want to achieve success, you must participate in the financial markets even though doing so will undoubtedly subject you to a great deal of volatility and perhaps even some sleepless nights.

Remember, having a portfolio that fluctuates in value has almost never prevented someone from meeting their financial goals. However, not benefiting from the power of compound interest and the long-term upward trend of financial markets has prevented many people from living the life they deserve.

Asset Class Returns

One of the main goals of much of the financial industry is to provide you with guidance about what security, sector, or asset class will serve you best in the coming months and years. This has always been the case and it makes sense. Undoubtedly, in the years to come, some sectors of the stock market will do better than others. Perhaps technology stocks will lead the way. Or maybe energy stocks will produce the strongest returns. Or it could be consumer discretionary companies or consumer nondiscretionary companies. Although we don't know which of the sectors will perform the best, we do know that some will do better than others.

It's the same with asset classes. Perhaps small-company stocks will do better than large-company stocks over the next decade. Maybe commodities will outperform real estate.

Figure 2.2 shows the performance of several asset classes and portfolio mixes over a 20-year timeframe (1999–2018). As you can

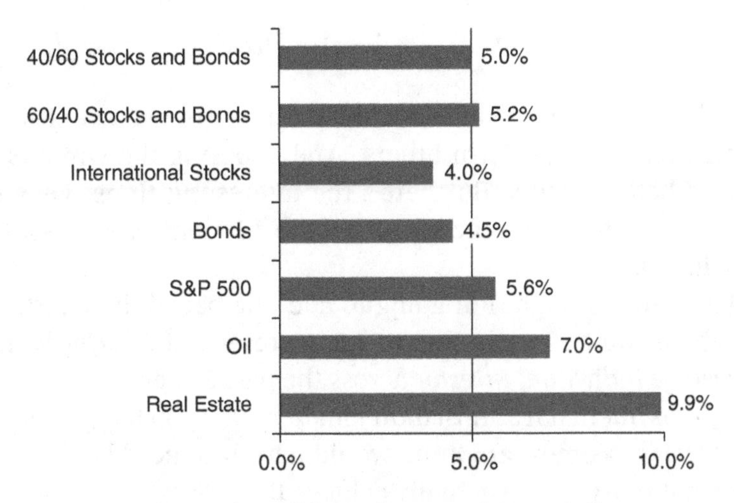

Figure 2.2 Asset Class and Portfolio Performance (1999–2018)
SOURCE: Analysis by Brian Perry. Data from JP Morgan Asset Management & Dalbar Inc.

see, some investments have done better than others. The cumulative affect has been that investors in say, real estate investment trusts (REITs) have grown their wealth significantly beyond that of investors who purchased bonds (at least during the 20-year time frame measured in Figure 2.2).

Consider that a $50,000 investment in REITs during that 20-year time frame would have grown to $330,311 while the same $50,000 invested in bonds would have turned into $120,585.

That, in one simple example, is why investors place so much focus on asset allocation, economic research, market forecasts, and the like. Picking the correct asset class, or mix of asset classes, can hold the key to financial success.

No wonder Wall Street churns out a constant parade of asset class forecasts!

No wonder the media talks breathlessly about the best or worst performing sectors!

Make no mistake: Buying the right sectors or asset classes can make an enormous difference in your investment returns and ultimately determine whether you achieve financial freedom.

A Twist in the Plot

Everything I wrote earlier is absolutely true. Some asset classes or sectors greatly outperform others. And choosing the winners will produce better results. But here's the interesting thing. Let's look again at that chart with the returns of the different asset classes and portfolio mixes.

This time, though, I'm going to add one bar to the chart. That bar, which you can see in Figure 2.3, represents the *performance of the average individual investor* across the past 20 years.

It turns out that it almost didn't matter what you bought over the past 20 years! Almost anything would have produced better results than what most people actually achieved!

Sure, buying real estate investment trusts (REITs) was better than buying bonds, and the S&P 500 did better than international stocks. But at the end of the day, buying and holding any of those would have outperformed the average investor's portfolio.

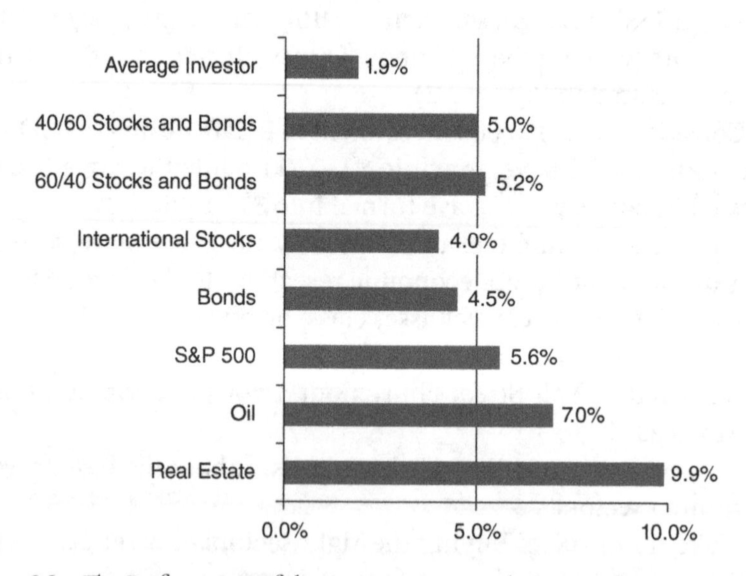

Figure 2.3 The Performance of the Average Investor (1999–2018)
SOURCE: Analysis by Brian Perry. Data from JP Morgan Asset Management & Dalbar, Inc.

The same holds true for asset allocations. Yes, different investors might want to have different investment mixes. And the asset allocation mix is one of the most critical decisions you need to make. But ultimately, *nearly any reasonable asset mix would have done better than the actual experience of the average individual over the past two decades.*

So, first I talked about the importance of asset allocation and selecting the best sectors or asset classes. But now I'm telling you it didn't matter what you bought, because almost anything would have done better than the average investor. So, what gives?

Time *in* the Market versus *Timing* the Market

The difference between asset class performance and investor performance comes about as a result of timing issues – namely, many people are getting in and out of sectors and markets at the wrong time, and all too often buying high and selling low. Moving in and out of the market and spending too much time on the sidelines prevents an investor from leveraging the most powerful tool at their disposal.

But what exactly is compound interest? Well, let's say you invest $10,000. One year later you've earned 10% on your investment, or $1,000. Now assume that in year two you also earn 10% on your investment. Have you earned another $1,000? No. You have in fact earned $1,100, because you earned 10% not only on your original $10,000 investment, but also on the $1,000 worth of gains you'd achieved in the prior year. (Please note that 10% annual returns year after year would be exceptional. I've selected that number simply for ease of math.)

This pattern would continue indefinitely; if in year three you again earned 10%, your dollar gain would come out to $1,210. Over longer periods of time, this compounding factor can produce truly immense gains.

In 10 years, $10,000 grows to $25,937
In 15 years, $10,000 grows to $41,772
In 20 years, $10,000 grows to $67,274
In 30 years, $10,000 grows to $174,494
In 50 years, $10,000 grows to $1,173,908

Figure 2.4 Growth of $10,000 with 10% Annual Returns
SOURCE: Analysis by Brian Perry.

For instance, using the initial $10,000 investment from the preceding example and assuming 10% annual returns, Figure 2.4 shows what your growth would look like.

As you can see, while the percentage returns remain consistent, wealth accumulates exponentially. That ability to convert small initial investments into vast sums reflects the power of compound interest.

That power in turn leads to a couple of important truths when it comes to organizing your finances.

First of all, time is your friend. The sooner you begin investing, the more likely you are to build wealth. In the earlier example, someone who had invested $10,000 shortly after graduating college would have accumulated more than $1,000,000 by their early 70s.

The second important takeaway is that compounding works in both directions. That same power that can build your wealth can also destroy it, if you allow yourself to become saddled with too much debt. The compounding effect of credit card, student loan, and other consumer debt can make it virtually impossible for some people to dig their way out.

The final takeaway is that, given that financial markets tend to go up more often than they decline, staying invested is vitally important. In other words, an investor needs to remain invested in order for compound interest to work its magic.

As we'll discuss in the remainder of this chapter, staying invested is something many individuals struggle to do. But for those who succeed, the rewards can be vast.

Why Are Las Vegas Casinos So Nice?

I need to be careful here in this section, because for many people, the idea that financial markets are similar to casino gambling strikes too close to home. So just to be clear in advance, I am not suggesting in any way, shape, or form that investing is akin to gambling. Speculating, short-term trading, and wading into markets you're unfamiliar with may very well represent a form of gambling. But long-term investing, when armed with knowledge and the intestinal fortitude to stay the course, represents a systematic endeavor with a high likelihood of success, which by definition is the exact opposite of gambling.

So, no, long-term investing isn't gambling. However, there is an important similarity between investing and gambling – namely, the importance of understanding probabilities.

Why are the casinos in Las Vegas and other large gambling centers so nice? Why do they have dancing fountains, rollercoasters, elaborate Egyptian or Parisian themes, or painted ceilings reminiscent of the Sistine Chapel?

The answer of course is that the reason casinos are so nice is that they can afford to splurge on decorations because they make a heck of a lot of money. Plus, the nicer or more elaborate the casino, the more likely people are to visit. And casinos, above and beyond all else, want to generate foot traffic to their location.

And why is that?

Well, it's because visitors might gamble, and gamblers, in the long run, *always lose money*. And when the gamblers lose money, the casino wins.

Yes, I realize that your Aunt Milly may have won $500 on a penny slot machine last week, and you may have had a good run at the blackjack tables last visit and gone home with an extra five grand in your pocket. Heck, sometimes casinos even get taken to the proverbial cleaners. Not that long ago, a group of high-stakes players went on a roll, and Wynn Casino in Macau lost $10 million! The loss was so large that Wynn was forced to disclose it publicly, because it had a material impact on their quarterly earnings.

But you know what? Despite the loss, Wynn opened its doors the very next day (or to be more accurate, the doors probably never closed in the first place). And Wynn would have been more than happy to invite those very same gamblers back at any point and give them another shot at winning big.

Why? Because while the probabilities don't mean that the casino is going to win every game, or every day, or even every month or year, they do mean that, *in the long run, the casino is absolutely, 100%, guaranteed to win. There simply cannot be any other outcome.*

After all, gamblers have the following odds on casino games:

- Roulette: 45%
- Slot machines: 35% (depending on the casino and game)
- Blackjack: 48%

Of course, that means that the house has the following odds on casino games:

- Roulette: 55%
- Slot machines: 65%
- Blackjack: 52%

So, if you're the casino, you stay open 24 hours a day, 365 days a year, come rain or snow or sun. Because the more you're open, the more people play, and the more you win.

The True Cost of Sitting on the Sidelines

The same principal applies in the stock market. Historically, stocks have risen on approximately 53% of trading days. The stock market has declined on approximately 47% of trading days. Of course, no one knows in advance which days stocks will rise, and nearly half the time they fall in value. Yet despite that fact, it still makes sense to stay invested, because over time, the odds are in your favor.

In a perfect world, an investor would participate in the market's upside while avoiding the downside. In this state of nirvana, the investor would perfectly time their moves in and out of the markets, thereby capturing the long-term upside while avoiding ulcer-inducing declines. The blissful investor would thereby meet their financial goals in a stress- and worry-free manner.

And that is precisely the goal of market timing, whose fundamental precept is to invest when markets are rising and then move to the sidelines prior to sharp declines.

Unfortunately, successfully timing the markets is an exceptionally difficult thing to do. After all, when markets are falling, how do you know if the decline will continue for six more months or if the rebound will start tomorrow? Similarly, although selling when markets seem overvalued might make sense on the surface, overvalued markets often continue higher for months or even years on end. And when the market does eventually decline, there is no guarantee that prices will fall below the level at which you sold in the first place.

And of course, a successful approach must be repeatable. And so, the challenge facing the market timer is not simply to move into or out of the market once or twice, but rather to do so again and again over the course of years and decades. And that ability to correctly anticipate when to buy and sell across different market environments, political regimes, and economic cycles, is very rare indeed.

If there were no cost to mistiming moves in and out, then perhaps the endeavor would make more sense. After all, a high-reward, low-risk strategy would be appealing. The problem, however, is that if your movements are anything less than perfect, market timing is one of the riskiest tactics you can employ.

That statement may sound odd. After all, isn't it risky to stay invested in an overpriced market that may eventually decline in value? Wouldn't prudently sitting on the sidelines make sense?

Well, for starters let's discuss two different types of investment risk. The first, and more commonly cited, is *volatility*. This is the figure you might see quoted in mutual fund reports or stock analysis websites. Commonly measured as standard deviation, volatility simply describes how bumpy an investment's path has been over time. And of course, the bumpier the ride, the more uncomfortable it is to hold on. This volatility is what many market timers attempt to mitigate by moving in or out of the market.

However, there is a second type of risk that I would argue is more dangerous than volatility. I'm referring to *shortfall risk*, which is simply *the risk that your realized investment returns fall short of the returns you require to meet your financial goals.*

This risk, in my opinion, is the far more important one. Think about it this way: if you go to Disney World, the route you take to get there and any delays you face along the way may very well impact the quality of your vacation. But wouldn't a far greater measure of how good or bad the vacation is simply be this: *Did you ever actually get to Disney World?*

Similarly, although you certainly want to minimize the bumps you face on your journey toward financial freedom, the far more important measure of success is whether you actually achieve that freedom. And that is why moving in and out of the market, with anything less than perfect timing, is so dangerous.

Consider two investors whom we'll call Jane and Tarzan. Both Jane and Tarzan started with $100,000. Both of them invested for

20 years. And most importantly, they both held exactly the same portfolio, allocated entirely to the S&P 500.

Jane put her $100,000 to work on day one and stayed invested through thick and thin for the entirety of her two-decade time horizon.

Tarzan did exactly the same thing, but with one important distinction. Tarzan sat out of the market for two months during that two-decade time frame.

Unfortunately for Tarzan, his timing was awful and those 60 days he missed out on turned out to be the best 60 days of the whole period. What kind of an impact do you think Tarzan's poor timing would have on his total investment returns, relative to Jane's total returns?

Jane stayed the course for the entire two decades and saw her $100,000 initial investment grow fourfold. On the other hand, Figure 2.5 shows that Tarzan missed the 60 best days during that period and saw his $100,000 drop by more than 70%! Keeping in mind that there were approximately 5,000 trading days during those 20 years, the difference between participating on 100% of

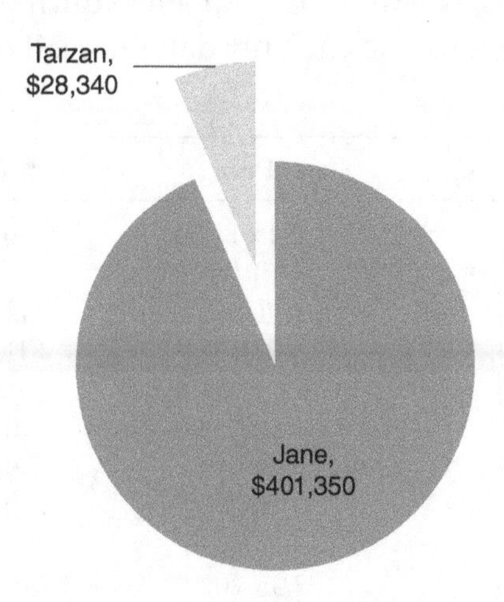

Figure 2.5 Growth of $100,000 Invested in S&P 500 for 20 Years
SOURCE: Analysis by Brian Perry. Returns provided by JP Morgan Asset Management with data from Bloomberg; time frame 1998–2017.

those trading days versus participating in 99% of those trading days was $370,000!

What do you think? Would an extra $370,000 one way or the other have an impact on the quality of your retirement? Again, keep in mind that Jane and Tarzan had the same time horizon and invested in exactly the same thing. The only difference was that Jane stayed the course and Tarzan did not.

Does Crisis Equal Opportunity?

Let me ask you a question: When do you think the best trading days have occurred? Have they been during robust bull markets as stocks powered ahead? Did those magic days come following great economic news or reports of strong corporate profits?

No, they did not. In fact, most of the best days have followed sharp declines. Take a look at Figure 2.6.

That list shows the 11 best trading days in the history of the S&P 500, as measured by percentage gain. Six of those days came during the Great Depression. Two of them happened during the global financial crisis. Two more happened during the depths of the COVID-19 pandemic. And the only date that fell outside of some of

Ranking	Date	% Gain
1	3/15/1933	16.61%
2	10/30/1929	12.53%
3	10/6/1931	12.36%
4	9/21/1932	11.81%
5	10/13/2008	11.58%
6	10/28/2008	10.79%
7	9/5/1939	9.63%
8	4/20/1933	9.52%
9	3/24/2020	9.38%
10	3/13/2020	9.29%
11	10/21/1987	9.10%

Figure 2.6 S&P 500 Largest Single-Day Percentage Gains
SOURCE: Analysis by Brian Perry. Data courtesy of S&P Dow Jones Indices LLC.

the worst economic periods of the past century came immediately following Black Monday. As a reminder, Black Monday represented the most cataclysmic drop financial markets have experienced, with major market averages down more than 20%. The important takeaway is that every single one of the 11 best trading days occurred precisely when the average market timer was perhaps most likely to be sitting on the sidelines.

And that brings me to another point. I've heard many people (presumably non-Chinese speakers) say that the Chinese use the same written character for both crisis and opportunity and that, therefore, "crisis equals opportunity." In fact, I used this slogan in dozens of presentations over the years before discovering that it is in fact not true. Nevertheless, there's merit to the concept so I'm sticking with it, because as investors, crisis *can* equal opportunity, and bad news can be your best friend.

When you are in the accumulation phase of your financial life, a crisis and the falling prices it presents allow you to accumulate additional shares while they are "on sale." In effect, falling markets help you to dollar-cost-average your portfolio, as your (hopefully) systematic contributions to retirement and other investment accounts purchase stocks at reduced prices.

The concept remains valid once you've retired and entered the distribution phase of your financial life. That is because you should be systematically rebalancing your portfolio during market declines, which means that you'll be selling assets that haven't fallen too much in value and using those proceeds to purchase additional amounts of the most beaten down assets. This is another form of dollar cost averaging, and although adhering to this discipline requires a level of mental fortitude, the results can be worth it, because the more stocks you can buy "on sale," the better off you'll ultimately be. And keep in mind that, even in retirement, many of your assets are ultimately earmarked not for next month or next year but rather for a decade or more into the future.

So, the next time there's blood in the streets and markets are in free-fall, try to take a deep breath, relax, and systematically rebalance your portfolio. Because individuals who do that, while staying the course with their stock exposure, ultimately have far better odds of meeting their financial goals than people who move in and out of the markets based upon recent price action.

Sadly, many people lack the discipline to set and follow an appropriate strategy, so let me repeat myself one more time: don't swim against the tide. Be disciplined. Let the long-term upward trend of markets propel you to your financial goals.

Or, instead, you could try to successfully trade based upon forecasts of what the future holds. So now let's shift our attention and take a closer look at how well that strategy has historically paid off.

Chapter 3
Guess What? A Forecast Is Just a Guess

Forecasting is very uncertain. Especially when it pertains to the future.

—*Mark Twain*

On October 4, 1957, the Soviet Union successfully launched Sputnik 1, the world's first artificial space satellite. The launch marked something of a turning point in public perception, as sentiment shifted toward a view that perhaps the Soviets had moved ahead of the United States in the race for technical and economic supremacy.

Of course, subsequent events proved otherwise. Sure, the Soviets managed comparable and sometimes even greater success than the United States in several areas, particularly around heavy industries such as steel manufacturing. But these surface victories masked, at least temporarily, the underlying cracks in the central planning system. Food shortages and breadlines, as well as an alarming lack of basic consumer goods, let alone "luxuries" like blue jeans, prompted social unrest, and eventually the complete collapse of the USSR.

But here is the really surprising thing about the collapse of the Soviet Union – no one saw it coming!

Literally every single forecast and analysis of what the world might look like going forward included the survival of the USSR and its continued competition with the United States.

Think about that for a moment. The collapse of communism was arguably the single most important geopolitical event of the second half of the twentieth century, and yet virtually no one saw it coming. Not the legions of PhDs at the world's greatest universities who'd made a career of studying Russian history or international affairs. Not the military hierarchy of the United States or NATO, whose job it was to closely track the enemy's capabilities. Not the State Department. Not the Treasury Department or Federal Reserve with their legions of financial experts. Not even the master spies of the CIA or MI6, whose lives revolved around trying to predict what was going to happen next in the Soviet Union.

That complete failure on the part of tens or perhaps even hundreds of thousands of the world's most intelligent, focused, and motivated people holds a valuable lesson for today's would-be superinvestors. And the lesson is simply this: *successfully forecasting the future is difficult, if not impossible, to do on a consistent basis.*

But Forecasting Is Fun

Ahh, forecasting. That glorious endeavor whereupon an ordinary person gazes deeply into the void and discerns the shape of things to come.

The prophet!

The seer!

What more wonderful and rewarding occupation could there possibly be?

Sadly, as I'll demonstrate, many economic and financial seers struggle to see past their very noses, and even those with a modicum of skill tend to struggle when it comes to timing and exactitude.

But first, let's be honest. There is something inherently empowering about pitting your wits against the masses and then proving that you, and you alone, are smarter than all the rest. Maybe it's a basic human condition, a little touch of hubris we all carry.

This basic human condition is exacerbated by the American ideal that everyone can be extraordinary. It's not for nothing that Lake Wobegon with its hordes of exceptional individuals has become such a successful archetype of the American psyche. Let's face it, in America anything is possible, which means that at times settling for average can feel a lot like losing.

The financial industry feeds on these twin desires to outsmart and outperform the masses. In fact, Wall Street has built an entire industry upon the basic premise that it is possible to accurately forecast the future. Brokerage firms issue buy and sell recommendations, as well as earnings estimates for individual companies. They also regularly forecast the level of the stock market or interest rates 12 months out. Pundits appear on television to opine on the future course of markets while enthralled viewers anxiously lean forward in their seats so that they might better internalize this sage advice.

Even the Federal Reserve has gotten into the act, publishing periodic updates and forecasts for future economic growth and inflation. Surely, the Fed, above all others, should be able to provide an accurate assessment, because, in addition to their legions of PhD economists, they have an additional advantage: they make the decisions that help shape the course of the economy. In sports terms, this would be like letting the starting pitcher forecast the score of his team's next game.

Given how enticing forecasting can be, as well as its popularity, let's take a look at how accurately various subsets of prognosticators have managed to predict the future.

Economists

The only function of economic forecasting is to make astrology look respectable.

—John Kenneth Galbraith

I love that quote. And it only gets better when you realize that the speaker was a long-time economics professor at Harvard, author of some four dozen books, and advisor to Presidents Roosevelt, Truman, Kennedy, and Johnson. The concept of one of the twentieth century's leading economists disparaging economic forecasting speaks to its difficulty.

Here's an example to validate Galbraith's quote. The *Wall Street Journal* regularly polls leading economists to ask their prediction on interest rates. The question is a simple one: Will interest rates be higher or lower 12 months from now?

Now while that question is simple, it is of course not easy. Fortunately, there are only two possible outcomes, and so a random coin flip allows for a 50% success rate.

Unfortunately, the world's leading economists aren't quite as accurate as a coin flip, boasting less than a 50% rate of accuracy. This lack of success is troubling, but the story goes deeper still.

In order to successfully time interest rates, you would need to get three things correct:

1. The direction (up or down) of rates
2. The magnitude of the move (how much higher or lower)
3. The timing of the move (or when it will reverse)

If you get all three of these things correct, you can successfully time interest rates.

But here's the kicker: *you actually need to get all three of those items correct twice* – once on the way out and once again on the way in.

Even if we allow for a 50% success rate on each of these decisions, the odds of correctly moving in and out still look daunting:

0.50 × 0.50 × 0.50 = 12.5% odds of moving out of market at correct moment

Multiplied by

0.50 × 0.50 × 0.50 = 12.5% odds of moving back into market at correct moment

Equals

1.56% odds of moving both out of and back into the market at the right times

Now obviously, to build a career around interest rate timing, you'd need to correctly move in and out of the market more than once. Given the preceding numbers, you can see that the odds of doing so are fairly prohibitive.

And remember, those are your odds if you're flipping a coin and getting things right 50% of the time. The world's leading economists, with decades of academic and professional training, are *less accurate than those random coin tosses.* That means that before you set out on this exercise you'd better have a good basis for thinking that you know more about the direction of the economy and interest rates than the world's foremost experts in the field.

Wall Street Analysts

It makes sense that this is where you have to go if you're looking for some successful forecasts. After all, the folks on Wall Street are smarter than most, work really hard, and have access to all available information. That's why they're paid so well.

Alas, even here we find that crystal balls tend to be muddy at best, and broken at worst. In fact, there have been studies that concluded that the stocks favored by analysts actually do worse than the overall market. For example, a recent academic paper with the exciting title of "Diagnostic Expectations and Stock Returns" reexamined and expanded upon prior research into the subject.

The study looked at analyst predictions made in December of each year, in order to measure how accurate those analysts' forecasts were. The forecasts were for a stock's performance over the ensuing three to five years, and the study covered 25 years of data. If you've been following your brokerage firm's buy and sell recommendation, the results of this research were depressing to say the least.

What the researchers found was that the stocks that the analysts were most optimistic about actually *underperformed* the stocks that they were most pessimistic about. In other words, *the stocks the analysts most wanted clients to buy did worse than the stocks they most wanted clients to sell*!

The performance differential between these stocks was startling. If you had ignored the analysts' forecasts and purchased their least favorite stocks, you would have earned a *15% return* the following year. If instead you had followed their sage advice, you would have earned *3%*. Making matters even worse, the analysts' favorite stocks also had more risk, were more volatile, and performed worse during market downturns!

So to summarize, if you want to take on more risk in your portfolio while also earning returns far worse than the market averages, you now know exactly how to do so. The key is simply to follow the buy and sell recommendations of your favorite Wall Street stock prognosticator.

If instead you'd like to get returns that are *five times higher* than those of the analysts' recommendations, and with less risk to boot, all you need to do is ignore what the stock forecasters say and instead buy their least favorite stock!

Let me soften this message slightly by saying that there is some value to Wall Street's stock research. That research might give you guidance into the company's financials and how the business is doing. Depending on the analyst's stance, reading such a research report can also help you evaluate an opinion contrary to your own so that you can make sure you aren't missing anything in your own analysis. This exercise can help you avoid a common behavioral trait known as confirmation bias, which we'll discuss in more detail later in the book.

But – and here is the key point – while there may be value to the *research,* the *forecast* is less than worthless. Numbers don't lie, and study after study has shown that Wall Street's stock analysts don't know, with any more certainty than you do, exactly what stock is going to do best next year.

Media Pundits

The impact of the financial media is important enough to have an entire chapter devoted to it later in this book, so for now I'll just point out one major problem with listening to media pundits (and here I'm including TV reporters, radio talk show hosts, newsletter writers, and other assorted public figures). The problem is simply this: even if the advice you get is correct, you may not be "tuned in" when the pundits revise their opinions and recommend a change in course.

For example, let's say you're watching a TV show and the host suggests selling XYZ stock at $50. And let's say you do so, and the stock does indeed fall in value, down to say $40. Great! You took what proved to be good advice and it worked out well for you.

But what if the TV host loves it now at $40, buys back in, and the stock goes to $75. Maybe the host never went back on the air to discuss XYZ. Or if he or she did, maybe you weren't tuned in that day. So, the result is that you sold a stock at $50 that is now trading at $75, which is not nearly as great.

The challenge just described is relatively unique to media pundits, who sometimes don't give you both sides of the story. Given that these folks also suffer from the same challenge all forecasters do (it's hard to predict the future), it makes sense to utilize media outlets for what they are intended for, which is information gathering or entertainment, rather than specific forecasts.

The Federal Reserve (the Fed)

The Federal Reserve is staffed by hundreds of PhD economists, all dedicated to tracking and steering the course of the U.S. economy. How well has this massive assembly of brains done at predicting the direction of the economy?

Well, fortunately, the Fed now publishes periodic estimates of future economic growth and inflation. We can then compare these forecasts to actual outcomes to give us a good look at exactly how accurate the Fed's forecasts have been.

As it turns out, the Fed's record has been mixed, at best. What makes this outcome particularly interesting is that the Fed not only forecasts future economic results, but subsequently plays a role in crafting those results, via its monetary policy. So, compared to other prognosticators, the Fed should have an even "easier" time successfully predicting the future, since it plays such a prominent role in shaping that future.

And yet we find that the Fed hasn't been particularly good at predicting things across time.

Now to be fair, there could be an element of gamesmanship to the Fed's forecasts. In other words, Fed forecasts play a role in public perception of both the economy and the future course of monetary policy. As such, the Fed may at times publish forecasts not solely in the interest of accuracy, but also to guide and shape public behavior as an additional tool of monetary and economic policy.

But despite this caveat, it does seem clear that the Fed has been no more proficient at predicting the future than the seers on Wall Street. The challenge the Fed forecasters face is similar to that encountered by all those who attempt to predict the future course of the economy and financial markets.

So, What's the Problem?

The first problem is that the economy isn't a closed science experiment with controllable variables. Ultimately, the economy is a collection of people, and the decisions those people make aren't always logical. For instance, how do you model out the following possibility: someone walks past a shop window and sees something she loves. It's an impulse purchase, but she decides she has to have it. So she goes into the store to buy it, gets up to the cashier, and discovers she accidently left her wallet at home. By the time she goes back home to get it, the urgency of the purchase has faded and she never buys what she saw in the shop window.

Or how about this one: someone has a good, secure job. It's Christmas time and tomorrow he is shopping for presents. That evening, he watches *It's a Wonderful Life*. He watches George Bailey nearly lose his job and his savings. This prompts irrational fear around all the things that could possibly go wrong with his own finances (remember, people don't have to be logical). The next day, Christmas shopping is scaled way back, just in case something bad happens at work.

Those are just two random possibilities, but the economy as a whole is made up of hundreds of millions if not billions of these sorts of decisions, so you can see how it's difficult to figure out what the end result might be.

Which brings us to the second big issue with forecasting. Chaos theory, or what is more commonly known as the Butterfly Effect, examines how small changes to complex systems can manifest unanticipated results. The term *Butterfly Effect* refers to a weather phenomenon, with the idea being that a butterfly flapping its wings in one corner of the world can prompt a chain reaction that ultimately leads to a devastating hurricane half a world away.

Of course, a butterfly isn't going to actually cause a hurricane, but the concept is what matters. This Butterfly Effect, or chaos theory, exacerbates all those decisions people make that are so difficult to predict. For instance, maybe because that consumer forgot her wallet and didn't make that purchase, the store went out of business and had to lay off its staff. Those unemployed workers then cut back their spending, which led to less economic growth elsewhere and so on. As you can see, trying to get an accurate handle on what is actually going to happen in the economy is a herculean task. Forecasters probably deserve a pat on the back just for trying!

But, even if they get an A for effort, the fact remains that forecasters, whether from the Fed, Wall Street, or elsewhere, mostly issue conversation pieces, rather than accurate estimates of what is actually going to happen. Use those forecasts as such, and your odds of meeting your financial goals will skyrocket.

The All-Star Team

But what about those shining stars who have gotten the big calls right, those famous folks who've successfully navigated uncertain waters and arrived at the promised land: the out-of-consensus, once-in-a-lifetime market call that turns out to be spot-on. How does the long-term track record of these modern-day prophets actually look?

Because, what could possibly be better than finding a seer who can warn you just ahead of a major market crash? I mean, wouldn't we all have loved to move to cash immediately before Black Monday in 1987 or right before housing collapsed and took the economy and financial markets with it in 2008 or before COVID-19 shut down the economy in 2020?

Believe it or not, there have been a fortunate few who've been skilled or lucky enough to predict such cataclysmic events. So, the question is, does it make sense to seek out this kind of advice?

For this advice to be useful, it must fit three criteria. First of all, it needs to be timely. Warning about an impending crash is useful if the advice is given immediately prior to the crash; moving out of the market months or even years prior to said event is a much less successful course of action. Here, the track record is mixed.

For instance, Meredith Whitney predicted trouble for the financial sector and the demise of Citigroup in October 2007. Her timing was nearly impeccable, and Citigroup declined more than 95% over the next 18 months. Investors in companies such as AIG and Lehman Brothers experienced similar results during that time frame. Elaine Garzarelli demonstrated similar timing when she predicted a stock market collapse the month prior to the 1987 Black Monday crash.

On the flipside, there are plenty of perennially pessimistic individuals (often referred to as "perma-bears") who have successfully predicted a sharp market decline, but who made their prediction so far in advance that you would have been better off ignoring their advice despite the fact that it eventually turned out to be correct.

Market seers also need to be able to tell you when to get back in. Advice to move toward the sidelines may be useful, but no one gets rich, or meets their financial goals, with a portfolio parked in neutral. So, the second key measurement of success is whether these legends not only warned people when to get out of the market, but also when to get back in. To the best of my knowledge, very few of the people that have gotten famous for predicting market collapses have ever correctly advised the public on when to get back into the market.

Finally, success needs to be repeatable. One-time calls might be the stuff of legend, but it takes repeated successes to build a fortune. So, what is the long-term record of some of the more famous market prognosticators?

This is where the trouble starts. Because the fact of the matter is that very few of the people who have gotten famous for a contrarian market call have been able to sustain that kind of success.

For instance, following her amazing prediction on Citigroup, Meredith Whitney started her own research firm in 2009. That firm closed in 2013. She then started a hedge fund, but that shuttered in 2015. Today, in addition to her 2007 Citigroup forecast, Whitney is best known for a 2010 interview on *60 Minutes* in which she forecast a massive wave of bankruptcies in the municipal bond sector. The result of that forecast was the polar opposite of her Citigroup call; municipal bankruptcies have been muted, and the sector as a whole has performed well.

The bottom line is that making an out-of-consensus call is a great way to get famous. Done correctly, you can also capitalize on your 15 minutes of fame and turn it into a lucrative career. But if you're looking for financial guidance that will help you meet your financial goals, you're likely going to need to be right more than once or twice in your lifetime. And sadly, even the most prescient of prophets have yet to demonstrate the ability to do that.

What Should You Do with Forecasts?

Hopefully, the last several pages have convinced you that predicting the future is difficult at best. What, then, should you do with all the information you gather about the state of the global economy and financial markets?

First of all, it's important to differentiate between strategy and tactics. Strategy is represented by your long-term financial plan, which is an outline of your financial goals and a roadmap for achieving those goals. Out of this will come your target asset allocation, or the mix of assets most likely to produce your required rate of return with the lowest possible level of risk.

Once you've established this target allocation, it should seldom change. Large-scale alterations to that allocation should generally come about because of changes to your goals or life circumstances (i.e., marriage, children, retirement, etc.). Market outlooks or forecasts should be incorporated, if at all, only at the margins. This is how institutional investors do it.

For instance, a pension fund might have a target mix of 50% stocks and 50% bonds. If they were optimistic about stocks, perhaps they would reduce their bond allocation to 45%, in order to slightly increase their stock holdings.

Contrast this with the behavior of many individuals, who, during a bull market, might completely abandon their bonds in favor of stocks. This is also true on the downside, with individuals panicking during market declines and fleeing stocks just when they should be buying.

So how can you avoid these mistakes? Well, instead of making wholesale changes to an allocation based upon your market outlook, consider smaller scale, tactical shifts.

Or better yet, utilize a disciplined rebalancing process for your portfolio. This practice forces you to sell what's gone up in value and buy what's declined in value, without relying on any guesses about what the future holds.

Huh. Buying low and selling high.

That sounds like a great game plan for long-term success, and one that will be discussed in far greater detail throughout this book.

Part II

If You Don't Know Where You're Going, You Probably Won't Get There

Chapter 4
You Must Know What Drives Investment Returns

Hopefully the previous chapter helped convince you that repeated attempts at forecasting markets likely wouldn't provide you with a path to investment success. With that in mind, let's explore some alternative methods for putting your money to work in the financial markets. We begin with a brief history lesson.

On December 31, 1975, Jack Bogle launched the First Index Investment Trust, a vehicle designed to track the performance of the S&P 500 *without trying to beat that index*. This innovation was originally lampooned by both the media and competitors, and was called "un-American" and "Bogle's folly." The chairman of Fidelity Investments at the time, Edward Johnson, was quoted as saying "I can't believe that the great mass of investors are going to be satisfied with receiving just average returns."

And yet today, a great mass of investors, both individual and institutional, has indeed piled into market tracking products, thereby sacrificing the opportunity to "beat the market." In fact, investors have moved something on the order of six trillion dollars into indexed products.

And why have they done that?

In order to answer that six-trillion-dollar question, let's start with a couple of questions I'd like you to answer for yourself.

Investment A: Would you be willing to invest your retirement account in something that has a 48% chance of success?
Investment B: Would you be willing to stake your family's financial future on something that has a 45% chance of success?
Investment C: Are you comfortable with an investment that has a 35% chance of success?

Okay, so the answers to the questions above are pretty obvious. If you are like most people, you probably aren't interested in any of those options, unless the reward for being right was far greater than the penalty for being wrong, which in these examples they are not.

Now let me ask another question with an obvious answer. Why aren't you interested in those investments?

Of course, the answer is because the odds of success are below 50%, which means that you expect to have a negative outcome from these investments. In fact, if you invest often enough, the negative odds mean that you'll likely lose a great deal of money.

The good news is that I'm not going to recommend that you pursue any of the preceding investment options. But in case you are curious about the list:

1. "**Investment A**" is blackjack.
2. "**Investment B**" is roulette.
3. "**Investment C**" is a slot machine.

The reason that you don't want to stake your future on a casino game is that the odds are heavily stacked in favor of the casino, and so the more you play, the less likely you are to win! By definition, that's not a great "investment"!

If you've followed me so far, let me throw out one more investment:

Investment D: Would you be willing to invest in something that has an 18% chance of success?

The correct answer to that question is a resounding "No!"

If you weren't willing to invest your IRA or 401(k) or children's college fund in a game of roulette with a 45% chance of success, why would you invest in something with odds far worse than that?

And what, you may be wondering, is that investment whose odds of success are only half that of a slot machine, and roughly a third of a roulette wheel or blackjack table? Well, you may be interested to know that *18% represents the percentage of actively managed stock mutual funds that outperformed their market benchmarks over a recent 15-year period.*

Eighteen percent! And in case you're thinking, "That's okay, I'll just focus on buying the winners," you should know that there is no evidence that the active funds that beat the market during one time period have the ability to do so during subsequent time frames.

You Can Beat the Dealer, But Can You Beat the Market?

Back in the 1960s, Edward O. Thorp wrote a seminal book called *Beat the Dealer*. In that book, Thorp laid out an approach to counting the cards in a game of blackjack. This card counting would shift the odds away from the casino and toward the player. In other words, when counting cards, time was a player's friend. The more he or she played, the more likely they were to come away a winner.

So, what happened?

Well, for starters, the book became a bestseller. And players able to incorporate the system were indeed able to shift the odds in their favor and beat the dealer.

Many did so. In fact, Bill Gross, who once ran the world's largest mutual fund, got his professional start as a card-counting blackjack player. Gross, and others, achieved varying levels of success.

But then what happened?

Since casinos remain some of the world's most lucrative businesses, and most players continue to lose money, you can probably guess what happened next. The casinos didn't like the idea that players had a statistical advantage, so they took steps to maintain their edge. They added more decks of cards to the blackjack table (the greater the number of decks, the more difficult it is to count cards). They "buried" cards, which simply means that rather than showing players every card, they hid some of the cards in each deck, in order to reduce the accuracy of the card counters.

And when all else failed, they simply banned the card counters from the casinos!

The result is that today, counting cards remains difficult, but not impossible. Some players do in fact manage to count cards successfully and tilt the odds in their favor. The problem, though, is that casinos track these players and ban them from the premises.

So, the players get more sophisticated, and sometimes resort to wearing disguises, fake noses and wigs and the like. But the casinos evolve, too, and with advanced cameras everywhere and facial recognition software in place, card counters have difficulty finding a table they can play at, even when disguised.

And that, my friends, brings us back to that startling statistic which demonstrates that over time less than one in five stock mutual fund managers have been able to beat their market benchmark.

It's Hard to Stand Above the Crowd in a Room Full of Tall People

One of the recurring themes of this book is the continued evolution of the financial markets. Whether due to the media, globalization, technology, broader access to data, the rise of the institutional investor, or any other factors, the bottom line is that financial markets today are perhaps the most competitive game on earth.

Remember, the skill of the blackjack card counters has not declined. In fact, their techniques have grown more sophisticated as they've taken to wearing disguises and working in teams. But the playing field of the casino has evolved, too, as cameras, software, and security guards combine to eliminate most if not all of the card-counter's edge.

The same holds true in the financial markets. I believe it is inarguable that the skill, resources, and dedication of professional investors have increased by leaps and bounds over the past three or four decades.

The problem is that the house has evolved, too. What I mean is simply this: in the short run, financial markets are a zero-sum game. When someone sells, someone else buys. When the price moves up or down, there is a winner and a loser. So, as the skill set and sophistication of all the players increase, it becomes more and more difficult for any one player to stand out from his peers.

And that, more than anything else, explains why most mutual fund managers fail to outperform their index. It's not that the fund manager isn't smart and talented. It's just that most of the other market participants are equally skilled. And so, it gets really hard to have an advantage over the other players. To use a silly example, it would be far easier for a basketball player to stand out in a high school game than in the NBA Finals.

So, What's the Solution?

Once we've established that it's really difficult to beat the market, what might an investor do to meet their financial goals? The solution, strange as it may sound, is to give up on *trying to beat the market* and start *trying to participate in the market.*

Maybe you're immediately saying, "Hold on, I don't want to sacrifice returns by just tracking the market!" Well, the good news (or the really sad news depending on how you look at it) is that by simply tracking the broader markets you'll find that your portfolio does better than the vast majority of investors.

In fact, over almost any reasonable time frame you measure, fewer than 20% of actively managed stock mutual funds outperform their indexes. That means that in all likelihood, accepting market returns means your performance will actually improve.

I want to be clear in stating that I don't think it's impossible to beat the market. Rather, my belief, which is supported by the evidence, is that beating the market is possible but extremely difficult to accomplish over the long run. There are managers out there with terrific track records. There are also some niche asset classes where indexing or broad market participation may not be practical or prudent.

But across the majority of the larger asset classes, the data is irrefutable: most active managers lag the market across time. And perhaps more importantly, even with regard to those managers who do outperform, it is exceptionally difficult if not impossible to predict in advance who they will be. Similarly, for those with strong track records, by the time they come to public awareness, their run of success may be at or near its end.

So, the bottom line is that if you are dead set on attempting to beat the market yourself or finding a manager to do it for you, then have at it. Just realize that you've set a difficult task for yourself, one at which most of the world's foremost experts fail.

If you reach the conclusion, based on the evidence, that market returns are your best option, you then have two choices of how to proceed. The first is to focus on market-tracking products such as index mutual funds or exchange-traded funds (ETFs). The second is to focus on mutual funds or ETFs that use a rules-based approach to gain broad market exposure to a given asset class.

We'll now take a closer look at each of those approaches in turn.

Indexed Products

As money has fled actively managed mutual funds over the past decade, much of it has found a home in indexed products. Regardless of whether you use a mutual fund or an ETF, the goal of any indexed vehicle is to track the returns of its index as closely as possible, and to do so at a low cost.

Costs matter, and you want to be cognizant of how much you are paying for your investments and what value you're receiving for your fees. By the same token, though, it's not all about minimizing costs. Your primary focus should instead be upon maximizing the value you receive relative to what you're paying.

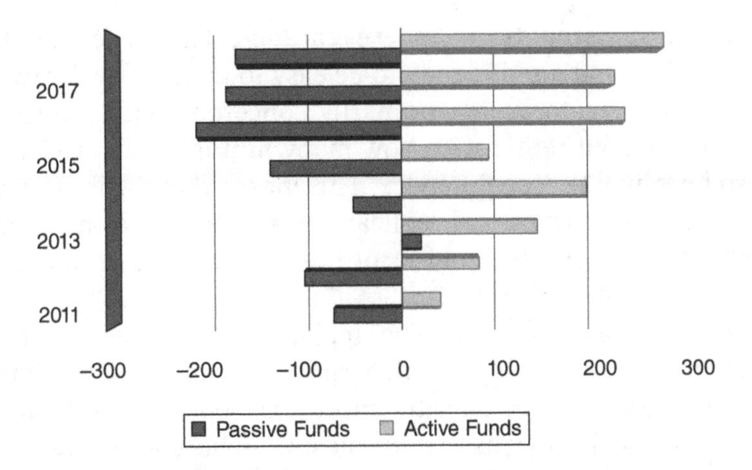

Figure 4.1 U.S. Stock Fund Flows (2011–2018)
SOURCE: Analysis by Brian Perry. Data sourced from Morningstar Direct. All figures are approximate.

After all, no one I've ever met has actively sought out the least expensive surgeon or the cheapest anesthesia prior to surgery. Similarly, investment fees matter, but don't forget to calculate the cost of not reaching your financial goals. I realize that it might be difficult to assign an exact monetary cost to not being able to send your children to college or having to work until the day you die because you cannot afford to retire. But we can all agree that the cost of those outcomes is exceptionally high from a quality of life and family perspective.

As I mentioned earlier, in addition to low costs, the primary benefit of an index fund is that it closely tracks its index and provides index-like returns. And the majority of active mutual funds underperform their indexes. So, by definition, the performance of many index funds is going to be superior to the performance of many actively managed mutual funds.

Voila! It's as simple as that. As Figure 4.1 shows, lower costs and higher returns have proven to be a successful recipe for driving flows into indexed products. Go figure!

For the reasons stated earlier **I think indexed products are great and can serve as a key foundational component of many portfolios**. However, there are a couple of drawbacks when it comes to indexed products, which I'll now discuss.

- **Index construction:** Indexes are created by commercial providers and are designed to be easy to track. In other words, an index creator is not primarily concerned with returns for investors, but rather with how many mutual funds, ETFs, and so forth will license the index. This means that the index needs to be easy to track and replicate. In practice what happens is that smaller or less liquid securities wind up underrepresented in commercial indexes.
- **Indexes are "dumb":** The majority of indexes are based on market weightings, which simply means that the largest securities or issuers have the most representation in the index. For stocks, this means that the most valuable companies get the highest weighting. In practice what occurs is that many indexes wind up being dominated by a small subset of their constituents with a disproportionate weighting. As an example, the Russell 3000 is a decent proxy for the broad U.S. stock market, and is comprised of three thousand small, mid-, and large-size U.S. companies. But in practice, the top 100 of those companies make up more than half of the index while the bottom 2,900 make up less than half the index. This approach might be fine when the largest companies are driving market returns, but it is less optimal when smaller corporations are outperforming.
- **Indexes can be gamed:** Indexes are based upon rules that determine what securities are appropriate for the index. Over time some securities that are in the index will no longer be appropriate while others currently outside the index will evolve to where they should be included. This process is known as reconstitution and, depending on the index, might happen on a quarterly or annual basis. The challenge is that because the index is rules based, people can estimate ahead of time what securities are likely to be added or deleted from the index.

But remember, index funds need to track the index as closely as possible, which means that they need to add new securities on the day the index adds them and sell old securities on the day they leave the index. Active traders can game this by buying or selling ahead of the index reconstitution. This can result in temporary price spikes and drops on the securities indexes need to buy or sell, which can slightly harm performance across time. One potential solution to this dilemma is a more flexible trading or reconstitution approach, which some indexes and funds are working on.

- **Style drift:** One final challenge indexes face is also related to the reconstitution process, and that's what is known as style drift. Basically, this means that you sign up for an index product with a set of characteristics, but between day one and the next rebalancing, the index contains securities that no longer fit the definition of the index. This may not sound like much, but with some indexes as much as 10% of the holdings may be "inappropriate" for the index prior to reconstitution.

Although I've just laid out some of the challenges indexes face, I want to reiterate that none of these mean that indexed funds and ETFs are not good products. On the contrary, *indexed products are a great way to build a portfolio, and can be building blocks for your financial success.*

Now let's take a look at the alternative to indexes, which is a rules-based approach to gathering broad market exposure.

A Rules-Based Approach

Trying to "beat the market" by timing its ups and downs is exceptionally difficult. Similarly, finding mispriced securities that are poised to increase in value is an endeavor at which few succeed.

Yet despite these long odds, the basic premise of active, assumptive management makes sense. The idea that an investor should overweight those securities with higher expected returns is a fundamentally sound concept. The problem, then, isn't the goal but, rather, the most common approach to achieving that goal.

The vast majority of market participants, upon setting out in their quest for superior returns, begin with an attempt at forecasting the future. And although forecasting the future may not be impossible, it is certainly quite difficult. And yet, like explorers headed into a vast and dark jungle, many investors plunge ahead into the darkness, convinced that their intuition, tools, or techniques will guide them into the light.

What these individuals fail to realize is that other explorers have ventured into the jungle ahead of them, and in doing so they've hacked out trails and left maps to guide today's voyagers. Now certainly, over time these trails can become overgrown and the maps outdated, so there is no guarantee our new explorers will safely navigate their way through the wild. But, *even if success isn't guaranteed, wouldn't our bold adventurers be foolish to ignore the clues their predecessors have left behind?*

It seems to me, then, that the sensible approach when seeking out superior returns isn't to try to blaze a bold new trail through the jungle, but rather to follow the route others have traveled with demonstrated success. In other words, while we can't be sure this route will work for us, we are certain *this route has worked for someone.* And if you ask me, I'd prefer a trail that has worked in the past and seems likely to work in the future over a stab in the dark at muddling my way through the unknown.

So, what if there was a way to combine the low costs and broad market representation of indexing while also incorporating efforts to overweight securities with more attractive risk-and-return characteristics?

Well, it turns out that in some cases such an approach does exist.

This approach, which I'll refer to as "rules-based," attempts to marry the best attributes of indexed products with the basic premise that there are some securities likely to perform better over time.

What is a rules-based approach?

There are a number of terms used for what I'm calling a "rules-based" approach. Some other common names for this approach include "factor based," "smart beta," and "enhanced indexing." Regardless of the name, the basic concept is the same. Rather than tracking a commercial index based on market weightings, rules-based vehicles follow formulas that determine how they will be invested and what securities will be included.

A simple example of a rules-based fund might be an S&P 500 fund that allocates its holdings equally, rather than by market capitalization. A more sophisticated example might be a large company stock fund that holds similar securities to the S&P 500, but which allocates its capital according to how "cheap" each company's stock is. In other words, the largest position would be in the stock that has the lowest relative price, and the smallest position would be in the stock with the highest relative price. The theory there would be that less expensive stocks tend to perform better across time.

Rules-based strategies can be accessed through both mutual funds and ETFs. One of the first and largest providers of these rules-based funds was Dimensional Fund Advisors, which offers a suite of mutual funds available primarily to institutional investors. Other firms with a quantitative, rules-based approach include the large hedge fund (and now mutual fund provider) AQR Capital Management, and Bridgeway Capital Management. More recently, large brokerage firms such as Charles Schwab have added rules-based vehicles to their suite of offerings, because the approach has increased in popularity and gained more widespread acceptance.

As with indexes, a rules-based approach will generally offer broad market representation. However, because they aren't measured solely by how closely they track an index, a rules-based vehicle can avoid some of the challenges indexed products face. For instance, rules-based managers might have more flexibility around trading, so they don't have the same degree of style drift and aren't as subject to pricing volatility around index reconstitution dates. Rules-based approaches can also hold any securities that "make sense" for their approach, rather than simply concentrating on those in a commercial index (and remember, the goal of an index isn't maximum returns, but rather ease of tracking).

At the same time, a rules-based approach will attempt to overweight securities expected to outperform their peers while underweighting or avoiding those expected to underperform their peers.

Remember, though, a rules-based approach by definition isn't relying on future forecasts. How then do they go about attempting to identify the "best" securities? It's simple really. Instead of attempting to peer into the hazy future, they instead learn from what is already known, by relying upon empirical research into past returns to identify securities that may outperform.

The key principle is that a rules-based approach begins with the same fundamental basis as indexing (low cost, broad market representation, no attempt to predict the future) but then attempts to add value through design enhancements intended to overcome some of the drawbacks of index construction while also utilizing empirical data gained from decades of academic research.

Fundamental Factors for Success

In the investment world, there are securities that have demonstrated superior returns across time. These securities share certain characteristics, which seem to contribute to these superior returns. And so, rather than guessing at the future in an effort to generate returns, I instead propose careful study of the past to identify the investments that historically have shown the greatest likelihood of success.

These characteristics, which I'll call factors, have been found through rigorous academic research and empirical analysis. In all, researchers have found over 300 factors that enhance security performance, but I suggest dismissing all but a few.

If we are going to consider a factor worth investing in, it needs to have a couple of characteristics. First of all, it needs to have a long track record. In other words, just because something has worked for a year or two doesn't indicate to me that it is likely to work into the future. Maybe it will and maybe it won't. I just don't know. But if on the other hand a factor has proven reliable across many decades, then I know its success isn't just a product of a specific market or economic environment.

Secondly, I'd like to see a factor that has worked in multiple markets and across multiple countries. For instance, if something works for U.S. large-growth stocks, but hasn't demonstrated success anywhere else, maybe it's just an anomaly. But if the factor has proven successful in U.S. large, medium, and small stocks, then maybe it's telling me something more. And if that success carries beyond U.S. shores to Canada, Germany, Japan, Thailand, or a host of other countries, then I'm more likely to think that maybe there is something to this characteristic that lends itself to security outperformance.

Finally, before I decide that I want to tilt a portfolio in the direction of a factor, that factor needs to make some sort of intuitive sense to me. In other words, the numbers are what they are, but even if the numbers indicate a positive relationship, I'm not going to invest unless the concept seems logical. As an absurd example, statistics might indicate that there is a correlation between sunspots and stock market movements, but I'll never invest based on what I see after staring at the sun!

With all that in mind, let's take a look at a couple of factors that seem to have contributed to security outperformance over the long run.

Stock Market Factors

Value Factor: Over time, value stocks have outperformed growth stocks. Some readers may find this surprising, since it might seem like a company that is growing quickly should have a stock that performs better. But investing success is largely a result of the price you pay, and often rapidly expanding growth stocks are simply too expensive. By definition, value stocks are less expensive than growth stocks, and this has led to superior performance over time.

Furthermore, value companies should provide higher returns than growth companies because they carry more risk. Their industries may be in decline or their business model may be dated. And relative to growth stocks, companies that fall into the value category may carry more debt on their balance sheet, have lower profit margins, or demonstrate slower revenue growth.

Think about it this way. If two borrowers go to the bank to take out a loan, will the borrower with perfect credit or the borrower with a low credit score get a better rate of interest? The answer of course is that the borrower with a low credit score will pay a higher interest rate. Phrased differently, the *expected rate of return to the bank will be higher for the loan to the less-creditworthy borrower*.

To be clear, I am talking about the entire market when I discuss value stocks or growth stocks; the performance of an individual value or growth company can vary widely, and there are plenty of growth companies that soar and plenty of value companies that sink into bankruptcy. But if we look at the entire cohorts, value has outperformed growth.

Here, according to Investopedia, are the definitions of growth and value stocks:

Growth Stocks

As the name implies, growth companies by definition are those that have substantial potential for growth in the foreseeable future. Growth companies may currently be growing at a faster rate than the overall markets, and they often devote most of their current revenue toward further expansion. Every sector of the market has growth companies, but they are more prevalent in some areas such as technology, alternative energy, and biotechnology.

Most growth stocks tend to be newer companies with innovative products that are expected to make a big impact in the market in the future, but there are exceptions. Some growth companies are simply very-well-run entities with good business models that have capitalized on the demand for their products.

Value Stocks

Undervalued companies can often provide long-term profits for those who do their homework. A value stock trades at a price below where it appears it should be based on its financial status and technical trading indicators. It may have high dividend payout ratios or low financial ratios such as price-to-book or price-to-earnings ratios. The stock price may also have dropped due to public perception regarding factors that have little to do with the company's current operations.

For example, the stock price of a well-run, financially sound company may drop substantially for a short period if the company CEO becomes embroiled in a serious personal scandal. Smart investors know that this is a good time to buy the stock, because the public will soon forget about the incident and the price will most likely revert to its previous level.

Of course, the definition of what exactly is a good value for a given stock is somewhat subjective and varies according to the investor's philosophy and point of view.*

*https://www.investopedia.com/articles/investing/080113/income-value-and-growth-stocks.asp.

What has this outperformance looked like over time? We have good data going back to 1928, so let's pretend that an investor had put one hundred dollars into the stocks of large U.S. companies at that time. Our investor didn't attempt to identify one particularly great company; they just bought the whole basket. Shortly after investing, the stock market crashed in 1929, followed by the Great Depression, Word War II, JFK getting shot, Watergate, the tech bubble and meltdown, the financial crisis, COVID-19, and a host of other major events. There was war, famine, upheaval, and a host of other plagues both at home and abroad. And, of course, there were good times, too, and bull markets and the like.

And our investor didn't do anything that whole time. She just stayed the course with her investment in large U.S. companies. Now to be clear, a few of the companies in her universe did well and prospered. But many did poorly, and some disappeared entirely. And so over time some companies faded away and were replaced by new entrants. And the whole time our investor just stayed the course, content in owning a slice of corporate America.

As a reminder, her "slice" of corporate America was focused on large companies. And her slice included both growth companies and value companies.

How much money do you think our investor would have now? Remember, she invested one hundred dollars back in 1928 and then just stayed the course. And now she would have ...

$600, 000

That is a lot of money, from an investment of only one hundred dollars. And that is the power of capitalism at work, as the growth of the economy and corporate earnings drove stock prices higher over time.

But what if instead of buying the entire large company universe, our investor had instead concentrated on large company stocks that also fall under the value umbrella? How do you think our investor would have done in that scenario? Would she have done better or worse?

Well, if she had invested the same one hundred dollars back in 1928, but instead had placed it in an index of large value companies, instead of $600,000, she would have ...

$1, 300, 000

That's more than twice as much money! So over time, value stocks have produced significantly higher returns, and built a lot more wealth, than the broader market.

Small-Company Factor: Another factor that has demonstrated strong performance for a long period of time is the small company advantage. Using the same data as the preceding scenario, since 1928 small-company stocks have outperformed large-company stocks. This, too, seems logical. Smaller companies have newer and less proven business models, so the risk of investing in them is greater than investing in larger, more established firms. Furthermore, "trees don't grow to the sky," and practically speaking there are limits on the growth of companies that are already huge. Smaller companies don't face that constraint.

Picking individual stocks in the small-company space would be an especially risky proposition, given the greater uncertainty these companies carry. But again, the goal isn't to pick individual winners. Instead, it's to buy the whole space, getting broad representation across the small-company universe.

Let's go back to 1928 again, except this time, instead of investing her one hundred dollars in the large companies, our investor correctly anticipates that small companies will outperform in the long run. How much would her investment have grown to?

Well, if she invested in the entire small-company universe instead of the entire large-company universe, she'd have turned her one hundred dollars into ...

$2, 700, 000

More than four times the return from the large stocks! So over time, small stocks have produced significantly higher returns, and built a lot more wealth, than larger stocks.

If smaller companies have historically outperformed larger companies, and value stocks have outperformed growth stocks, what do you think would have happened if our investor had combined those two factors and purchased **small value stocks**?

Do you think she would have wound up with more or less money?

If you guessed more, you're right. And not just a little bit more, either. It turns out that if our investor had concentrated her holdings in small-value stocks, her one-hundred-dollar investment back in 1928 would have turned into ...

$7, 800, 000

Amazingly, even though large U.S. companies posted strong returns and fantastically multiplied her initial investment, if she'd been more selective in the types of stocks she purchased, she could have wound up with more than a dozen times more money!

Remember, those additional gains didn't come by picking the best stocks but, rather, by *identifying the right kind of stocks and then buying all of them.*

Interestingly, this is similar to what the most famous investor of all time has done. Studies have demonstrated that although Warren Buffett buys individual stocks and companies, the majority of his gains have not been achieved through picking the right stocks and companies. Instead, the bulk of Warren's amazing success has come about because he was selecting the right kinds of companies and stocks to purchase. In other words, it wasn't primarily that he was a great fisherman (though to be fair he is a really good one) but rather that he was fishing in the right pond!

That conclusion doesn't take away from Warren Buffett's genius or detract at all from his remarkable track record. After all, he was smart enough to find the right ponds to fish in, and then he became a really good fisherman. Those are two things very few investors have ever accomplished.

But shifting the narrative does provide a different lesson for readers to take away from Buffett's success. If instead of trying to find the **best stocks** to buy, individuals instead identify and purchase the **best kinds of stocks**, their odds of success skyrocket. Buffett himself alluded to this, in a famous speech he once gave at Columbia University. In that speech, titled "The Super Investors of Graham and Doddsville," Buffett talked about how so many of the investors with the best long-term track records employed similar strategies and techniques.

And what were those strategies and techniques? Well, primarily that *they tended to focus on value stocks, and usually didn't buy the largest companies around.*

Is it too good to be true: Of course, as with anything in life, there are caveats to everything I've just discussed. For starters, in any given time period, there is no guarantee that small companies or value companies are going to outperform. What you might get are better returns over time, but not every time.

Take a look at the two charts in Figures 4.2 and 4.3, which show how frequently the small and value premiums have outperformed over different time horizons. Figure 4.2 demonstrates how often value stocks have outperformed growth stocks.

Figure 4.3 shows the frequency with which small companies have outperformed large companies.

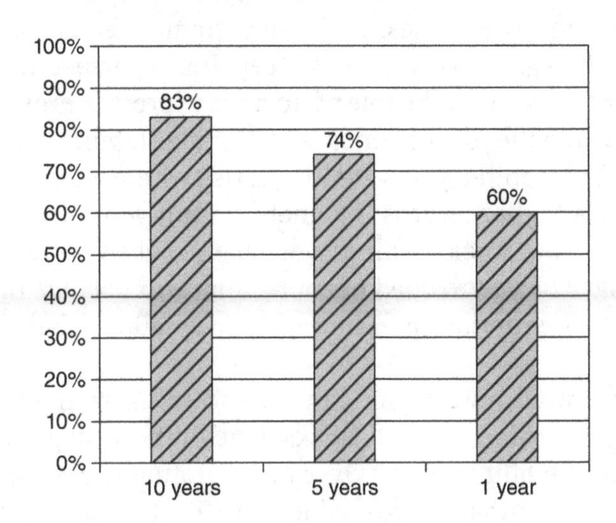

Figure 4.2 Frequency with Which Value Outperforms Growth
SOURCE: Based on data from Dimensional Fund Advisors.

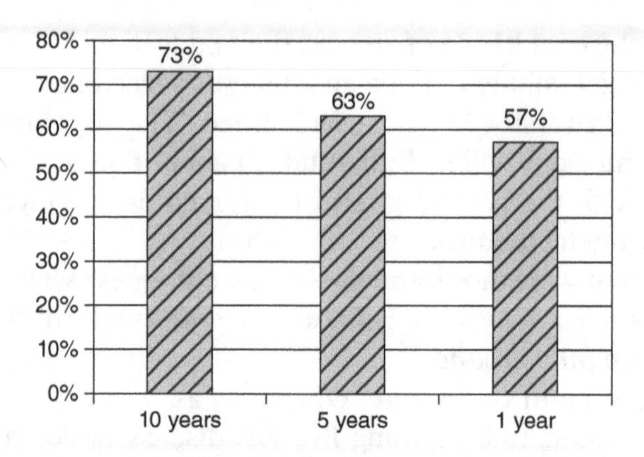

Figure 4.3 Frequency with Which Small Outperforms Large
SOURCE: Based on data from Dimensional Fund Advisors.

As you can see, there is no guarantee that small companies, even over long periods of time, will do better than large companies or that value companies will do better than growth companies. But the odds suggest that, at least historically, the longer your time horizon, the greater your odds of success, and that's about all you can hope for when it comes to investing.

Another caveat is that small companies generally carry more risk than large companies, and value companies generally have more risk than growth companies. Keep this in perspective, though. At the most basic level, the role of stocks is to provide growth to your portfolio while the role of bonds is to provide stability and income.

With that in mind, you want to take risk where it can be compensated for via higher returns – namely, within your stock portfolio. So, if within your stock holdings, you take a slightly more aggressive stance, that's okay. Provided of course that you balance this out by holding an appropriate measure of high quality, relatively stable bonds.

There are also steps you can take to mitigate the inherently greater risk of value or small stocks. One of those steps is to incorporate a profitability screen. Over time, profitable companies tend to perform better than unprofitable ones. That sounds obvious, but the problem is that in a search for profits, many investors overpay for the companies that produce them.

The key is to still fish in the value and small company universe, where prices are inherently more reasonable, and then to apply a profitability screen in order to weed out the garbage and overweight the better companies. Doing this can help you avoid some of the companies that are cheap for a reason (i.e., they are losing money or about to go under) and make sure you are buying reasonable businesses at attractive prices.

So, there you have it. In your stock portfolio, focus on securities with higher expected returns over time – namely, smaller companies and more value-oriented companies. And then use a profitability screen to narrow your focus further toward quality companies at attractive prices.

Bond Market Factors

Term Premium Factor: Let me ask you a question. What do you think entails greater risk: Lending someone money for 30 days or lending them money for 30 years? The correct answer is 30 years.

Why? Well for starters, there is greater uncertainty of repayment over 30 years. If you lend a creditworthy borrower money for 30 days, the odds of their finances deteriorating so badly in just a month that they can't repay you are fairly low. But a lot can happen over the course of three decades. In municipal bond land, Detroit went from the auto capital of the world to bankruptcy in roughly that length of time. In the corporate bond space, think of once mighty titans that no longer exist: Eastern Airlines, Pan Am, Kodak, Radio Shack, Blockbuster, the list could go on.

Another source of uncertainty when it comes to long-term investments is inflation. Because principal and interest payments on many bonds are fixed, the possibility of inflation eating away at the value of those payments is a significant concern. And the longer a loan is outstanding, the greater the possibility that the economic environment changes, and that inflation takes more of a toll than initially expected.

Finally, lending money for a long period of time involves opportunity risk. Opportunity risk refers to the possibility that while your money is locked up for 30 years earning say, 4%, new loans become available that would yield 6%. However, you cannot access those loans because you're locked into your existing contract.

For all these reasons and more, longer-term bonds (and remember, a bond is really just a loan) tend to be riskier than shorter-term bonds. And if you accept that lending money for a long time is riskier than lending for a shorter period of time, then it makes sense that a lender should get paid more for taking on the added risk.

And it turns out that longer-term bonds generally provide higher returns than shorter-term bonds. There are exceptions to this, and in certain environments shorter bonds may provide higher returns than longer bonds. However, these tend to be the exception that proves the rule, and we will focus here on the circumstances that prevail 90% of the time.

But just because you can get paid more for investing in longer-term bonds doesn't mean you should invest as far out as possible. As it turns out, there is a sweet spot when it comes to where you want to invest.

The Yield Curve: The term *yield curve* refers to a graph depicting the yield that bonds of various maturities produce. For example, you could take all different maturities of Treasury bonds (3 months, 6 months, 1 year, 2 years, 3 years, 5 years, 10 years, and 30 years) and then plot their yields. You then draw a line connecting those points, and that gives you your yield curve.

The yield curve then shows you how much additional compensation you can receive if you invest in bonds of longer maturities. The steeper the curve, the greater the amount of additional yield you receive as you buy bonds of longer and longer maturities.

The shape of this curve varies greatly over time and can be very steep or quite flat. Sometimes the curve is even inverted, which means that shorter-term bonds pay more interest than longer-term bonds. But the most common shape, which can be seen in Figure 4.4, resembles something like an upside-down fish hook, with the steepest part of the curve represented from approximately one to 10 years, and the curve then flattening out from there.

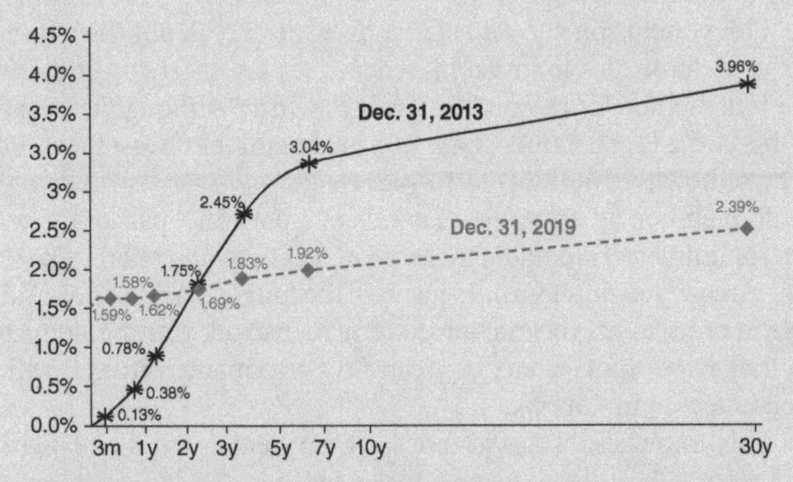

Figure 4.4 U.S. Treasury Yield Curves (Year-End 2013 and Year-End 2019)

SOURCES: FactSet, Federal Reserve, J.P. Morgan Asset Management, Guide to the Markets (`https://am.jpmorgan.com/us/en/asset-management/gim/adv/insight/guide-to-the-markets`). U.S. data are as of December 31, 2019.

Professional bond traders and managers focus closely on the yield curve and there are a variety of strategies they employ depending on the curve's current and projected shape. But for the purposes of this book, simply remember that there is a benefit to investing where the yield curve is steep, because you are receiving more compensation for each incremental unit of risk you take.

Do you notice anything on the chart in Figure 4.4? One obvious takeaway is that the 2013 curve is steeper in the beginning and then flattens out beyond 10 years or so. On the other hand, the curve from 2019 is relatively flat. Because longer maturities equal more risk, as you move left to right across the graph you are taking on additional increments of risk. *The important takeaway then is that the steeper the curve, the more compensation you are receiving for each additional unit of risk you take on.* So, for instance, in 2019, bond investors were receiving less compensation for taking on risk than they were in 2013.

This conclusion should lead an investor to seek out the optimal range of maturities to invest in, where they are receiving attractive levels of income for reasonable levels of return. Although the shape of this curve is constantly changing, in general that *sweet spot* tends to be somewhere in the 1- to 10-year range.

Remember, when you own bonds in a portfolio, part of the reason for doing so is to add a measure of safety to your portfolio. For that reason, you don't want to just buy the longest-term bonds available in order to get the maximum return. Instead, you should focus on that sweet spot, where you can find reasonable returns with a moderate amount of risk.

This emphasis on the steepness of the yield curve is one reason that global diversification may make sense in the bond market as well as the stock market. The ability to scour the globe for regions demonstrating the greatest reward for the term premium can be a significant advantage. Bonds are a little bit different than stocks, and so with global bonds I often recommend using a currency-hedged approach. This simply means that your foreign bonds are hedged back into U.S. dollars. Doing so will greatly reduce the volatility of your investment (this currency volatility is less impactful in the stock market, so using currency hedges for your foreign stocks is often not necessary).

Note: If you invest in global bonds through a mutual fund, you can search for one that hedges its currencies. Both hedged and unhedged vehicles abound, so make sure to choose wisely.

So, there you have it: one way to receive attractive returns in the bond market is by focusing on the term premium factor. But in doing so, you'll want to be cognizant of the risk you are taking, and make sure to appropriately balance the risk and return in your bond portfolio.

Credit Premium Factor: The second way to generate returns in the bond market is via the credit premium factor. "Credit premium factor" refers to the fact that the less creditworthy the borrower, the higher the expected return for lending them money.

This makes sense of course; a less creditworthy borrower is less likely to pay back a loan under the terms laid out. Here we are talking about the bond market but this also holds true with consumer loans. Just imagine two potential homebuyers visiting their local bank for a mortgage. The individual with pristine credit is going to get a significantly lower rate than the borrower with a low FICO score and a recent default on their credit report. The bond market works the same way.

It makes sense that if you buy bonds issued by less creditworthy issuers, you'll get a greater potential return than if you invest in bonds from very highly rated issuers. Similar to FICO scores, the bond market has its own system for rating the safety of borrowers, which can be seen in Figure 4.5. Bonds rated AAA thru BBB are

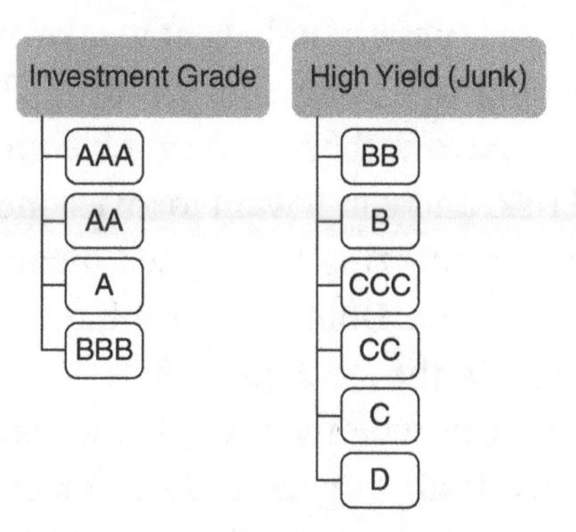

Figure 4.5 Standard & Poor's Bond Rating Scale
SOURCE: Analysis by Brian Perry. Information courtesy of Standard & Poor's.

considered Investment Grade and are generally of high quality. Bonds rated BB or below are considered high yield. High-yield bonds are also sometimes referred to as junk bonds.

Again, remember that the role of bonds in a portfolio isn't simply to generate returns, but also to keep your money safe and provide diversification from your stocks. Lower rated bonds can be riskier than highly rated bonds, and their prices can be more closely correlated to stock market movements. This correlation ("correlation" refers to how closely linked the movements of two assets are) can reduce the diversification benefits you are seeking.

So, you need to strike a balance between risk and return when it comes to incorporating the credit risk premium. There are two keys when doing this. First of all, in many situations the majority of your bond holdings should be concentrated in higher rated, investment-grade issues because they provide greater diversification than lower quality bonds.

The second thing to remember is that successful investing is all about balancing risk with reward. In this context, that means that you'll want to take the most credit risk when it provides the most reward. Credit risk is measured by "spreads," which are a way of comparing the return of a bond with the risk-free Treasury rate.

As Figure 4.6 demonstrates, these spreads tend to vary quite a bit. When this spread is wide, you'll want to take on more credit risk, because you are being well compensated for it. On the other hand, when the spread is narrow, there isn't much compensation for taking on additional risk, and you'll want to invest more conservatively. In other words, when utilizing these fixed income premiums, you also want to focus on value. Doing so can enhance your risk-adjusted returns, just as it can in the stock market.

But remember, even when you are being relatively aggressive, make sure you keep it all in perspective. For many investors, the role of bonds remains safety, diversification, and income; don't lose sight of those first two goals in your quest to maximize your returns.

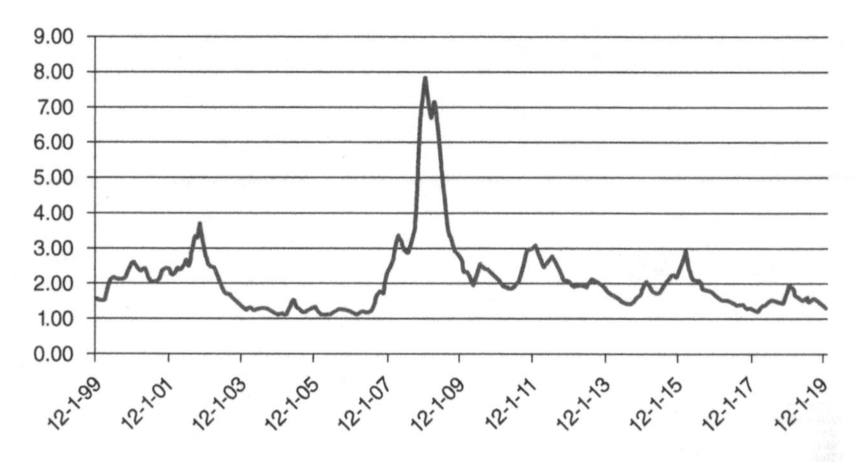

Figure 4.6 Corporate Bond Option-Adjusted Spread (OAS) from 1999 to 2019
SOURCE: Data courtesy of Federal Reserve Bank of St. Louis (ICE BofAML US Corporate BBB Option-Adjusted Spread, Percent, Monthly, Not Seasonally Adjusted).

The Bottom Line on Factor Premiums

There you have it: factors that have historically led to higher returns in both the stock and bond markets. Again, tilting your portfolios to capture these premiums doesn't guarantee that you'll outperform the broader market. But, as opposed to speculating about what the future might hold, following an approach that has historically worked makes sense to me.

Empirical research and common sense have shown that focusing on securities with certain characteristics has led to strong returns over time. And given that these factors have proven successful for many decades, it seems reasonable to expect that these characteristics might continue to enhance portfolios into the future.

Chapter 5

You Must Have a Specific Financial Goal

In order to achieve financial success, you need to begin with the end in mind. And the more precisely you can define what that end looks like, the more likely you are to reach your desired outcome. Once you've crystalized your financial goal, you need to plot out the necessary steps to achieve that success and consider how each of the steps you take will impact other facets of your finances. Finally, you need to put your plan into action, and adjust as appropriate over the course of your working career and retirement. Get all this right and you can achieve victory, in the form of a successful and prosperous financial future. But fail at any of those tasks, and your future may not look so bright.

Success begins with planning, so this is the part of the book where I sound like an annoying teacher as I remind you, "Failing to plan is planning to fail." Yes, I realize that you've probably heard something similar before. And yes, the concept is self-evident. And yet, when it comes to their finances, the vast majority of individuals fail to plan appropriately.

Think about that for a moment. Almost no one you know would head out on a summer road trip without at least some sort of planning in place. At the very least, people usually have a destination in mind! Not to mention a map or GPS to tell them how to get where they want to go. And they usually have a general sense of how long it will take them to reach their destination, and what they'll do when they get there.

And then, when it comes to something that will determine the quality of approximately one-third of their years on this planet, those same people don't plan at all! In fact, many of them don't even know what their destination is, let alone how long it will take to get there, or what things will look like when they arrive.

I'm talking of course about retirement. Statistics show that the average American retires in their 60s and lives well into their 80s. Given increasing life expectancy, for many retirees the golden years may last three or four decades.

A 35-year retirement, for someone who lives into their mid-nineties, represents a third of their time on this planet. And the entire course of those years will be determined by financial decisions that person makes in the years leading up to retirement. Sadly though, many people fail to make any decisions at all, and fewer still follow a practical approach to defining and planning their retirement goals.

With that in mind, let me walk you through a process that should allow you to determine, with a reasonable degree of accuracy, what retirement will look like for you and what you need to do to get there. The following approach is not as precise as completing in-depth financial planning where you map out future cash flows, expenses, taxes, and the like. But it does represent a good starting point and completing this exercise will at least give you a sense of whether you're on track to retire.

Step One: Determine Your Vision of Retirement

The first step in the retirement planning process is to determine what type of retirement you want to have. This may seem obvious, but many, many people fail to complete this basic task. Oh, sure, they know they want to "retire" someday, but they lack a clear vision of what that might look like. For many busy professionals, the result is a lack of satisfaction early in retirement, as the day-to-day challenges of the workplace give way to an open schedule and empty calendar. To be fair, many of these people do eventually find productive and enjoyable outlets for their time and energy, but wouldn't you rather get started on the right foot immediately, rather than enduring a lengthy transition process?

Furthermore, determining what sort of lifestyle you want in retirement can have important financial planning implications. Think of the following questions:

- When are you planning to retire?
- Where are you going to live? Are you going to stay in your current home? Are you going to move out and downsize? Are you planning to relocate to a new city, state, or country?
- Are you going to work part-time in retirement? If so, is it for personal satisfaction or because you need the extra money?
- Do you have children or grandchildren you want to move closer to or visit regularly?
- Do you want to travel more? If so, what does that look like and how much will it cost?
- Do you have new hobbies or activities you plan to pursue?
- What about volunteering? Is that something you always wanted to do?
- How is your health? Do you expect to have a long and healthy retirement, or for some reason do you have cause to suspect that health concerns may play an issue in your retirement?
- Does your spouse or significant other share your views on these and other important lifestyle issues? Have you even discussed them together?

Things can change over the course of a lengthy retirement, but having some vision of your end goal will help your planning process immensely. At the most basic level, doesn't it make sense to have an idea of *when you want to retire*? And wouldn't the rest of those questions have an impact on *how much money you'll be spending in retirement* or *how long you'll need your retirement funds to last*?

So just to reiterate, the first step in retirement planning is to come up with a vision for what your retirement will look like, and the clearer that vision is, the better your chances of bringing your dream to fruition.

Step Two: Determine How Much You Spend Today

I personally don't believe that it's necessary to calculate exactly how much you spend on lattes, dry cleaning, movies, and so forth. If you want to do so, or if it helps you stay on track, that's fine. But when it comes to determining how much you spend today, the important thing is to get the big picture right.

How much do you spend on housing, cars, utilities, and the like? And don't forget about the "oneoffs" that seem to recur pretty much all the time. Be honest, you may not go on that cruise to Alaska again, but you're likely to go *somewhere*. And while a new car for you may be a one-time purchase, your spouse may need a new car in two years. And at some point in the future, maybe you'll upgrade again. The same holds true for home repairs and even home improvements. One-time purchases are by definition one time, but you should try to incorporate them into your spending and average them out. For instance, if you spend $30,000 on a new car every six years, you spend an average of $5,000 per year on new cars.

Again, the key is to get an estimate of how much you spend. The more accurate you can be the better. If you're not sure, here is a simple exercise. How much income did you have last year? You probably know the answer to that. How much did you pay in federal, state, local, and Social Security taxes? You can get that off of your W2 form or tax return. Finally, how much did you save? You can figure this out by looking at your brokerage, retirement account, and savings account balances. Did they go up or down? By how much? (Don't forget to subtract market gains or add back market losses as you do this. You are only interested in determining your contributions and withdrawals.)

Once you know how much you made, what your taxes were, and how much you saved, you also know how much you spent, because the answer is simply this: **Your income minus your taxes minus your savings equals your spending.**

It's that easy. Money comes in. Some of it goes to the government in the form of taxes. Some of it (hopefully) gets saved. Whatever is left over got spent, unless there is a giant hole in your pocket, which I'm guessing there isn't.

Note: The only additional complication is that if possible you should try to separate your spending on liabilities (mortgage, car loans, student loans) from the rest of your spending. The easiest way to do this is to figure your total spending, then subtract out your spending on liabilities, which should be easy to calculate. You'll see why we do this when we get to Step Four.

Step Three: Determine When You Want to Retire

This step is as straightforward as it sounds. The date you come up with doesn't have to be written in stone, but you need to have at least a rough idea of when you'd like to retire from full-time employment.

Note: If your intention is to "work forever," then in Step Three you should instead choose a date for when you want to achieve financial independence. In this case, financial independence would mean that you no longer have to work for money and instead have the choice of whether you want to continue working.

Step Four: Determine How Much Income You'll Need in Year One of Retirement

Okay, now you know how much you are spending today, and when you want to retire. Let's put those two together to determine how much you will spend your first year of retirement.

To start, take the number of years until you retire and figure out the impact of inflation over that time. Inflation has historically been around 3.5%, so that's a good number to use. An online calculator or Google search of, say, "cost of living adjustment 15 years from now with 3.5% inflation" should give you that impact. So can most handheld calculators or an Excel spreadsheet.

If retirement were in 15 years, you would need to increase your spending by a factor of 1.67-fold in order to maintain the same standard of living. Importantly, you only apply this inflation increase to your nonliability spending. Fixed liabilities like a mortgage shouldn't increase with inflation over time, which is why we separated those out in Step Two.

Say you spend $100,000 today, and $20,000 of that is your mortgage payment (the other $80,000 is nonliability spending). If you wanted to calculate your spending 15 years from now, you'd multiply 1.67 × $80,000 to come up with $133,600, and then add the $20,000 mortgage payment on top of that. (For this exercise your mortgage only includes principal and interest. If you escrow taxes and insurance with your monthly payment you should include them with "regular" spending, since they could increase with inflation.)

By the way: If you plan to retire prior to age 65, you won't be eligible for Medicare. So unless you have attractively priced continuing medical coverage from your former employer, don't forget to add in the cost of private medical insurance. Prices on these policies vary widely, but in many instances they can run $1,000 a month or more for each person in your household. Even worse, the cost of these policies has historically increased at a faster pace than the general rate of inflation. So the bottom line is that medical insurance, and how you'll pay for it, is an important consideration if you plan to retire prior to Medicare eligibility.

So, there you have it. A $100,000 lifestyle today will cost $153,600 upon retirement 15 years from now, based upon the preceding example. Of course, everyone's particulars are going to be a bit different, but the exercise remains the same.

A Note About Spending in Retirement

There is a pervasive belief that spending tends to decline in retirement. The thought is that you cut back on spending for commuting, clothes, and keeping up with the Joneses.

For some people this is true. For instance, some studies estimate that 41% of Baby Boomers have zero dollars saved for retirement. Sadly, those individuals will likely have no choice but to cut back on their retirement spending, because they don't have any money to spend.

But for those who have accumulated some retirement savings to augment Social Security, or those with strong pension income, my experience, as well as the experiences of my colleagues, has been that the idea that people spend less in retirement **is fundamentally not true**.

This makes sense. Think about it this way. If you are currently working, ask yourself: Do you tend to spend more money during the week or on Saturdays? When do you play more golf, do more shopping, take more day trips, engage in more hobbies, do more yard or home projects? For the vast majority of people, the answer to that question is of course, Saturdays, for no other reason than that they have more free time on the weekend.

Well, guess what? Once you retire, every day is Saturday! And particularly earlier in retirement, people tend to engage in all the activities they never had time for while working, so spending tends to increase. I call those the Go-Go years, and that is the time when newly retired folks are traveling more, visiting their kids or grandkids, taking up new hobbies, buying an RV, and trying to improve their golf games.

(*continued*)

(*continued*)

At some point of course, you might get tired of traveling. Or you might accept that it's not the golf clubs, the golf balls, the golf course, or the weather. The truth of the matter is that golf is just hard, and you aren't very good at it. And so you throw your clubs in the lake, quit the game, and slide somewhat gracefully into the Slow-Go years. Maybe you stay home a bit more, read a few more books, and generally take it easy. Spending might even decline during this period.

So, what follows the Slow-Go years? Why, the No-Go years of course! You probably know someone at this stage of life. They've given up snowboarding and dirt biking, and maybe even more mellow activities like going out to eat or to the movies. So you'd think spending would be pretty low. And you're right. Spending in the No-Go years tends to be pretty low across most categories of expenses.

But if you know anyone in their late 80s or 90s, they (or their caretakers) probably wear grooves into the asphalt driving endless loops to a couple of particular destinations.

Where are they going?

They're going to the doctors. They're going to the pharmacy. They're going to physical therapy.

So, just at the point when most other spending declines, medical expenses tend to increase significantly.

Of course not everyone follows the pattern I've described. But I've seen it enough that my best advice is to assume you'll spend as much, if not more, in retirement. If it turns out you spend less, so what. Then you'll have to figure out what to do with the extra money.

And that's a significantly better problem than running out of money midway through your retirement, because the job market for folks in their 90s isn't very good, and doesn't appear likely to improve anytime soon.

Step Five: Determine Your Sources of Retirement Income

Will you receive a traditional defined benefit pension when you retire? What about Social Security or other government-sponsored income sources? Do you own rental properties that will provide you with cash flow?

Congratulations! These fixed income sources represent money you'll have coming in each year in retirement and will reduce the amount you'll need to withdraw from your savings and investments.

For some folks, the goal isn't complete retirement, but rather stepping back from a career they are no longer passionate about. Maybe the work has grown dull, or you just want a little less stress in the office. Maybe you still want to work, but on your own terms and at your own pace. Perhaps 40 or 50 hours a week no longer fits your lifestyle, but 20 or 30 hours can keep you engaged while leaving time to pursue your passions.

If any of these applies to you, you'll also want to consider any income you generate from working. Importantly, you'll need to keep in mind that though you may enjoy your new work, you're unlikely to do it forever. Even the best of us often reach a point where we are physically unable to work. With that in mind, my advice is to include income from your new employment for the first portion of your retirement, but to also run the numbers with that income sliding off during the later stages of your life.

Step Six: Determine How Much You'll Need from Your Savings and Investments

Once you've completed Step Five and determined the aggregate amount of fixed income you'll have, subtract it from the retirement spending number you came up with in Step Four. The remainder is the amount you'll need to withdraw from your accumulated savings in order to fund your retirement lifestyle.

In Step Four, we hypothetically determined that our retiree would need $153,600 the first year of retirement. If we further assume that in Step Five our retiree had $75,000 a year coming in from Social Security and pensions, they would need to generate the difference ($78,600) from their portfolio in order to live their desired lifestyle in retirement.

Step Seven: Determine a Sustainable Distribution Rate

The term *sustainable distribution rate* refers to the rate at which you can draw down your portfolio without running out of money before you run out of breath. To use extreme examples, a 70-year-old pulling $500,000 a year from a $1,000,000 portfolio (a 50% distribution rate) is obviously going to run out of money well before they reach average life expectancy. On the other hand, if that same individual were only withdrawing $10,000 a year from that same portfolio (a 1% distribution rate) it seems quite likely that their money would last for the remainder of their lifetime.

Anytime you are making forecasts, there is, of course, an element of uncertainty involved. Nevertheless, a sustainable distribution rate can be calculated with some degree of accuracy by engaging in cash-flow planning, which involves running simulations that model your income, expenses, taxes, inflation rate, and investment returns for each year of your projected life expectancy.

A simpler though less accurate method of determining a sustainable withdrawal rate is to use a rule of thumb. The most common rule of thumb is that a portfolio distribution rate in the neighborhood of 4% gives a retiree a high probability of not running out of money. There are numerous assumptions that go into this, and opinions vary as to the accuracy of the 4% number. Some argue that 5% may be sustainable, as long as investment returns are reasonably strong. Others postulate that 3% is a better number, particularly if you retire earlier or have a longer life expectancy.

For the purposes of this book we'll stick with the 4% estimate, but do keep in mind that it could be a bit too high in some circumstances, whereas for others a portfolio may be able to withstand a distribution rate slightly north of 4%.

Step Eight: Determine How Much Money You Need to Retire

All right, now the rubber hits the road and we come up with the number you've been waiting for: *How much money do you need in order to retire*?

The answer to this vital question is actually quite simple to calculate if you've been following the steps laid out in this chapter. All you need to do is take the annual amount of income you need from your portfolio, which we calculated in Step Six, and divide that by your sustainable distribution rate.

Our hypothetical retiree in Step Six needed $78,600 per year from their retirement account. So, we'll divide that by a sustainable distribution rate, which we'll assume to be 4%.

$78,600/.04 = $1,965,000

So, our retiree needs just under $2,000,000 in savings in order to be able to live the lifestyle they desire in retirement, with a relatively high degree of confidence that they will not run out of money or need to reduce their standard of living later in life.

Step Nine: Determine Your Plan to Accumulate the Money You Need to Retire

This is a chapter on planning, after all, and so now that you've determined exactly how much you need to retire, you'll need to come up with a plan to accumulate that amount. The bad news is that, in the earlier example, $1,965,000 is a lot of money. The good news is that you won't need to save that entire amount.

If you properly invest the money that you save, market growth and compound interest will play a large role in accumulating the amount you need. In fact, depending on when you begin to save and invest, and when you plan to retire, it may turn out that you only need to save half, or even a quarter, of the total amount.

That is because, at a growth rate of 7%, $500,000 invested for 10 years will grow to approximately one million dollars. In 20 years, a $500,000 investment growing at 7% would turn into approximately two million dollars. That is the power of compound interest, and it is why one of the most important steps in planning for any financial goal is to properly invest your savings.

The key point is that once you've identified the amount you need for retirement, you'll want to evaluate where you're at today, and then come up with a game plan for getting to where you want to go.

Remember, failing to plan is planning to fail! But the good news is that if you follow the steps laid out in this chapter and summarized in Figure 5.1, then at least you have, for perhaps the first time in your

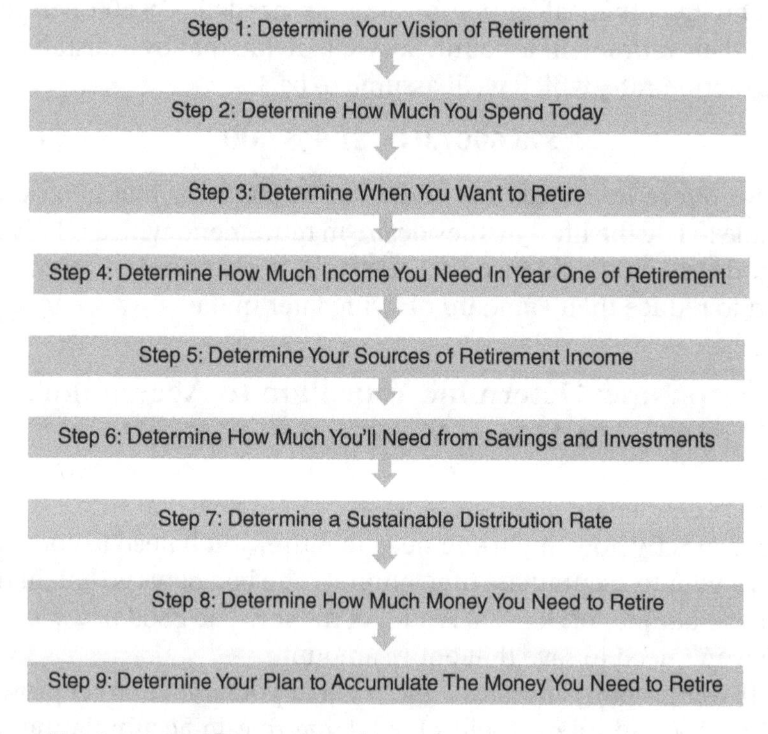

Figure 5.1 Summary of Retirement Planning Steps
SOURCE: Analysis by Brian Perry.

life, a clear vision of what your destination actually is. And having that clarity around your goal is a vital necessity if you're going to achieve success.

Putting It All Together with a Step-by-Step Example

Because correctly identifying how much money you need is such an important element of your financial planning, I'd like to review this process again using a step-by-step example.

For this exercise, let's use a hypothetical married couple named Susan and Bob Smith. Bob is 57 and Susan is 54. Bob makes $120,000 a year working as an engineer, and wants to retire at age 67. Susan is a teacher making $65,000 a year, and would like to retire at the same time as Bob. They live in a home they own, valued at $600,000, with 17 years left on their mortgage. Given this profile, let's run through the steps Bob and Susan should take in order to determine how much money they will need to retire.

Step One: Determine their vision of retirement: To begin, Susan and Bob will sit down together and discuss exactly what they want from retirement and how they want to spend the next three or four decades of their life. Let's assume that they have this conversation and decide that they want to stay in their current home, and that neither wants to work once they retire from their full-time jobs. Instead, they'd prefer to travel more, and Bob would like to improve his golf game while Susan wants to explore volunteer opportunities.

Step Two: Determine how much they spend today: Susan and Bob do not keep a strict budget, and to begin, they do not know how much they are spending each year. But they do know that their combined incomes are $185,000 per year. They also know, from looking at their tax returns and pay stubs, that last year they paid $50,000 in taxes, spread across federal, state, Medicare, and Social Security. Furthermore, Bob contributed the maximum allowable amount to his 401(k), which at the time was $24,000. Susan didn't quite max out her retirement plan, but she did contribute $14,000. The Smiths also have a savings account they've been building up, so they check last year's beginning and ending balances. At the start of the year, the balance was $85,000 and at the end of the year the balance was $105,000. So they saved $20,000 there. When we combine the retirement accounts and savings account, we get:

$24,000 + $14,000 + $20,000 = $58,000 in total savings

The Smiths earned $185,000, paid $50,000 in taxes, and saved $58,000, which means that the difference, or what they spent, was $77,000. However, upon closer inspection, the Smiths also have a credit card that they carry a balance on, and last year that balance increased from $12,000 to $22,000. That $10,000 increase represents additional spending, so we need to add it to the previous figure to get:

$77,000 + $10,000 = $87,000 in total spending

So, the Smiths have now determined that they spend $87,000 per year. Furthermore, by looking at their mortgage statement, they have determined that $24,000 of that spending comes from their monthly mortgage principal and interest (P&I) payments. The remainder, or $63,000, represents spending on everything else. This breakdown will be important in Step Four.

Step Three: Determine when they want to retire: This one is important, but in the case of the Smiths, easy to determine. They are both quite clear that they want to retire in 10 years. Of course, things can always change and many people wind up retiring earlier or later than planned, which is why ongoing financial planning and the ability to adjust according to circumstances is so important. But for the purposes of this basic exercise, we'll assume the Smiths do indeed retire on schedule.

Step Four: Determine how much they will spend in year one of retirement: The Smiths now know that they are currently spending $87,000 a year, and that they want to retire in 10 years.

They also know (because they read this book!) that using an estimate of 3.5% for annual inflation increases is a reasonable assumption. So, they do some math and calculate that 3.5% inflation, compounded over 10 years, increases their cost of living by a factor of 1.41.

The Smiths apply this factor to their nonmortgage spending, which in Step Two they determined was $63,000 ($87,000 total spending minus $24,000 for principal and interest payments). When they multiply 1.41 times $63,000, they come up with $88,830. This represents their spending in year one of retirement, on everything other than their mortgage P&I. They then add the mortgage P&I back in, but *do not inflate* those amounts, because for most people one of the benefits of home ownership is that it "fixes" a portion of housing costs so that they are not subject to inflation.

Once they've done the math, the Smiths come up with $88,830 + $24,000 = $112,830.

That figure, $112,830, represents the amount that the Smiths can expect to spend the first year of their retirement.

Step Five: Determine their sources of retirement income: Bob has been paying into Social Security his entire career. He logs onto the Social Security website and determines that his projected annual award at age 67 would be $32,000. Of course, he has options around when to take Social Security and there are pros and cons to each choice, but for this exercise we'll assume Bob takes Social Security at his full retirement age of 67. Susan has mainly worked as a teacher, and has not paid into Social Security. However, as a teacher she is eligible for a pension. She speaks with her HR administrator and determines that her annual pension if she retires in 10 years would be $17,000 per year.

So, between Bob and Susan they have $32,000 + $17,000 or $49,000 in annual income scheduled to come in during retirement.

Step Six: Determine required portfolio distributions: In Step Four, the Smiths determined that they'd need $112,830 the first year of retirement. In Step Five they figured out that they would have $49,000 coming in from Bob's Social Security and

Susan's pension. The difference, or $112,830 – $49,000 = $63,830, will have to come from their accumulated savings and investment portfolio.

Step Seven: Determine their sustainable distribution rate: As previously discussed, 4% is a general rule of thumb for a sustainable spending rate. Since the Smiths are retiring at a relatively "normal" age, they decide to use the 4% number, but they understand that they will have to monitor that and adjust as necessary.

Step Eight: Determine how much money they need to retire: Now Susan and Bob need to figure out how much money they need to retire. They'll start with their projected portfolio withdrawals for the first year of their retirement, which in Step Six they determined was $63,830. Then they'll divide that number by 4%.

So, $63,830/0.04 = $1,595,750.

That amount, $1,595,750, is the amount the Smiths should accumulate prior to retiring in 10 years if they want to have a high probability of not running out of money while living a similar lifestyle to what they enjoy now.

Step Nine: Determine their plan to accumulate the money they need: The final step Bob and Susan will take is to formulate a plan to get to that $1,595,750 they need to retire. Their plan going forward will take into account the savings they've accumulated so far, projected savings in the years to come, and reasonable investment growth rates. Then they'll take a look and see if they are on track or not. If it appears that they'll have a bit more than $1.5 million in 10 years, then great! They are on track.

If it looks like they'll have a significant surplus, they can consider retiring earlier or enhancing their lifestyle. If, on the other hand, they're coming up short, then Bob and Susan will need to have a further discussion and make some difficult choices. Possible solutions to a projected shortfall might include:

- Retiring later
- Cutting expenses and saving more today
- Working part time in retirement
- Altering the projected retirement lifestyle, such as by spending less or relocating

In reality, when faced with a potential retirement shortfall, the optimal solution depends on individual priorities, but usually involves some combination of the aforementioned options. The important point is that it's better to know about a potential shortfall, because it can then be managed or corrected. Sticking one's head in the sand is seldom a successful strategy, regardless of how hopeless your finances may feel.

Already Retired?

What if you're already retired? Does this exercise apply to you? Well, if you're already retired you can reverse engineer the preceding steps in order to determine how much money you can spend each year without running out. Basically, you add up your fixed income sources and then add in 4% of your accumulated savings.

The concept is the same, it's just that you aren't working anymore and so the amount of your accumulated savings is locked in. So rather than starting with how much you *want* to spend, if you're already retired, you start with how much you have and then figure out how much you *can* spend.

The Bottom Line

The bottom line is that financial success, like anything else in life, requires careful planning and implementation. The good news is that it really isn't that hard to crystalize your vision of what you want from your finances, or to create a roadmap to get you to your destination. Then, when life happens, as it inevitably will, you'll have a plan to fall back on in order to see if you're still on track. You'll also have a compass to measure your progress against, one that is far more relevant to your future than some arbitrary conception of the market. Best of all, when you combine a clear vision of your goals with careful planning and periodic checkups, taking a long-term approach while ignoring the chaos around you becomes far, far easier.

Chapter 6
You Must Invest to Meet Your Goal

The previous chapter's exercise for specifically identifying your financial goal is vital to the planning process, because if you don't have a clear vision of what you're attempting to accomplish, you'll find that it is nearly impossible to craft an appropriate approach for getting where you want to go. However, as you just learned, specifically targeting your financial destination really isn't that hard to do. Better still, once you've identified and clarified your financial goal, the next step logically falls into place.

Basically, after you determine how much money you need to accumulate and distribute, you'll need to build a portfolio to accomplish your goals. Building that portfolio can be as simple or as complicated as people want to make it. The approach that follows does have a dash of science behind it, but the real focus is on making it as logical as possible.

Remember, once you build out your portfolio, you're immediately going to walk into a financial haunted house. Financial boogeymen and other nasties are constantly going to jump out and surprise you, trying to get you to abandon your carefully constructed plan. The media and the public at large aren't evil, and they aren't out to ruin your finances. But even when they have the best of intentions, the end result of the mayhem around you will be to make it extremely difficult for you to stay the course.

That's where the logic comes in. Having a portfolio that *makes sense* can help you hold on when times get tough and your emotions threaten to get the best of you.

With that in mind, it's time to go deeper and explore the process of building and implementing your investment portfolio.

How Much Money Do You *Want* to Make?

Question: How much money do you want to make?

Answer: As much as possible!

If I were to ask 100 people how much money they want to make from their investments, I'm pretty sure most would respond with the same answer. But is that actually the right answer?

I'd like to suggest that you *do not actually want to make as much money as possible from your investments.*

I know. I know. I'm a blasphemer, and you're probably about to burn me in effigy right now. But bear with me a little longer.

Of course, on the surface it's obvious that you'd want to make as much money as possible. Who wouldn't? But let's dig deeper on this.

What if I gave you two choices? The first choice is an investment that *should* make you 15% returns over time. The second investment *should* make you 5% returns. Naturally, you prefer the 15% returns, particularly if your neighbor and your co-workers are all getting 15%. Because it would feel dreadful to know that you aren't doing as well as all your friends. You must, of course, keep up with the Joneses in all things.

But what if I also told you that the first investment is going to experience nausea-inducing ups and downs and that there will be times when you're spending your retirement worried about whether you'll have to go back to work because you lost all your money? Would that first investment still sound like a good idea?

Imagine, too, that in the scenario just described you don't actually need to make 15% in order to maintain your retirement lifestyle. Sure, it would be nice to see your portfolio balloon in value. But it's not necessary for it to do so. And therefore, those sleepless nights of financial uncertainty are also unnecessary.

Would you still want that 15% investment?

How Much Money Do You *Need* to Make?

There is a logical progression in the steps you must take to achieve financial independence. For instance, you must first identify and clarify your financial goal and determine how much money you need to meet that goal. That information in turn will guide you to one of the most important figures in determining your financial future: your **required rate of return**.

A required rate of return is simply the minimum return on your investments that you must achieve in order to meet your financial goal. In other words, it tells you **how much money you need to make.**

At the most basic level, there are two types of risk you face when investing. The first is known as shortfall risk. *Shortfall risk* is simply the risk that you don't generate sufficient returns to meet your financial goal. In other words, this is the risk that you run out of money. I'd strongly argue that shortfall risk is the greatest danger you face, because ultimately the measure of any journey's success is whether you reached your destination.

In order to avoid shortfall risk, you must generate returns equal to or greater than your required rate of return. If you do this, you'll meet your goal. If you fail to do this, you'll fall short of your goal. It's as simple as that.

Your returns need to meet your required rate of return. In other words, that required rate of return tells you how **much money you need to make**.

Note: The required rate of return is a figure that you need to average over time. In any given year, or even over the course of several years you are unlikely to generate returns that exactly match your target. Some years your returns may be greater and in others your performance may trail your required rate. Depending on how you are invested, there is a high probability that sometimes your returns will be negative, maybe even substantially so.

This is okay. You don't need to meet your required rate of return every year. You simply need to average that number over the course of years and decades.

Here is an interesting stat to demonstrate just how much your returns are likely to deviate from your long-term goal. Over the past century, the Dow Jones Industrial Average has returned roughly 8.5% per year. However, it turns out that there was actually only one year in which the return was between 8% and 9%. In fact, there were only five years in which the annual return was anywhere between 7% and 11%!

The takeaway is that financial markets are volatile and fluctuate greatly. Again, however, your goal is to build a portfolio likely to generate your required return over time.

How Much Risk *Should* You Take?

If you've been investing for a while, you probably remember at least a couple of the events shown in Figure 6.1. And how about the market turmoil prompted by the COVID-19 pandemic? What were you feeling while major stock market indexes plunged more than 30% in the course of a month?

Black Monday in October 1987, when the Dow fell 22% in a single day
The Dot-com Meltdown and Bear Market of the early 2000s
The Financial Crisis of 2007–2009
The "Flash Crash" of 2010 when the Dow fell and rose 1,000 points in 15 minutes
December 2018, when stocks dropped approximately 20%

Figure 6.1 Major Market Events of the Last Three Decades
SOURCE: Analysis by Brian Perry.

Here's a silly question: Did you have fun investing during any of those periods? Probably not, unless you happened to have a large chunk of money you were waiting to put to work and were able to buy stocks when they were on sale.

As you get closer to, and eventually transition into, retirement, market volatility becomes even less "fun." Let's face it; from a financial perspective, retirement requires a pretty significant mindset shift. After all, you've spent decades working to accumulate money. Your goal has always been (at least from a financial perspective) to have as much money as possible.

And then, when you retire, you realize that you might never again contribute to your accounts. In fact, rather than continuing to grow your pile of money, you'll now begin spending down your accumulated savings. Instead of growing, your financial resources may start to shrink.

Now couple this scenario with a situation in which market volatility is causing a sharp drop in your portfolio. Not only do you have to spend down the money you worked so hard to accumulate, you also have to lock in losses by selling into a declining market. And you're likely seeing your savings decline (through a combination of withdrawals and market declines) at a rate beyond what you're comfortable with.

There is a simple solution to this. It's not perfect, because you'll likely still see some of your savings periodically subjected to steep market selloffs. Nevertheless, once you determine your required rate of return, determining how much risk to take is actually quite simple. Basically, you want to take as little risk as possible in achieving your required returns. After all, no one ever got on an airplane and rooted for turbulence. So why would you want to experience a ride that is bumpier than necessary in your investment portfolio?

Remember, first you determine your required rate of return. Then you need to identify portfolios likely to meet that required rate over time. Doing so will help you to manage shortfall risk. Once you've done this, the next step is choosing which of the available portfolios you want to invest in. In general, your choice should then be the portfolio with the least risk.

	Expected Annual Return	Standard Deviation	Maximum Drawdown
Portfolio 1	4%	7%	12%
Portfolio 2	6%	12%	20%
Portfolio 3	8%	20%	30%

Figure 6.2 Sample Portfolio Risk and Return
SOURCE: Analysis by Brian Perry.

It is important to realize that choosing the portfolio with the least amount of risk will likely result in lower returns than if you chose a more aggressive portfolio. You may not keep pace with the S&P 500, or with your brother-in-law or co-workers. As with many things in life, there are trade-offs here. Basically, you are sacrificing potentially higher returns for a higher degree of certainty that you won't run out of money. *You are also choosing fewer sleepless nights.*

Let's take a closer look at Figure 6.2 in order to get a better sense of some of the trade-offs you'll have to consider. Remember, the first thing you need to accomplish when investing is to achieve a rate of return sufficient to meet your financial goal. This number is your required rate of return, and meeting that requirement is not optional. With that in mind, if you've done your financial planning and determined that your required rate of return is 4%, you can choose from any of the portfolios shown in Figure 6.2.

But what if your required rate of return is higher? What if it's 6%? Well, in that case, you can no longer choose Portfolio 1, because that portfolio is unlikely to generate sufficient returns for you to meet your financial goal. In other words, because your required rate of return is 6%, and the expected return of Portfolio 1 is only 4%, you must eliminate that portfolio from consideration because you **must achieve your required rate of return over time**. And if I sound like a broken record on that point, it is only because it is so important to achieving the future you desire and deserve.

Okay, so you need at least 6% from your portfolio, and you've therefore eliminated Portfolio 1 from consideration. Which portfolio, from among the two remaining, should you then choose? Portfolio 3 certainly sounds good. After all, who wouldn't want to get 8% a year from their investments? And more is always better than less, isn't it?

I'll grant you that more is better than less, as long as everything else is equal. But look again at the chart, because in this case everything else is most certainly not equal. Yes, Portfolio 3 is expected to generate significantly higher returns than Portfolio 2. But it also carries more risk.

The standard deviation of Portfolio 3 is 20%, whereas the standard deviation of Portfolio 2 is only 12%. That means that you can expect Portfolio 3 to bounce around a lot more than Portfolio 2. Furthermore, the maximum drawdown of Portfolio 3 is 30%, as compared to only 20% for Portfolio 2.

Maximum drawdown measures how large of a decline the portfolio is expected to suffer in a worst-case scenario. In other words, at some point you can expect Portfolio 2 to drop by 20%. And at some point you can expect Portfolio 3 to plummet by 30%. If you are like most folks, a 30% decline is likely to be a far more painful experience than a 20% fall, especially when you are retired and unable to add any more money to your investment portfolio.

So, although Portfolio 3 offers higher expected returns, which are nice, the correct choice of a portfolio might be Portfolio 2. That investment mix generates sufficient returns to meet your financial goals, but is also safer and will cause less financial stress and fewer sleepless nights.

Choosing the portfolio with the least risk is a general rule of thumb, and of course there are exceptions to this. For example, if your situation is such that you are unlikely to run out of money, and you have a legacy goal of leaving money to family or charity, you may choose to take on more risk than necessary in order to generate higher returns over time. After all, in that situation you aren't only investing for yourself, but also for your family or favorite charity, either of which might have a much longer time horizon than you do.

The type of risk I am focusing on now is generally referred to as *volatility*. This is the risk you are probably most familiar with as an investor. It is also the type of risk you see highlighted any time a news headline screams about a stock market decline.

Volatility can be unnerving, and it has caused many investors to panic and abandon their portfolios at inopportune times. That is why you want to minimize the volatility within your portfolio.

> A note about volatility: Volatility refers to the fluctuations in financial markets. The most common measure of volatility is standard deviation. The higher the standard deviation, the more the investment fluctuates. However, it is important to understand that standard deviation measures volatility both to the downside and to the upside. In other words, if a security is moving sharply higher, it has a standard deviation greater than that of a security that is not going anywhere. In my experience, very few individuals mind volatility to the upside, as that means they are making money. It's downside volatility, or market declines, that people care about. Of course, it's always important to remember that anything that can go up a lot can also go down a lot.

Remember, however, and this is one of the most important points in this book, you only want to minimize the volatility of your portfolio from among the choices that will still get you to your financial goal. In other words, **volatility hurts. But shortfall risk is what will kill your financial dreams.**

Sleeping on a Bed of Money

Okay, so you want to build a portfolio that will generate the returns you need with the least amount of risk. But how do you go about doing that? Well, there are a number of different ways to build such a portfolio, but let's take a look at an approach that makes a lot of sense. This approach is based on the simple, fundamental concept that the *less time you spend worrying about market volatility, the happier you're likely to be.*

Remember how earlier in the book you learned that certain securities have higher expected returns than others. Well, hopefully, you intuitively grasp the idea that you want to own more of the securities with superior risk-and-return characteristics. Now let's put together a hypothetical example of how selecting those investments can help you build a portfolio that will get you the returns you need while still allowing you to sleep at night.

Let's consider a scenario in which you have only two investment options. Option one is that you can buy stocks, and option two is that you can stick your money under the mattress.

When you stick your money under the mattress, you know that it isn't going anywhere. Your money isn't going to disappear in a market crash. You don't have to worry about what the economy is doing or who wins the next election. You know exactly where your money is at all times, with the result that you sleep better at night.

What's the bad news though? Well, that's obvious. The bad news is that your money won't grow in value when it's under the mattress. Therefore, if all of your money goes under the mattress, you won't generate the returns necessary to meet your financial goal. In fact, you might actually be losing money as inflation eats away at your purchasing power.

With that in mind, you can't simply put all of your money under the mattress. Doing so would cause you to fall short of your financial goal. But on the other hand, it sure is nice knowing you have that money under the mattress. And I'll bet you sleep better knowing that you're lying down on a bed of money. Therefore, the idea is to have as much money under the mattress as possible, while still meeting your financial goal.

Adding Some Stocks to the Mix

So, the goal is to have as much money as possible under your mattress. The more money you're sleeping on, the better you'll sleep. But the problem is that if all of your money goes under the mattress, you won't generate the returns needed to meet your financial goal. That's where stocks come into play.

The stocks you are going to buy are going to boost your overall returns, hopefully enough so that you meet your goal. Remember, the first step in building your portfolio involves calculating your required rate of return, which is done by projecting out your future income and expenses. Rule number one of building your portfolio is that you must achieve this required rate of return over time. Failure to do so means failure to meet your financial goals. The required rate of return is unique to each person's situation and goal, but for this example let's assume you need 6% from your portfolio.

Please note that there is no magic to the 6% number here; so don't assume that your portfolio has to generate that return. You might need more or less. I'm only choosing 6% for ease of math. In fact, all numbers in this section are designed to make the math clean, so please focus on the concepts and not the numbers.

In attempting to achieve that 6% return that you need to generate *over time*, you'll put some money under your mattress and some money into stocks. In order to sleep well at night, you want to put as much money as possible under your mattress, but keep in mind that the portion that goes under the mattress will not grow at all. The portion that goes into stocks will generate different returns depending on what stocks you buy.

For our simple example, you have two choices of stocks to buy.

1. If you buy Stock A, you expect to get 8% returns over time.
2. If you buy Stock B, you expect to get 10% returns over time.

We've previously established that more is better than less, so obviously 10% returns sound better than 8% returns. But which of these stocks is riskier? Maybe Stock A represents larger, more established companies. Maybe Stock B represents the stocks of smaller, less established companies.

So again, that important question: Which of these stocks is riskier? The correct answer is Choice B, every time. You never get something for nothing in the financial markets, and if an investment promises higher returns, it generally does so because it carries commensurately higher risk. Importantly, the kind of risk

I am talking about here is volatility risk, or the threat that your investments will bounce up and down more violently.

However, our story doesn't end there. Yes, Choice B carries more risk than Choice A. But let's look at what happens when we put these investments together with some money under the mattress.

Portfolio A

Let's assume for the moment that you've decided that you're going to put your stock money in Choice A, which you expect to generate 8% returns over time. The remainder of your money will go under the mattress where it will be nice and safe. But unfortunately, your mattress money won't be growing while it is staying nice and safe.

Remember, and this is crucial, for this example you need to build your portfolio so that you expect to generate 6% returns over time in order to meet your financial goals. Also remember that 6% represents your required rate of return, and achieving this is not optional. It is called your **required** rate of return for a reason.

So here's the important question: If the remainder is going under the mattress and earning zero, what percentage of your wealth needs to go into Choice A?

Well, you need 6% from the whole portfolio, and the portion that goes under the mattress won't generate any returns, so you need to do some third-grade math, as follows:

6% divided by 8% = 75%

So, if you go with Choice A, 75% of your money goes into stocks, and the remainder, or 25%, goes under the mattress.

Importantly, you expect that this portfolio will achieve the returns you need over time.

Portfolio B

Let's run through that same exercise, except using Choice B. Remember, these are the stocks with the higher expected returns, but in the financial markets you seldom get something for nothing. With greater return potential comes greater risk, and Choice B is more volatile and will fluctuate more in value.

You still need 6% returns from the overall portfolio, and the money under your mattress still earns nothing. But now, you expect 10% from your stocks. Using the same math as we used for Choice A, we find:

6% divided by 10% = 60%

So, if you go with Choice B, 60% of your money goes into the stocks, and the remainder, or 40%, goes under the mattress. As with Choice A, this option is also expected to generate the returns you need in order to meet your financial goals.

But remember, while you need to meet your required rate of return, you also want to enjoy as smooth of a ride as possible. The stocks in Choice B are more volatile and will fluctuate more in value than those in Choice A.

Does this mean that Choice B is a poor one?

Not necessarily.

What Portfolio Do You Want?

Both of these portfolios are expected to return 6% over time, thereby getting you to your goal. This is the first, and most important, consideration when building your investment portfolio.

And as stated earlier, Stock Choice B is riskier than Stock Choice A. There is no getting away from that. You don't get more return without more risk.

But here is the absolutely vital point. **Even though its stocks are more volatile, I might still prefer to have the B portfolio**!

Think about it this way. Although the stocks in B are riskier, they also have higher expected returns. Because of that, you're able to hold fewer stocks in your mix while still attaining the rate of return you require. Holding fewer stocks allows you to hold commensurately more of your money under the mattress.

Portfolio B has fully 40% under the mattress, allowing you to sleep more comfortably at night. And, once you make sure your portfolio will allow you to meet your goal, the second thing you want to do is minimize your risk. Or, to put it in more human terms:

- Retirement Rule #1 = Don't run out of money
- Retirement Rule #2 = Enjoy your retirement (by not worrying about money)

The way you obey these two rules is by building a portfolio with an expected return that matches or exceeds your required rate, and by then taking on the least possible risk in order to get that return.

And one of the best ways to minimize your risk is to keep as much of your money as possible under the proverbial mattress, where you don't have to worry about it.

The important takeaway here is that risk shouldn't just be measured on an investment-by-investment basis. The risk that really matters is at the portfolio level. Your goal then is to put together a collection of investments, some of which may be risky on their own, into a portfolio that meets your financial goal with the least risk possible. That, in a nutshell, is the art of portfolio construction.

Note: You shouldn't literally keep your money under the mattress of course, because doing so will prevent you from even keeping pace with inflation, let alone seeing your money grow. In the financial markets, high-quality bonds are the equivalent of money under the mattress. Those are the kinds of bonds discussed in Chapter 4, and they will serve as the money under your mattress as you build out your portfolio.

Still Not Convinced?

Here's another way of thinking about why you want more of your money under the proverbial mattress. Remember earlier in the book when we ran through your calculations for determining how much money you need to retire?

Well, just for this example lets pretend that you want to spend $100,000 per year in retirement and that you'll have $60,000 a year coming in from various fixed income sources. So you need $40,000 each and every year from your portfolio. Let's further assume that you've accumulated $1,000,000 for retirement.

Now let's reconsider the portfolios we built. Remember, portfolio B has 60% in stocks and 40% under the mattress. With a $1,000,000 portfolio that means you would have:

- **$600,000 in stocks**
- **$400,000 under the mattress**

For this example, you need to draw $40,000 per year from your portfolio. If you divide 400,000 by 40,000 you get:

400,000 divided by 40,000 = 10

Remember, you have $400,000 under your mattress and you need to draw $40,000 annually from your portfolio. So, what does the number 10 represent?

Ten is the number of years of living expenses you have sitting under the mattress before you have to use any of the money sitting in stocks.

In other words, in this example, you have an entire decade's worth of spending sitting under your mattress before you ever have to worry about what your stock portfolio is doing.

That is why you want to construct a portfolio with as many safe assets as possible. Doing so frees you from having to worry about the gyrations of the stock market, or the constant barrage of economic, political, and market headlines.

Let me ask you, how would you like to be able to have the following exchanges in retirement?

- **Your friend:** Are you worried the stock market's down 15%?
- **You:** Nope, ask me again in a decade.

- **Your co-worker:** Does the upcoming election make you nervous about your portfolio?
- **You:** Nope, I don't need to worry about my portfolio for the next ten years.
- **Your cousin:** They say there's a recession ahead. Are you worried about your investments?
- **You:** Nope, not unless the recession lasts for a dozen years.

Obviously, knowing that you have several years or more of spending locked into relatively safe investments can reduce the stress you feel when the more growth-oriented segment of your portfolio fluctuates.

The truth is that at the end of the day, there are a number of ways to manage risk in a diversified investment portfolio and the method I've laid out is only one of them. But it is effective, primarily because it focuses on the emotional aspects of retirement investing. This peace of mind then makes it easier to ignore the mayhem around you and stay on track toward your goals.

Enjoy Your Retirement!

You've worked hard, and you want to enjoy your retirement. And let's face it; it's never fun losing money. Bear markets are always frightening. This fear gets exacerbated when you enter retirement. At least when working you can tell yourself that if your portfolio falls too much you can always postpone your retirement and give your investments time to recover while you continue to contribute to your accounts.

But in retirement that's no longer the case. The amount you've saved is your nest egg, and there aren't going to be any more inflows to top it off (assuming you don't go back to work). As such, it's natural for retirees to worry about their portfolio when markets are falling.

The problem is that life is short, and retirement should be enjoyable. The last thing you want is to be using the mediocre Wi-Fi on your cruise ship to check your stock portfolio when you could be having fun at the pool bar. Similarly, financial worries can cause you to squander time spent with children, grandchildren, or treasured friends.

The combination of determining your required rate of return and then using financial research to determine where to focus your investments can then allow you to own as many safe assets as possible. In turn, having money socked away in safe investments can improve the quality of your retirement. The peace of mind factor is key here, and the idea that you have years or even decades of spending sitting in relatively stable assets can free you from financial worry, allowing you to get on with the important business of maximizing your retirement fun!

Chapter 7
You Must Practice Smart Diversification

Do you remember the decade of the 2000s? That was back when folks with the gift of perfect foresight were finally rewarded! After all, back at the turn of the millennium, your neighbor, Bob, whom you've nicknamed The Oracle, was correctly able to peer into the future and foresee that the next decade would offer two wars, two horrendous bear markets, two recessions, 17 consecutive interest rate increases by the Federal Reserve, and the worst financial crisis since the 1930s. Why, the only thing missing were plagues of locusts!

Those 10 years were the very definition of a difficult environment. Under those conditions, stock markets would undoubtedly collapse. Bond markets, buffeted by Federal Reserve rate increases, would suffer. And investors couldn't hope to make a profit. The savviest investors would definitely choose to sit on the sidelines and wait for a period characterized by less turmoil and more certainty.

Your lucky neighbor, blessed as he was with clairvoyance, surely would have profited from his priceless gift by completely avoiding the financial markets and sticking his money under the mattress.

The interesting thing, though, is that your neighbor, despite his gift, would have been far worse off for having avoided the markets.

In fact, all those poor fools who couldn't foresee the wars and recessions and financial crisis would have ended the decade in a far better spot than The Oracle.

So, your neighbor, Bob, saw the future, saw the turmoil it contained, and chose to sit on the sidelines and avoid the mayhem. And he suffered for this seemingly prudent choice.

So, what should he have done instead?

Well, instead of avoiding the markets, he should have practiced **smart diversification**.

What Is Smart Diversification?

You've probably heard of *diversification* in the past, and you likely agree it's a good thing. After all, I don't need to remind you not to put all your eggs in one basket, since diversification represents something of a free lunch in the financial markets, and you'd be wise to partake of it.

And, if you've read this book up to this point, I'm going to go out on a limb and assume that you like the idea of being *smart*.

So, then, what do I mean by *smart diversification*?

In order to answer that question, let me begin by *examining some of the behaviors that do not constitute* ***smart diversification***. In doing so, I think you'll start to get a sense of what does and does not make sense when it comes to diversifying your investment portfolio.

You Don't Want to Be a Pig!

There is an old adage on Wall Street that bulls get rich, bears get rich, but pigs get slaughtered. The idea is that bulls (or those optimistic about stock prices) can make money, as can bears (investors who think stocks will fall). But pigs, or investors who get too greedy, invariably lose out in the long run.

With that in mind, the first kind of behavior you want to avoid in your quest for smart diversification is an overconcentration in a single asset class. The most common way this comes about is when someone holds too many stocks. Now, in some instances this can make sense, but if you think back to the previous chapter, most investors don't need to attain astronomical returns in order to meet their financial goals. But, people being people, it's only natural to want to do as well as possible, especially during periods when stock prices are rising.

A typical example of this is an investor who starts with a balanced portfolio of 50% in stocks and 50% in bonds. The stock market then begins to do well, and embarks on a multiyear bull market. The investor's stock portfolio grows at a far faster clip than his or her boring old bonds. As such, the percentage held in stocks creeps toward 60%, then 70%. Maybe the situation even gets exacerbated as the investor complains to his or her advisor that diversification (in the form of bonds) is holding the investor back and harming returns. For a time, the advisor talks the client out of abandoning bonds in favor of stocks. But eventually the client grows tired of watching other investors do better, and the client fires their advisor, sells his or her remaining bonds, and moves entirely into stocks.

Predictably, the stock market crashes soon after.

The end result of it all is that the client owned fewer stocks while the market was marching higher, and then more stocks right near the market top. They are then far too exposed when the market suffers its next reversal. And remember, these reversals are inevitable. It is the nature of markets to move both higher and lower, even though it can be easy to lose sight of this when times are very good or very bad.

If our hypothetical client still owned an appropriate (for them) mix of stock and bonds, he or she would have several advantages over our investor who had concentrated too heavily in stocks.

- The client would have more money, because losses in a diversified portfolio would have been less than those of our all-stock investor.

- They would have some money in safe assets, which they could then sell to buy more stocks. Buying stocks when they are on sale would lead to higher returns over time. This process is known as rebalancing.
- They wouldn't face the psychological challenge of the aggressive investor in trying to hold on and not abandon stocks. And, of course, if the investor does abandon stocks, there is then the psychological challenge of trying to get back into the market.

The bottom line is that the investor who maintained a disciplined allocation and avoided committing too heavily to a single asset class now has far greater odds of achieving his or her financial goals than a less disciplined colleague.

Sadly, this simplistic example occurs far too often. Therefore, the first rule of smart diversification is to own a combination of asset classes in proportions likely to accomplish the rules discussed in the previous chapter:

- Rule #1: Meet your required rate of return.
- Rule #2: Take the least amount of risk possible.

Owning What You Know May Not Be Best

The famous mutual fund manager Peter Lynch wrote a book titled *One Up on Wall Street*, in which he suggested that investors could do well by owning what they know. The basis of this advice is sound; an intimate familiarity with one's investments could enhance the probability of success.

The problem is that many investors take this advice too literally. The result is that they load up on companies or industries they are familiar with. Consider, for example, the doctor whose investment portfolio is full of drug stocks, or the real estate broker whose investments consist of rental properties and publicly traded stocks linked to the real estate industry (these stocks are often known as real estate investment trusts, or REITs). In both of those examples, there are at least a couple of reasons that the investment approach might not make sense.

First of all, if someone's investments and their livelihood both come from the same industry, they have put themselves in a position in which an industry downturn can impact both their paycheck (from their job) and their savings (from their investment portfolio). For instance, think back to the early 2000s and the bursting of the dot-com bubble. Many technology companies declared bankruptcy, which led to numerous tech industry layoffs. At the same time technology stocks cratered, with the tech-heavy Nasdaq Index falling by 80%. A similar set of circumstances hit the financial sector in the 2007–2009 financial crisis.

The second problem is that different industries perform well at different times. If you concentrate your holdings in a single industry, you may miss out on better performing sectors. Consider an investor whose familiarity with the oil industry caused him to concentrate his holdings in that sector. There are certainly times when this might have paid off. For example, there was a period in the mid-2000s when energy stocks posted strong returns. But as with all industries, the performance of oil stocks ebbs and flows.

So consider the plight of our hypothetical individual back in 2017. That year, the U.S. stock markets soared, with the S&P 500 up approximately 22%. Those are the kinds of years in which large retirement accounts are built.

But alas, Figure 7.1 shows that things weren't so rosy for our energy investor.

Although the broader market was up nearly 22%, energy stocks posted poor returns that year. In fact, not only did our energy investor's portfolio not increase by 22%, the portfolio actually declined in value.

What do you think, would the difference between **positive** 22% and **negative** 1% make a material difference in your retirement planning?

Just to be clear, the takeaway from the 2017 example is not that you should have only owned the tech stocks that were up nearly 40%. Sure, that would have been nice, but doing so would expose you to the same risks our oil investor faced.

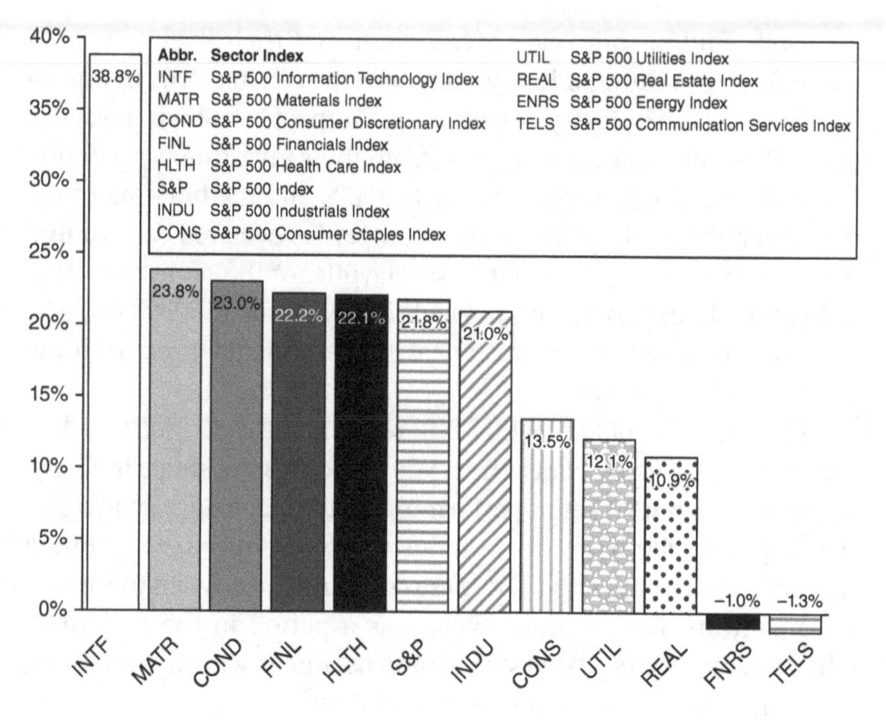

Figure 7.1 Example of Differences in S&P Sector Performance
SOURCE: Based on data from NovelInvestor.com.

At some point, technology will go from first to worst, and investors too heavily concentrated there will see their portfolios underperform, or worse. This is exactly what happened in the early 2000s. Technology stocks soared during the 1990s, and led the stock market to record gains. That party eventually came to a screeching halt, and tech stocks were decimated during the bear market rout at the turn of the millennium. Figure 7.2 shows the performance of some tech industry titans during that period.

And those were the winners! Microsoft, Cisco, Amazon, Intel, and QUALCOMM all survived the wreckage, eventually recovered, and today are thriving corporate titans. Many tech stocks suffered total losses as companies disappeared forever. I could continue with examples from the financial industry in the mid-2000s, or energy

	Dot-com Boom High	Dot-com Crash Low	% Decline
Microsoft	$58	$27	–53%
Cisco	$80	$10	–88%
Amazon	$70	$10	–86%
Intel	$73	$13	–82%
QUALCOMM	$100	$12	–88%

Figure 7.2 Representative Performance of Tech Titans During Dot-com Meltdown
SOURCE: Analysis by Brian Perry. Data from Yahoo Finance.

stocks in the 1990s, or a host of others, but you get the point. Overexposure to a single industry is great when it works, but catastrophic when it doesn't. And I am going to work off the assumption that you'd like to avoid catastrophe on the road to meeting your financial goals.

With that in mind, a better approach for those lacking the power of clairvoyance would be to own all the sectors. Such an approach would have ensured that in our 2017 example, the investor owned tech and energy, as well as everything else. That combination of the best and the worst, as well as everything in between, would have generated those 22% returns for the investor. And although that's not as good as just owning tech would have been, it's a heck of lot better than only owning energy.

Importantly, it's that middle ground between the extreme highs and lows that most folks need to capture in order to meet their financial goals. Remember, though, the media and financial industries will often encourage you otherwise. They'll tell you they know what will do best and what will do worst. And they'll shout that if you don't own the "right" sectors, your finances are doomed.

It's hard to ignore this noise! But you must! Like Odysseus lashing himself to the ship's mast to avoid the Sirens' call, you must put processes in place to protect you from the insidious influence of the world around you, a world unintentionally designed to keep you from meeting your financial goals.

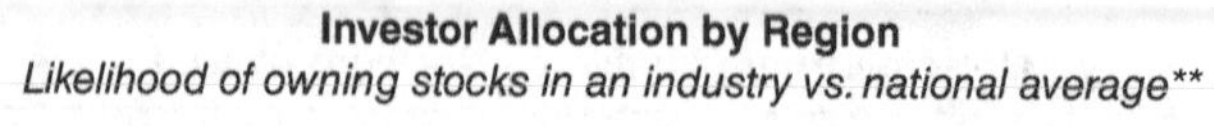

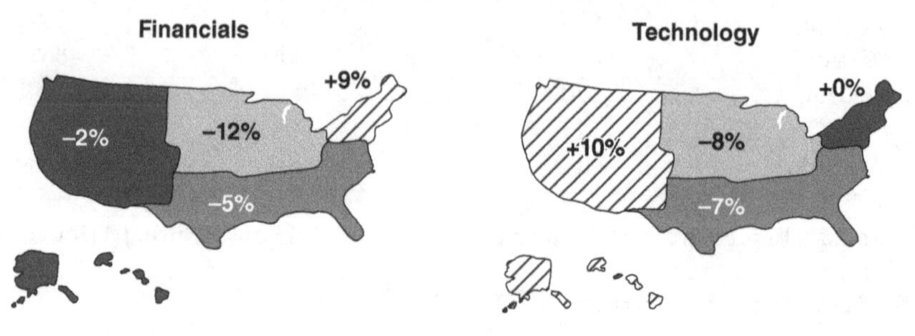

% +/– National Average

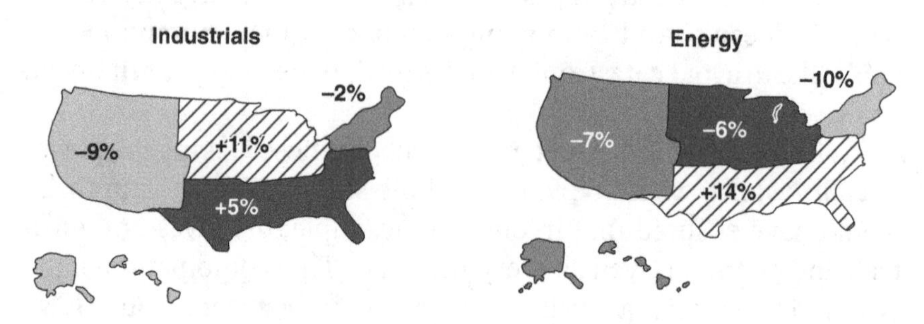

Figure 7.3 Propensity of Investors to Own What They Know Best
SOURCE: Adapted from J.P. Morgan.

Even the very environment you live in will encourage you to concentrate in certain types of investments. Don't believe me? Check out Figure 7.3.

Across the United States, investors tend to concentrate on their region's dominant industry, which is the industry they or their neighbors work in, the industry most frequently discussed in the press, and the industry they are likely most familiar with.

- Investors in the Northeast overweight financial companies.
- Investors in the South overweight energy companies.
- Investors in the Midwest overweight industrial companies.
- Investors in the West overweight technology companies.

This approach might not make sense, though. Think about it this way: if you live in the Northeast, even if you don't work in finance, you are impacted by the industry's performance. When the financial industry suffers, its employees spend less on entertainment, travel, and eating out. They are less likely to buy bigger homes, or new furniture for their current homes. They are less likely to put their children in private school or sign up for golf lessons. In other words, when the financial industry is in turmoil, the economy of the Northeast is greatly impacted.

Now, hopefully this doesn't affect you too much, but it might. Maybe your company has layoffs and you're out of work. Or maybe you own a small business, and your revenues drop. These difficult situations would be exacerbated if your investment portfolio were concentrated in the stocks of the very companies dragging the local economy down. And needless to say, this situation can become even more problematic if you actually work in the struggling industry.

The common rationale for owning too much of an industry is that the person *knows* that industry. I wish I had a dollar for every tech-industry employee I've met who's told me they own tech stocks because they *know* tech!

Yes, I'll agree that you may have knowledge about your industry. In fact, I hope you do! But a better hurdle might be this: Do you have more knowledge than the other 5–10 million people working in that industry? Do you have greater insight than all but a handful of people in the world? Because that's what it takes to prosper from a concentration in a single industry. Remember, although you might know about upcoming product launches and the hot new company, so do hundreds of thousands or millions of other folks, and that information is already baked into stock prices.

So unless you can honestly claim to be one of the world's handful of foremost experts in your industry, diversification is going to greatly enhance your odds of financial success.

It's a Big World

The United States is home to many fantastic companies. And its economy is the biggest in the world. Its financial markets are home to thousands of securities, and it enjoys the rule of law and few restrictions on trading in and out of securities. In other words, it's great to be an investor in the Good Old U.S. of A.

But that being said, one of the most common mistakes people make is failing to take advantage of opportunities open to global investors. Generally speaking, a different country leads the way almost every year, and there is no real pattern to predict what country might do best going forward. Figure 7.4 shows annual performance for a number of developed country stock markets over a 20-year period. Each year, the country that had the best performance is highlighted.

As you can see, there is only a single year (2014) in which the United States was the world's best performing market. In every other year, an investor focused only on the United States would have missed out on better performance somewhere else.

A U.S.-centric focus also results in excluding a number of great companies. For instance, the most commonly used international stock index is the MSCI EAFE, which includes companies from Europe, Australia, Japan, and other developed markets. Its top holdings include corporate stalwarts such as:

- Nestlé
- Novartis
- Toyota
- SAP
- British Petroleum (BP)
- LVMH
- Royal Dutch Shell
- Allianz
- Unilever
- Sony

The bottom line is that it's a big world out there, full of opportunities to find attractive investments. If you fail to incorporate global investing into your portfolio, you're choosing to exclude a number of the world's leading companies. You're also choosing to pass up the opportunity to enhance your portfolio's diversification, and potentially it's returns.

	1999	2000	2001	2002	2003	2004	2005	2006	2007	2008	2009	2010	2011	2012	2013	2014	2015	2016	2017	2018
Australia	17.6	−10.0	1.7	−1.3	49.5	30.3	16.0	30.9	28.3	−50.7	76.4	14.5	−11.0	22.1	4.2	−3.4	−10.0	11.4	19.9	−12.0
Austria	−9.1	−12.0	−5.6	16.5	57.0	71.5	24.6	36.5	2.2	−68.4	43.2	9.9	−36.4	25.9	13.4	−29.8	3.5	11.3	58.3	−27.4
Belgium	−14.3	−16.8	−10.9	−15.0	35.3	43.5	9.0	36.7	−2.7	−66.5	57.5	−0.4	−10.6	39.6	27.6	4.1	12.1	−7.6	18.6	−26.9
Canada	53.7	5.3	−20.4	−13.2	54.6	22.2	28.3	17.8	29.6	−45.5	56.2	20.5	−12.7	9.1	5.6	1.5	−24.2	24.6	16.1	−17.2
Denmark	12.1	3.4	−14.8	−16.0	49.3	30.8	24.5	38.8	25.6	−47.6	36.6	30.7	−16.0	31.3	25.2	6.2	23.4	−15.8	34.7	−15.4
Finland	152.6	−14.2	−38.2	−30.3	19.4	6.1	16.7	29.9	48.7	−55.2	11.1	10.3	−31.9	14.6	46.0	−0.7	2.0	−4.7	22.5	−3.4
France	29.3	−4.3	−22.4	−21.2	40.2	18.5	9.9	34.5	13.2	−43.3	31.8	−4.1	−16.9	21.3	26.3	−9.9	−0.1	4.9	28.7	−12.8
Germany	20.0	−15.6	−22.4	−33.2	63.8	16.2	9.9	36.0	35.2	−45.9	25.2	8.4	−18.1	30.9	31.4	−10.4	−1.9	2.8	27.7	−22.2
Hong Kong	59.5	−14.7	−18.6	−17.8	38.1	25.0	8.4	30.4	41.2	−51.2	60.2	23.2	−16.0	28.3	11.1	5.1	−0.5	2.3	36.2	−7.8
Ireland	−12.6	−12.7	−2.8	−26.2	43.8	43.1	−2.3	46.8	−20.1	−71.9	12.3	−18.1	13.7	5.7	41.2	2.3	16.5	−7.1	18.1	−25.3
Italy	−0.3	−1.3	−26.6	−7.3	37.8	32.5	1.9	32.5	6.1	−50.0	26.6	−15.0	−23.2	12.5	20.4	−9.5	2.3	−10.5	28.4	−17.8
Japan	61.5	−28.2	−29.4	−10.3	35.9	15.9	25.5	6.2	−4.2	−29.2	6.3	15.4	−14.3	8.2	27.2	−4.0	9.6	2.4	24.0	−12.9
Netherlands	6.9	−4.1	−22.1	−20.8	28.1	12.2	13.9	31.4	20.6	−48.2	42.3	1.7	−12.1	20.6	31.3	−3.5	1.3	4.8	32.2	−13.1
New Zealand	12.9	−33.5	8.4	24.2	55.4	35.2	1.7	16.6	8.9	−53.8	50.4	8.3	5.5	29.3	11.3	7.3	−6.3	18.4	11.7	−4.0
Norway	31.7	−0.9	−12.2	−7.3	48.1	53.3	24.3	45.1	31.4	−64.2	87.1	10.9	−10.0	18.7	9.4	−22.0	−15.0	13.3	28.3	−8.6
Portugal	−8.9	−10.3	−22.0	−13.8	43.0	24.7	−1.9	47.4	24.0	−52.2	40.4	−11.3	−23.1	3.5	11.0	−38.2	0.9	3.6	23.8	−11.1
Singapore	99.4	−27.7	−23.4	−11.0	37.6	22.3	14.4	46.7	28.4	−47.4	74.0	22.1	−17.9	31.0	1.7	3.0	−17.7	1.4	35.6	−9.4
Spain	4.8	−15.9	−11.4	−15.3	58.5	28.9	4.4	49.4	24.0	−40.6	43.5	−22.0	−12.3	3.0	31.3	−4.7	−15.6	−1.0	27.0	−16.2
Sweden	79.7	−21.3	−27.2	−30.5	64.5	36.3	10.3	43.4	0.6	−49.9	64.2	33.8	−16.0	22.0	24.5	−7.5	−5.0	0.6	20.6	−13.7
Switzerland	−7.0	5.9	−21.4	−10.3	34.1	15.0	16.3	27.4	5.3	−30.5	25.3	11.8	−6.8	20.4	26.6	−0.1	0.4	−4.9	22.5	−9.1
United Kingdom	12.5	−11.5	−14.0	−15.2	32.1	19.6	7.4	30.6	8.4	−48.3	43.3	8.8	−2.6	15.3	20.7	−5.4	−7.6	−0.1	22.3	−14.2
United States	21.9	−12.8	−12.4	−23.1	28.4	10.1	5.1	14.7	5.4	−37.6	26.3	14.8	1.4	15.3	31.8	12.7	0.7	10.9	21.2	−5.0

Figure 7.4 Best performing stock market by year (1999–2018).

SOURCE: Data from MSCI World Indices. Returns measured in U.S. dollars.

Sometimes You're Trapped by Your Own Success

There are times when, whether through luck, skill, or some combination of both, you might find yourself heavily concentrated in one investment. Hopefully, the balance of this chapter has convinced you not to intentionally place yourself in such a position. There are instances, though, in which having a concentrated position is a good thing. If you've owned an investment that generated very large returns, it may have enhanced your overall wealth and improved your financial position. The challenge of course is how to maintain your newfound wealth. After all, you've undoubtedly heard nightmare stories of people who were too heavily concentrated in a single stock or market sector. Those individuals may have accumulated large gains when times were good, but all too often they were left without a chair when the music stopped playing.

I'm thinking here of folks with large holdings of technology stocks in the late 1990s, who saw their wealth soar as they generated huge returns for a couple years, then lost everything in the dot-com bust.

Similar tales exist from the housing bubble and collapse of the mid-2000s. Maybe you know someone who leveraged their way to a "portfolio" of a half dozen condos in Vegas, only to be forced into bankruptcy several years later when they found themselves far underwater on those mortgages.

And what about the employees at Enron, the failed utility supernova? Many of them piled into their employer's stock and watched their 401(k) balances skyrocket, only to lose both their jobs and their savings when that company's success turned out to be a sham.

And yes, your investment might be different, and it might continue doing well forever. But, then again, at various times prospects were also bright for:

- America's largest retailer (Sears)
- The world's largest automaker (GM)
- America's largest utility (Enron)
- America's wealthiest and fifth-largest city (Detroit)
- One of the wealthiest countries in the world (Argentina)

Still not convinced that things change, even if it is difficult to see a future in which your investment does not thrive? Consider the following company, which was the largest in the world during its time. In fact, the company in question was the largest the world has ever seen. At its peak, its inflation-adjusted market value was *$7.9 trillion*. To put that in context, that's **equal to the combined market value of all of the following**:

- The maker of the iPhone (Apple)
- The dominant search engine (Google)
- The maker of Windows, Word, and Excel (Microsoft)
- The world's biggest online retailer (Amazon)
- The number-one social media network (Facebook)
- China's leading online marketplace (Alibaba)
- America's largest energy company (ExxonMobil)
- America's second-biggest bank (Bank of America)
- Warren Buffett's company (Berkshire Hathaway)
- America's fourth-biggest bank (Wells Fargo)
- America's biggest retailer (Walmart)
- The largest credit card company (Visa)
- America's second largest energy company (Chevron)
- The maker of baby powder and Band-Aids (Johnson & Johnson)
- China's leading technology company (Tencent)
- America's largest phone company (AT&T)
- South Korea's largest company (Samsung)
- The seller of 100 billion Big Macs (McDonalds)
- The company that popularized electric cars (Tesla)
- The company that introduced streaming video (Netflix)

What company, you ask, could possibly be worth as much as all of those corporate titans combined?

The company I'm talking about, which you can see in Figure 7.5, is, of course, the *Dutch East India Company*.

Now, you probably haven't thought about the Dutch East India Company since high school history class. And you definitely don't shop there or use their products. And yet, when this leviathan was

Figure 7.5 The True Scale of the World's Most Valuable Company
SOURCE: Visualcapitalist.com.

the largest company the world has ever known, is it safe to assume that its future was pretty bright?

Of course it is. Investments do well because they have a bright future. That doesn't mean an investment can't continue to thrive. But it does mean that simply "doing well" doesn't guarantee the investment will continue to succeed. That is because of the following important principle of financial markets:

Good and **Bad** don't matter nearly as much as **Better** and **Worse.**

In other words, it's not so much a matter of a company, sector, or market posting good news or strong financials. What's really important is how those numbers look relative to expectations. At the height of the financial crisis in the Spring of 2009, the financial and economic news was not good. Markets began to rally, however, simply because the news was "less bad."

This same concept holds true in the context of investments that have performed well. If a stock, a sector, or a market has performed well, a lot of good news is already priced in. Therefore, continued good news is not sufficient to sustain an indefinite upward trend. Instead, the news needs to be even better than expectations. And of course those expectations are already quite lofty, or else the investment wouldn't have already soared in value. The phenomenon is not unlike pushing a snowball uphill.

The bottom line is that if you are fortunate enough to own an investment that has performed well and now represents a large portion of your overall net worth, you face a unique challenge. The first step is that you need to accept that no matter how well the investment has done, and no matter how bright its future prospects might be, success is never guaranteed.

Once you've accepted that the future isn't inevitable, the second step is figuring out what to do about that inflated position.

Dealing with Concentrated Positions

So what can you do when you find yourself holding a concentrated position? Maybe this came about through stock options in your employer, or from an inheritance, or an investment you bought that turned out to be a homerun. Regardless of how it came about, you now find that a single investment has grown to represent an outsized proportion of your portfolio. This is often referred to as a **concentrated position**, and dealing appropriately with this situation can be challenging.

For all the reasons already discussed, if a position becomes too large relative to your other holdings, you need to consider ways to reduce it. Otherwise you are exposing yourself to the risk of a catastrophic hit to your finances if the investment reverses course and performs poorly. There is an old saying, "Concentrated positions can be good for building wealth, but they are terrible for maintaining wealth."

But selling may not be easy. If the investment has been good to you, or if it is inherited from a loved one, you may have emotional attachment to it. And even if you don't, selling may be complicated by potential tax implications.

A deeper discussion of tax minimization comes later in this book, but for now you should be aware that if you hold an investment outside of a retirement account, you might be subject to capital gains tax when you sell that investment. When you purchase or inherit an investment, the price at that time establishes a basis. Basis is essentially what you paid for the investment. Any increases in value between what you paid and what you sell the investment for are taxed at special capital gains rates. These rates are lower than ordinary income tax rates, but they are still substantial, and need to be taken into account prior to disposing of a large position.

Despite the tax implications of a sale, it is important that you don't let a potential tax bill outweigh prudent investing. In other words, if it makes sense to sell the investment, you should do so in the most tax-efficient manner possible, but the important thing is that you make the sale. Saving money on taxes does you no good if it is accomplished by watching the value of your investment crater.

When dealing with concentrated positions, there is no one right answer about how to proceed, but in general it is best to develop a systematic plan for reducing your position in a tax efficient manner. If that plan indicates that the reduction in the position will take place over an extended period of time, it may make sense to consider hedging the position.

Hedging refers to methods of reducing risk, often at the expense of sacrificing some of the potential upside. Hedging strategies can be complicated and might involve the use of options in order to protect the gains you've accumulated in the stock while you gradually reduce your position.

One common method of hedging is to purchase a put option on the stock or investment that you own. That put option works a lot like insurance, in that you pay a premium to purchase the option, but in exchange you get downside protection if the value of your investment falls. There are also more complex strategies where you can essentially get the insurance for free by selling call options. Selling the call options caps your upside, but the proceeds from the sale pay for all or most of your downside insurance. In this scenario, which is referred to as a collar, you've essentially put a ceiling on your upside and a floor on your downside. You then have confidence in the price you'll sell the investment for, and can systematically sell a portion of it each tax year in the most efficient manner possible.

Please note that the strategies just discussed are commonly used in the financial markets, but they do take a certain level of sophistication to utilize appropriately. Used incorrectly, options can expose you to great risk. Used correctly, though, they can help protect your net worth and allow you to be savvier in your tax planning. The important point is that these are relatively advanced instruments and should only be used carefully, or with the guidance of a trusted financial professional.

The bottom line is that although a detailed discussion of the disposition of concentrated positions, hedging strategies, and tax considerations is beyond the scope of this book, if you have a concentrated position in a single investment, it may make sense to research these topics further or discuss your situation with your financial professionals.

Smart Diversification Enhances Your Odds of Success

Now that you've gained a better understanding of some of the ways people fail to practice smart diversification, let's take a closer look at how smart diversification can help you reach your financial goals.

Even before reading this chapter, you probably already knew that you should own an appropriate mix of stocks, bonds, and other asset classes, in proportions determined by your financial goals and required rate of return. And you've probably heard enough horror stories to convince you to avoid large concentrations in a single company or sector. Hopefully this chapter has further reinforced these concepts and left you convinced that proper diversification holds the key to successful investing.

With that in mind, though, I want to discuss the benefits of diversification from a different perspective. Because, although *many people focus on how diversification can help you reduce risk,* I instead want to *focus on how diversification can help you improve returns.*

If you've ever been to the fair or visited an amusement park, you may be familiar with the game where you throw darts at a wall of balloons. And behind every balloon, the host reminds you, lies a winner! Of course, most of those "winners" are a lousy plastic whistle or its equivalent, and the prize isn't worth nearly as much as the dollar you paid to throw that dart.

But behind some of those balloons lies treasure! Maybe it's a gigantic stuffed panda bear or something like that. And if you can win one of those, your kids or grandkids will think you're a hero. So, you pay a couple of dollars and you throw a couple of darts.

And what happens? Well, predictably, you pop two balloons and you win a cheap plastic whistle. Remember, there are only a small number of giant pandas on the board and your odds of popping the right balloon were commensurately slim.

Think about this, though: If you threw more darts, wouldn't you have a better shot at getting that stuffed panda bear? Of course you would. As with any endeavor involving probabilities, the more tries you have, the greater your odds of eventually succeeding.

So, let me ask you a question: Why should investing be any different? If you accept that some investments are likely to do well in the future and some are not, then doesn't it make sense that the more investments you own, the greater the odds that you'll own those that do well?

Now to be fair, if you were clairvoyant and knew precisely which balloons hid the giant panda, you'd be best off by paying for only a single dart, popping that balloon, and winning the big prize. That analogy, carried over to the financial markets, is the equivalent of loading up a sizable percentage of your portfolio in a single type of investment.

When that approach works well, it can be massively rewarding.

The problem is that no one knows in advance which balloon is hiding the giant panda, just like no one knows with certainty which investments are going to perform best in the years ahead. Therefore, the approach most likely to lead to success is to throw as many darts as possible, or in an investment context, to own a wide variety of investments, thereby dramatically increasing your odds of owning the winners and achieving acceptable investment results.

This type of diversification will not, I repeat, will not allow you to generate massive returns. What it will do, though, is drastically increase your chances of achieving the kind of returns that allow you to meet your financial goals.

So, although concentration is a feast-or-famine proposition, and the equivalent of rolling the dice with your future, diversification is very much a steadier approach, designed to produce more consistent, though sometimes less spectacular, results.

Remember, though, that in the famous race between the tortoise and the hare, the hare finished last.

That parable remains as relevant today as when it was written 2500 years ago.

Winning the Lost Decade

To draw this chapter on smart diversification to a close, let's return to the story of our friend Bob. You remember Bob, the guy with perfect foresight into the future. As discussed at the beginning of this chapter, the decade of the 2000s was a difficult one for investors. As the new millennium dawned, the ebullience of the dot-com boom turned into a sharp market selloff, highlighted by the collapse of many previously high-flying tech stocks. By the middle of the decade, markets had recovered, but a credit crisis soon ensued, followed by the Great Recession. Newspapers referred to a "Lost Decade" during which the S&P 500 had produced negative returns.

In retrospect, market declines shouldn't have been a surprise. After all, if you'd visited a fortuneteller in 2000 and they'd told you the ensuing decade would contain the headlines in Figure 7.6, you might have guessed that the S&P would be weak. Perhaps you'd have even been *smart enough to avoid markets completely, just as Bob did.*

But would avoiding markets completely have been the best approach? Well, at first glance, avoiding "the market" appears that it would have been a great idea. After all, Figure 7.7 shows that

Two Wars

"U.S. and Britain Strike Afghanistan"
–New York Times, October 8, 2001

"Bush Orders Start of War on Iraq"
–New York Times, March 3, 2003

Two Recessions

"Will There Be a Double Dip?"
–The Economist, August 8, 2002

"How Today's Global Recession Tracks the Great Depression"
–Financial Times, June 17, 2009

Two Periods of High Unemployment

"Welcome to the Amazing Jobless Recovery"
–Bloomberg Business Week, July 28, 2003

"U.S. Unemployment Rate Hits 10.2% Highest in 26 Years"
–New York Times, November 6, 2009

Housing Crisis

"U.S. Home Prices Continue Record Slide"
–Los Angeles Times, February 25, 2009

"2009 Foreclosures Hit Record High"
–Wall Street Journal: Market Watch, January 14, 2010

Credit Market Meltdown

"Crisis on Wall Street as Lehman Totters, Merrill is Sold, AIG Seeks to Raise Cash"
–Wall Street Journal, September 14, 2008

"Corporate Bond Defaults Hit Record"
–Financial Times, August 20, 2009

Figure 7.6 Representative Headlines from the Lost Decade
SOURCE: Analysis by Brian Perry. Headlines sourced from the *New York Times, Financial Times, Wall Street Journal, Bloomberg BusinessWeek, The Economist,* and *Los Angeles Times.*

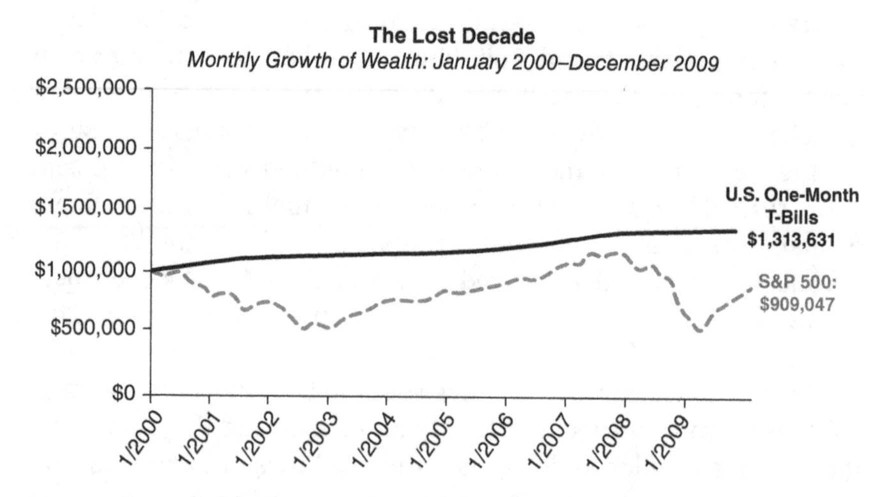

Figure 7.7 Growth of Wealth for S&P 500 and U.S. One-Month T-Bills
SOURCE: Based on data from Dimensional Fund Advisors and Standard & Poor's.

investors in Treasury bills outearned the S&P 500 during the 2000s, and with a heck of a lot less volatility, too.

But let's look more closely and broaden our definition of "the market" a little bit. Many folks have a tendency to think only of large U.S.-based companies when talking about "the market." And, to be fair, the postfinancial crisis years have been good to investors in the stocks of those types of companies, which makes it easy to forget why diversification makes sense.

But would a focus on large U.S. companies have made sense during that Lost Decade? Back then, while the S&P 500 was limping along to a **(–9.10%)** total return, other asset classes performed as follows:

- U.S. Small Company Value Stocks **+231.3%**
- U.S. REITs **+175.6%**
- U.S. Government Bonds **+82.0%**
- Emerging Markets Stocks **+202.3%**
- Emerging Markets Value Stocks **+413.8%**

So, on closer examination, maybe that decade wasn't so lost after all, provided investors broadened their definition of what exactly constituted "the market."

As shown in Figure 7.7, between January 2000 and December 2009, investors in the S&P 500 lost money. In fact, a $1,000,000 portfolio invested in the S&P at the beginning of that period would have declined to $909,047 by the end of the decade. But, on the other hand, the globally diversified portfolio of stocks and bonds shown in Figure 7.8 would have grown from $1,000,000 to $1,866,681.

Consider those two portfolios. The globally diversified portfolio is owned by an investor still on track to meet their goals.

The S&P 500 portfolio belongs to someone who may have to seriously reevaluate their retirement timeframe and lifestyle.

Which portfolio would you rather have? Which of those people would you rather be?

The past is never a perfect prologue to the future, and the bottom line is that no one can predict the future with absolute certainty.

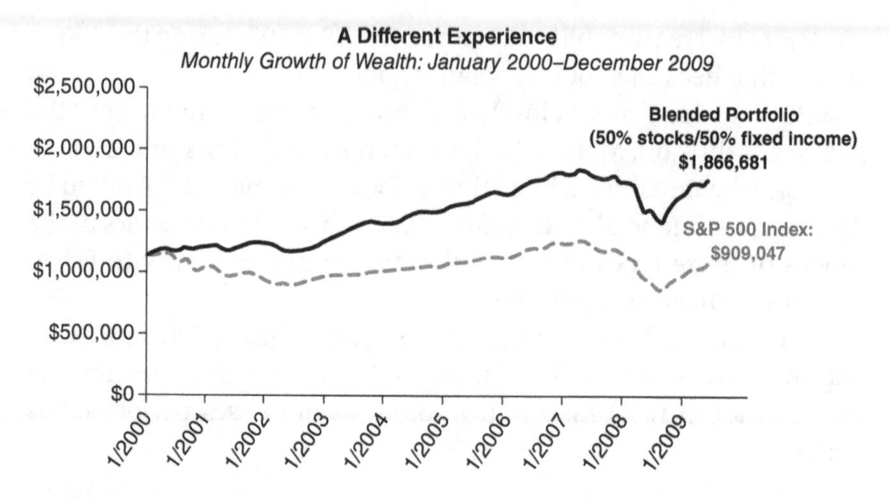

Figure 7.8 Growth of Wealth for S&P 500 and Diversified Portfolio
SOURCE: Based on data from Dimensional Fund Advisors and Standard & Poor's.

The best we can do is hypothesize probabilities, and then arrange portfolios to perform well across the widest range of outcomes.

To me the important question is this: If you're now two decades closer to retirement than you were in 2000, can your retirement plan really survive another Lost Decade?

Can your retirement plan really survive the increased risk that comes from focusing on a narrow subset of the global capital markets?

If not, maybe it's time to consider the benefits of smart diversification.

Chapter 8
You Must Learn How You'll Be Taxed

Let's pause for a moment and consider what your biggest future expense might be.

Will it be healthcare? Well, you'll likely pay a lot for medical expenses. Estimates vary, but it's safe to anticipate that a 65-year-old couple retiring now will spend somewhere between $285,000 and $385,000 during their retirement. That's a lot of money, but its not going to be your biggest expense.

What about travel? Maybe if you're lucky, and if that's your answer I salute your optimism and hope you're correct.

Housing could be a big expense, depending on whether you anticipate carrying a mortgage or paying rent for the majority of your retirement.

But for many people, the answer to the question of what their biggest future expense will be lies in the title to this chapter. That's right, taxes. The taxman always cometh, and over the course of your retirement taxes are quite likely to be your largest expense. This is also generally true when working, but as you'll soon see you probably have more control over the taxes you pay in retirement than during your working years.

Now, I don't know you personally so I'm not sure what your precise financial goals are. But at the end of the day, money can only go four places. When you have money, you can:

- **Spend it on yourself**
- **Give it to your family**
- **Give it to a charity**
- **Give it to the government (taxes)**

As I said earlier, I don't know what your goals are. Almost everyone wants to make sure they don't run out of money in retirement. Maybe you want to spend more money on yourself. Maybe you want to treat your family to a vacation, or help your children with a home purchase, or pay for a grandchild's college education, or leave an inheritance. Maybe your goals are charitable, and you want to increase your tithing, or leave a bequest to your favorite charity when you pass. Again, I don't know you, so I'm not sure exactly what it is that you want to accomplish.

But, I'm here to tell you that no matter what it is that you want to do, you're going to be far more successful at it if fewer of your dollars go to the government. Because the bottom line is that **the less you pay in taxes, the more money you'll have to spend on yourself, or give to your family, or give to a charity**.

As such, efficiently accumulating, investing, and distributing your assets in order to minimize your lifetime tax burden is a crucial step in securing your financial future and helping you live the lifestyle you desire.

However, and this is the crux of the matter, taxes are another area of your finances where you'll need to ignore the hype and pursue financial strategies outside of the mainstream. That is because, to be blunt, much of the common wisdom you've heard around saving for retirement is either incorrect, outdated, or both.

As with so much of your financial life, navigating your way to a tax efficient future is going to require a mindset shift, and you might have to adopt practices different than those you've used so far. Your reward for doing so could be a future in which you have more control of the taxes you pay, a higher likelihood of not running out of money, and a better chance of accomplishing your financial goals. It's up to you to decide if that reward is worth ignoring the hype and charting your own path.

If you've decided to chart your own course, let's take a closer look at how you can keep the taxman at bay.

But First, *the Hype*

Before we talk about what you should do to lower your future tax bill, let's take a moment to address some common misperceptions about what your future might look like. Some of these are addressed elsewhere in this book, but I want to summarize them here since its important to understand exactly where the prevailing wisdom comes from as well as why it might not make sense for you to follow that wisdom.

1. **You'll spend less in retirement:** As discussed in Chapter 5, many people spend as much or more in retirement. This is particularly true if you want to live a comparable lifestyle in retirement as you did when working, which is a reasonable definition of a successful retirement.
2. **You'll be in a lower tax bracket in retirement:** Maybe, if you spend far less money. But if you're living a similar lifestyle, you'll need a similar amount of money coming in which would lead to similar tax bills. Besides, ask yourself this: *Over the next 10 or 20 years, do you think taxes are going lower*? Do you think taxes are going higher?
3. **Defer, Defer, Defer:** Prevailing wisdom, based in large part on the misconceptions mentioned earlier, is that you should defer as much of your tax bill as possible during your working years. This may not make sense, for reasons we will explore in much greater detail.
4. **Taxes are inevitable, and beyond your control:** With proper planning you can control your taxes.

And Now, *the Truth*

If you're ready to ignore the hype and take control of your taxes, the starting point is to focus on diversifying the tax status of the assets you own and more importantly, *the future income streams you will receive.*

I know, I know. You probably read the words "tax status" and immediately tuned out. In fact, I'm impressed you're still reading. But I think your perseverance will be rewarded, because what I'm about to discuss isn't really about taxes. It's about quality of life later on in life. It's about living large while paying less to the taxman. And that, my friends, is a very exciting topic indeed.

Best of all, the taxation of your future income streams is something very much within your control. So, if the idea of maximizing your lifestyle and minimizing your future tax bills sounds appealing, read on!

Income Taxes: A Quick Primer

Living like a king while paying taxes like a pauper requires a basic understanding of how the U.S. tax system works. So, just like vegetables must be eaten before dessert, we'll have to cover some rather bland material before getting to the good stuff.

Picture a staircase. Staircases are great visuals for income taxes, because rates step up at successive income levels. Figure 8.1 shows the 2020 tax brackets for a single filer.

Tax rates are progressive, meaning that the higher your income, the higher the rate at which it's taxed.

There's a 10% rate, and 12%, 22%, 24%, 32%, 35%, and 37% rates – these are the federal rates. There are also state taxes, but since these vary widely, we'll focus on federal income tax for this discussion.

As an example, in 2020, the top of the 22% bracket was $85,525 of taxable income for a single filer ($171,050 for a married couple filing jointly). This is income after all deductions and can be found

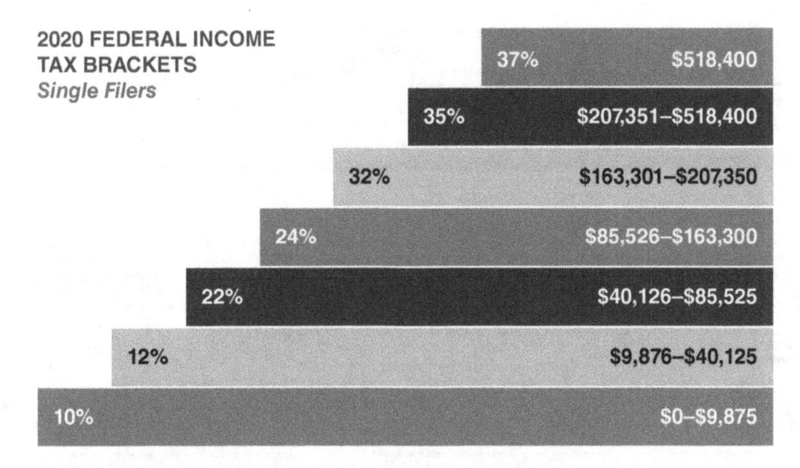

Figure 8.1 Federal Income Tax Brackets for a Single Filer
SOURCE: Analysis by Brian Perry. Information sourced from Internal Revenue Service.

on line 11b of tax form 1040. A sample of tax form 1040 is shown in Figure 8.2. This number on line 11b represents your taxable income and determines your marginal tax rate.

For instance, if you are married and filing jointly, and your taxable income on line 11b were $152,000, then your income would be taxed as shown in Figure 8.3.

As you can see, your income is taxed at marginal rates. This means that even though you're in the 22% tax bracket, you don't pay 22% of your taxable income to Uncle Sam. The total blended percentage you end up paying is what's called your effective tax rate.

To calculate your effective tax rate, you divide your income taxes by your taxable income. So, for the married couple earlier, you'd divide the taxes due ($25,020) by the taxable income ($152,000) and come up with an effective tax rate of approximately 16.5%.

The above refers to federal income taxes. There are different rates that apply for qualified dividends and capital gains, and these rates become very important as you move into retirement and begin to distribute income from your portfolio.

As a rough estimate, Figure 8.4 shows you what capital gains rate you might be subject to (keep in mind, these levels are approximate, not exact).

Form **1040** Department of the Treasury—Internal Revenue Service (99)
U.S. Individual Income Tax Return **2019** OMB No. 1545-0074 IRS Use Only—Do not write or staple in this space.

Filing Status ☐ Single ☐ Married filing jointly ☐ Married filing separately (MFS) ☐ Head of household (HOH) ☐ Qualifying widow(er) (QW)
Check only one box.
If you checked the MFS box, enter the name of spouse. If you checked the HOH or QW box, enter the child's name if the qualifying person is a child but not your dependent. ▶

Your first name and middle initial	Last name	**Your social security number**
If joint return, spouse's first name and middle initial	Last name	**Spouse's social security number**

Home address (number and street). If you have a P.O. box, see instructions. Apt. no.
City, town or post office, state, and ZIP code. If you have a foreign address, also complete spaces below (see instructions).
Presidential Election Campaign Check here if you, or your spouse if filing jointly, want $3 to go to this fund. Checking a box below will not change your tax or refund. ☐ You ☐ Spouse
Foreign country name | Foreign province/state/county | Foreign postal code | If more than four dependents, see instructions and ✓ here ▶ ☐

Standard Deduction **Someone can claim:** ☐ You as a dependent ☐ Your spouse as a dependent
☐ Spouse itemizes on a separate return or you were a dual-status alien

Age/Blindness **You:** ☐ Were born before January 2, 1955 ☐ Are blind **Spouse:** ☐ Was born before January 2, 1955 ☐ Is blind

Dependents (see instructions):

(1) First name	Last name	(2) Social security number	(3) Relationship to you	(4) ✓ if qualifies for (see instructions): Child tax credit	Credit for other dependents
				☐	☐
				☐	☐
				☐	☐
				☐	☐

1	Wages, salaries, tips, etc. Attach Form(s) W-2			1
2a	Tax-exempt interest	2a	b Taxable interest. Attach Sch. B if required	2b
3a	Qualified dividends	3a	b Ordinary dividends. Attach Sch. B if required	3b
4a	IRA distributions	4a	b Taxable amount	4b
c	Pensions and annuities	4c	d Taxable amount	4d
5a	Social security benefits	5a	b Taxable amount	5b
6	Capital gain or (loss). Attach Schedule D if required. If not required, check here ▶ ☐			6
7a	Other income from Schedule 1, line 9			7a
b	Add lines 1, 2b, 3b, 4b, 4d, 5b, 6, and 7a. This is your **total income** ▶			7b
8a	Adjustments to income from Schedule 1, line 22			8a
b	Subtract line 8a from line 7b. This is your **adjusted gross income** ▶			8b
9	**Standard deduction or itemized deductions** (from Schedule A)	9		
10	Qualified business income deduction. Attach Form 8995 or Form 8995-A	10		
11a	Add lines 9 and 10			11a
b	**Taxable income.** Subtract line 11a from line 8b			11b

Standard Deduction for—
- Single or Married filing separately, $12,200
- Married filing jointly or Qualifying widow(er), $24,400
- Head of household, $18,350
- If you checked any box under *Standard Deduction*, see instructions.

For Disclosure, Privacy Act, and Paperwork Reduction Act Notice, see separate instructions. Cat. No. 11320B Form **1040** (2019)

Figure 8.2 Example of U.S. Individual Tax Return Form 1040
SOURCE: Internal Revenue Service.

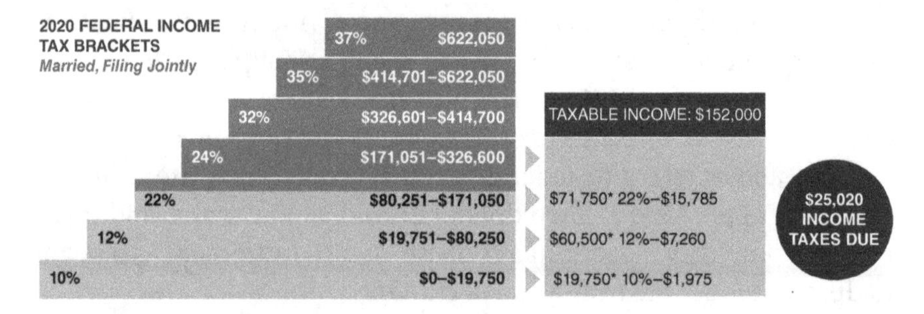

Figure 8.3 Example of Income Tax Calculation for a Married Couple
SOURCE: Analysis by Brian Perry. Tax brackets courtesy of Internal Revenue Service.

If taxable income falls below the 22% tax bracket	0%
If taxable income falls at or above the 22% tax bracket but below the 37% rate	15%
If taxable income falls in the 37% tax bracket	20%

Figure 8.4 Federal Capital Gains Tax Brackets
SOURCE: Analysis by Brian Perry. Information from Internal Revenue Service.

Both your effective tax rate and your capital gains tax rate are important figures to incorporate into your overall tax planning. But for the discussion to follow, it's your marginal rate that is most important, because that is the rate you will pay on your next dollar of income.

Are Taxes Going Higher?

The truth of course is that no one knows for sure, but the general consensus among people I meet is that yes, taxes are eventually going higher. In fact, it seems inevitable that taxes will increase, given the challenges facing the country: funding for entitlement programs like Social Security and Medicare, a huge national debt, an aging population, and so forth.

But all of those circumstances existed a couple of years ago, and at that point, instead of going higher, tax rates actually fell. The Tax Cut and Jobs Act, put into place at the start of 2018, lowered both business and personal income tax rates. The corporate tax cuts are permanent, but the individual tax cuts are not.

Because the personal income tax reductions were forecast to add more than one trillion dollars to the national debt, they could not be made permanent without a supermajority of 60 votes in the Senate. The Bill passed along partisan lines (shocker there!) without a supermajority, and so the personal tax cuts are only temporary and sunset after 2025. In other words, we know for a fact that, absent an act of Congress, taxes are going higher after 2025.

Congress could act of course, and the reversion to the old tax rates may not occur as scheduled. But ask yourself this: If Congress does act to alter tax law, do you think it would be to lower taxes further? Or would the more likely outcome be a reversion to higher tax rates? Given that uncertainty, taking advantage of a bird in hand to do some strategic tax planning at a time when you have the lowest tax rates in your lifetime could make a lot of sense.

Tax Diversification

Just as diversifying your investments makes sense, it's also wise to practice tax diversification. There are three different sources of cash flow in retirement, and as you can see in Figure 8.5, they are all taxed differently.

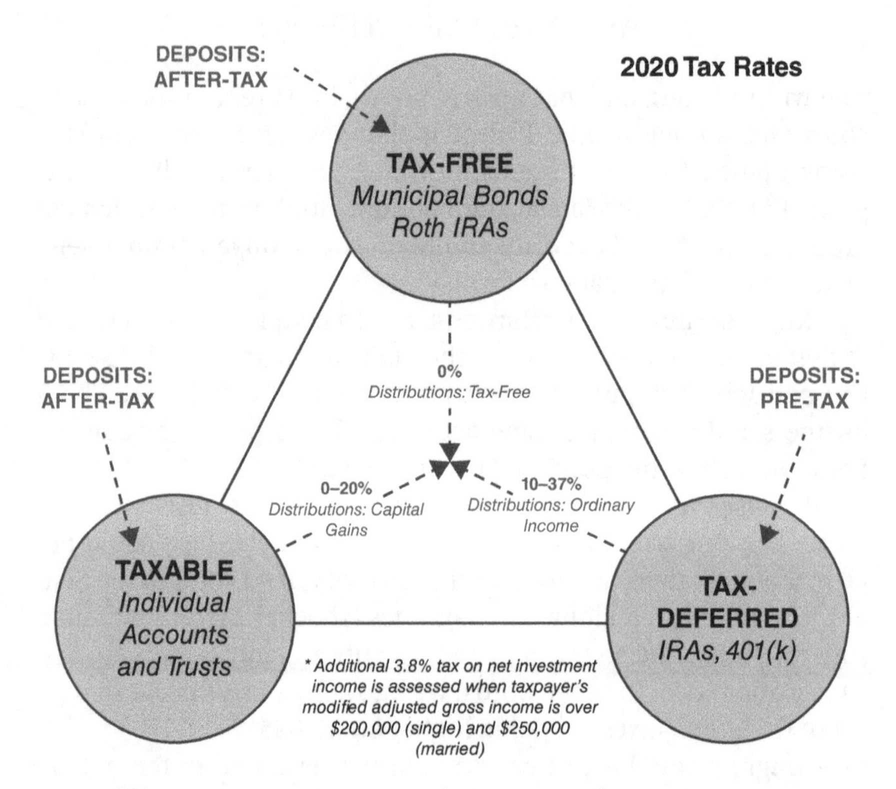

Figure 8.5 How Retirement Income Sources Are Taxed
SOURCE: Analysis by Brian Perry.

One source of income gets distributed tax-free. This pool includes any assets held in a Roth account or a Health Savings Account (HSA) as well as municipal bonds. Income derived from the second pool includes capital gains and dividends received from stocks, bonds, real estate, and so forth. The tax treatment of these assets varies, but careful planning can often result in a 15% rate for these funds; some folks might even avoid taxes here completely.

The final pool consists of tax-deferred assets, and the defining characteristic of this bucket is that when you take money out, it's taxed at your ordinary income rate, which can be as high as 37%. This bucket includes most of your retirement accounts, such as IRAs, 401(k)s, TSPs, 403(b)s, and 457s. Income derived from pensions and Social Security, as well as from any part-time work you, do also falls in this bucket.

One of the keys to a successful retirement is to manage the tax efficiency of your income by drawing from the appropriate pool at the appropriate time. Doing so can slow down the rate at which your assets are depleted, or phrased differently, can increase the length of your retirement. Alternatively, tax efficiency can allow you to retire sooner, or perhaps enhance your lifestyle in retirement.

Do You Know Who Your Partner Is?

If I asked you if you have ever run an investment partnership, how would you answer that question? Before you give me your answer, let's define an investment partnership as follows:

> *An investment partnership is an arrangement wherein you do the investing and your partner receives a slice of your profits.*

With that definition in mind, I'll ask you again whether you have ever run an investment partnership.

How'd you answer that question? If you replied no, let me ask you a couple of additional questions:

- Do you have an IRA?
- Do you have a 401(k), 403(b), TSP, or similar employer-sponsored plan?

If you answered yes to either of those questions, then you have in fact run an investment partnership. In fact, you're running one right now. Your investment partner is ... the **IRS**!

Think about it. If the definition of an investment partnership is that you do the investing and someone else gets a share of your profits, then an IRA or 401(k) is the very definition of an investment partnership. You invest the money, and the IRS gets a share of any profits when you withdraw funds from the account at some future date.

Let's broaden our discussion beyond investment partnerships to talk about partnerships in general. When you enter into a business partnership of any sort, there are a couple of things you probably want to sort out right upfront. *Chief among those would be who gets what share of the profits.*

Think about it. The guys who started Google never would have waited until it was a multibillion-dollar business to determine who owned how much of the company. At the start of any business partnership, the partners need to determine who owns what. This way there are no future disagreements, and everyone involved has a clear idea of what the fruits of their labor might look like. The more important the partnership is to your future, the more important it is to nail down this ownership structure so that you know what to expect going forward.

If you believe (and I hope you do!) that saving for your retirement is pretty important to your future, then that only serves to heighten the following irony:

> *Your IRA or 401(k) is the only business partnership you'll ever enter into in which you've given the other side unilateral ability to change the partnership terms anytime they want!*

Remember, the IRS owns a share of your account. But even worse is that with the flick of a pen they can raise tax rates, **which effectively increases their ownership share in the partnership you are running with them.**

And there's nothing you can do about that.

No wonder planning for retirement is so difficult. You don't know what the economy will be like, or what stock market returns will be, or what inflation might do to your future cost of living. You don't know if you'll stay healthy, or what your family situation will be, or how long you'll live.

And now you don't even know how much money you have saved for retirement.

Because you know that the IRS owns some portion of your savings, but you don't know how much, because you don't know what future tax rates will be.

That is why it's so important to build some tax diversification and take back control of your future financial situation.

Let me be clear that there is nothing wrong with deferring taxes. As with so much financial advice, the suggestion to defer taxes rests on a solid foundation, at least while you are accumulating assets. But as your portfolios grow in size, and as you move closer to retirement, your strategy should evolve, and your goal should shift from tax deferral to tax optimization. And by tax optimization, I mean that you should seek not just to minimize your taxes in the current year, **but rather to pay the least amount of tax possible over the course of both your working years and your retirement.**

And unfortunately, having the bulk of your assets tied up in a tax-deferred pool whose distribution will result in the highest of tax rates just isn't optimal, particularly when you don't know what those future tax rates will be. This situation is only exacerbated by the fact that taxes seem likely to increase in the years ahead.

Careful planning can help fix this situation. If you take only one of my suggestions, please do the following: **Give as much care, effort, and attention to protecting and distributing your wealth as you did to working for and accumulating your wealth.** That, dear reader, is the key to enjoying your golden years and to leaving the sort of legacy you desire.

As If That's Not Enough ...

As if the lack of clarity around how much of your money will end up in your partner's pocket weren't bad enough, there are several other issues you'll face if the bulk of your assets are tied up in tax-deferred accounts.

The first challenge you'll face is that all of the one-offs in life will cost you significantly more than they otherwise would. Think about it this way. Your core lifestyle (housing, food, travel, etc.) is going to require a certain level of income. That income will generate taxes, and you'll find yourself in whatever tax bracket you fall into based on that income.

Then you decide to remodel the bathroom. Or you want to take a once-in-a-lifetime six-month cruise. Or you have a medical emergency or need long-term care.

Let's look at what occurs if you need a new car. Just because you're buying a new car doesn't mean that you can stop paying the mortgage or cell phone bill. And you probably won't stop eating, either. So your core lifestyle will remain similar, and hence your taxable income will remain consistent, too.

But now you need $30,000 for a new car. If all of your money is in a tax-deferred IRA or 401(k), where are you going to pull the money for the car from? The answer of course is that tax-deferred account.

The problem is that the $30,000 you pull from that account represents additional taxable income. So not only do you have to pull the $30,000 for that new car, you also need to pull money to pay the taxes on the money you pulled to pay the car. And to take that one step further, you also need to pull money to pay the taxes on the money you pulled to pay the taxes on the money you pulled to pay for the new car. The effect is not unlike a snowball gaining speed downhill, and the result is that your $30,000 new car can easily wind up costing $40,000 or more.

Oh, and by the way, this situation becomes even worse when you consider that the funds you're pulling from that deferred account might actually be pushing you into a higher tax bracket to boot.

Inflation causes a similar situation to occur with your core living expenses. With inflation, your cost of living increases as time goes by, which means that you need more dollars to live the same lifestyle. And, you guessed it. Those additional dollars needed mean you'll have to pull more funds from your tax-deferred accounts, leading to higher tax bills and declining account balances.

So, the bottom line is that a life paid for with funds from your tax-deferred accounts is likely to be a very expensive life indeed.

What's Certain in Life?

Let's summarize where we are so far. For starters, having all your funds in a tax-deferred account means you'll be carrying around the IRS as an investment partner for the rest of your life, which is a bit like running a marathon with a gorilla on your back. Then, your tax bills are going to increase over time as you withdraw money to keep pace with inflation or pay for the one-offs in life. But, that has to be the end of the bad news regarding the predicament you're facing.

Right?

Nope.

Just to make things even better, your tax-deferred investments come with a wonderful cocktail of rules and requirements designed to make you miserable. Let's take a look at three of them now:

Required Minimum Distribution (RMD) – Sure, the IRS owns part of your deferred account and they are going to collect taxes when you pull money from that account. But maybe you don't need the money and aren't ever planning on pulling it out. So you're good, right?

Wrong.

Remember, the IRS essentially gave you a loan when you put money in this account. You should have paid taxes at that point, but the IRS "loaned" you the money for the taxes and let you put it into your retirement account. Bu unfortunately, those pesky Internal Revenue Service agents aren't the forgetful sort. They lent you money, and they want it back.

Required Minimum Distribution Table		
Participant Age	Distribution Period (Years)	Required Minimum Distribution (% of balance)
72	25.6	3.91%
73	24.7	4.05%
74	23.8	4.20%
75	22.9	4.37%
80	18.7	5.35%
85	14.8	6.76%
90	11.4	8.77%
95	8.6	11.63%
100	6.3	15.87%
105	4.5	22.22%
110	3.1	32.26%
115+	1.9	52.63%

Note: The chart above is based on the Uniform Lifetime Table for use by: 1) Unmarried owners. 2) Married owners whose spouses are not more than 10 years younger. 3) Married owners whose spouses are not the sole beneficiaries of their IRAs. Percent of balance for required minimum distribution is approximate due to rounding.

Figure 8.6 Required Minimum Distributions
SOURCE: Information from Internal Revenue Service.

When you turn 72 the IRS decides its time to start collecting on what you owe them. They do this by forcing you to begin taking withdrawals from your deferred account, regardless of whether or not you actually need or want the money. And then of course they tax you on these forced distributions.

Required Minimum Distributions (RMDs) start when you turn 72. They then increase each year, as you get older, according to the following schedule in Figure 8.6.

So, at age 72 your RMD is approximately 4% (3.91%, to be precise). And then that withdrawal amount increases each year because the IRS wants you to deplete the assets before you die so that they can collect their tax money.

Required Minimum Distributions are inevitable, and if the majority of your assets are held in tax-deferred accounts, your 72nd birthday might start to look like a looming cliff.

There's only one real way to avoid those RMDs. However, it's quite a dramatic step, and I don't necessarily recommend it.

The reason I don't necessarily recommend avoiding your RMDs is because the best way to do so is to die!

That's right, if you die, you don't have to take RMDs. But it is, as I said, a draconian step, and one I can't really recommend.

And besides, don't forget that old saying about how the only two certainties in life are death and taxes. Because ...

Income in Respect of a Decedent (IRD) – Even if you die, you still can't really avoid the taxman. Or, to be more precise, your heirs can't avoid him. That's because, in the event that you die while there are still funds in your retirement account, your heirs will be forced to pay taxes via Income in Respect of a Decedent, which effectively acts like RMDs for those who inherit IRAs.

That's right, you die and then the taxman comes along with a shovel and a crowbar. The taxman digs up your grave, uses a crowbar to pry open your casket, reaches into your pocket, and takes some more taxes in the form of IRD. Because even in death the taxman cometh!

There was a positive here, however. Remember, RMDs are based on life expectancy. And often times you wind up leaving your accounts to someone younger than you, like a son or daughter, or niece or nephew. And that younger person has a longer life expectancy, so their RMDs are less each year than yours would have been. For instance, if you pass away at 80, and your daughter is 40 at the time, the ensuing distributions she must take (assuming she sets this up correctly) would be much less than those you had been taking, since she has a much longer assumed life expectancy. This concept is known as a stretch IRA because the distributions are stretched across a greater number of years. This stretching results in more time for the funds to grow tax deferred with the result that your daughter receives more of an inheritance. This was a very good thing and could potentially save your heirs a great deal of money.

Let me pause for a moment and ask you a question. When you think of Congress, is the first word that comes to mind *bipartisan*? Probably not.

Which makes it truly impressive that in 2019 the House of Representatives voted 417 to 3 on a bill. Now, I'm not sure you could get that kind of consensus from the House around things as noncontroversial as:

- Having food poisoning isn't fun.
- Puppies are cute.
- Bell bottoms were a bad idea.

And yet that august body was able to join together in brotherly and nearly universal harmony as they agreed to a bill that included, among other things, the abolition of that lovely stretch IRA I discussed earlier.

So now, instead of taking those distributions over the next 40 years of her life, your daughter is forced to deplete the account you left her over a 10-year time frame. Which means far more of that money will go to the IRS, and far less will go to your loved ones.

But at least we finally got Congress to come together in bipartisan unity!

Penalties – So to summarize, the IRS wants you to get older (72) or they want you to die (IRDs). There's also a third thing they want you to do, and it's equally unappealing. Because basically, the IRS wants you to screw up!

That's right, your partners over at the Internal Revenue Service are hoping you make a mistake and miscalculate or forget to withdraw your RMD, because, if you do so, the IRS assesses a penalty of 50% of the amount you neglected to take.

In other words, if your RMD was supposed to be $20,000, and you neglected to take it, you'd owe a $10,000 penalty!

Making matters even worse, you'd still owe taxes on the entire $20,000 you were supposed to withdraw. In that scenario, you'd see your IRA balance decline by $20,000, but might only wind up with $5,000 in your pocket. The remaining $15,000 could easily have gone to your friends at the IRS in the form of penalties and taxes.

So, to summarize the details of the partnership you've entered into with the IRS:

- Your "partner" wants you to get older and reach age 72.
- Your "partner" wants you to pass away so they can tax your heirs.
- Your "partner" wants you to screw up so they can shift 50% of your partnership stake to their side of the ledger.

And of course, in any of the these scenarios, as well as in those instances in which you're withdrawing funds simply because you need the money to live on, the distributions are taxed as ordinary income, which represents the highest rates available.

When you look at it that way, you've unwittingly entered into quite the devil's bargain when it comes to how you're going to fund your retirement.

Fortunately, there is a solution.

Part III

Just Because You're Paranoid Doesn't Mean They Aren't Out to Get You

Chapter 9
How to Avoid the Taxman Without Going to Jail

As you might suspect by now, the solution to your tax problem lies in moving as much money as possible into the tax-free and taxable pools. Doing so has several benefits. First of all, moving money out of your tax-deferred accounts now will minimize your future distributions from those accounts, which will reduce your future taxes. Secondly, distributions from the tax-free and taxable accounts either don't generate taxes or are taxed at much lower rates. So, if in retirement you are primarily living off funds in your tax-free and taxable accounts, you can be living like a king (or at least a prince) while paying taxes like a pauper.

Think about it like this. In retirement you'll wind up pulling cash from all three pools. For example, let's say you want to live off $100,000. You pull funds from your tax- deferred pool up to the top of the 12% tax bracket. You then pull the rest of the money you need from your Roth account at a zero percent tax rate and from your taxable account at a 15% or lower capital gains rate. You're now living at an income level that should put you in the 22% tax bracket. But you're paying taxes at closer to 12%. That means you can:

- Make your money last longer.
- Enjoy a higher standard of living.
- Both of the above!

The key, then, to enhancing your retirement is to create the ability to pull more of your income from the tax-free and taxable pools while minimizing the amount of money you need to pull from your tax-deferred accounts.

Building Your Tax-Free Pool of Money

Let's start by focusing on the tax-free pool and getting money into a Roth account. There are two main ways to get money into a Roth IRA – *contributions* and *conversions*. Let's start by looking at contributions.

There are several different ways that you can *contribute* to a Roth account. Let's take a look at each of these in turn:

Roth IRA Contributions: For 2020, you can contribute up to $6,000 to a Roth IRA account. If you are over age 50, there is an additional $1,000 catch-up provision, so you can contribute a total of $7,000 if you are 50 or above. Roth IRA contributions are always made with after-tax dollars, and there are no tax benefits at the time you make the contribution. However, the money you put in, as well as any gains, are free from taxation when you take them out.

There are several restrictions regarding Roth IRA contributions. First of all, you need to have earned income in order to contribute. Earned income comes from employment, so you need to be working to contribute to a Roth. Alternatively, you can make a spousal contribution if you are married and your spouse is working. Because you need to be working to contribute, retirees generally cannot contribute to a Roth account, unless they have a part-time job.

Social Security and pension income, rental income, and investment income do not represent earned income and are not eligible for contributing to a Roth IRA.

Secondly, there are income limits that determine eligibility for Roth IRA contributions. For 2020, if you are single and make more than $124,000 or married and make more than $196,000, your ability to contribute to a Roth IRA begins to get phased out. Once you get above $139,000 single or $206,000 married, you are ineligible to contribute because you make too much money.

If you fall into this category, though, there is a workaround.

Backdoor Roth IRA Contributions: If your income falls above the IRS eligibility limits for Roth IRA contributions, you still may be able to move money into a Roth IRA account. That is because anyone, regardless of income, is eligible to make *after-tax contributions* to a traditional IRA account. This process involves taking dollars you have already paid taxes on (hence the term *after-tax*) and contributing those dollars to an IRA account.

Of course, the benefit of making contributions to a traditional IRA account is that you get an immediate tax deduction. If you were just using after-tax dollars to make those contributions, you'd be losing the main benefit of contributing to a traditional IRA. But the strategy doesn't end there.

Once you've made your after-tax contribution, you then immediately take those dollars and convert them to a Roth IRA account. Because you're using after-tax dollars, there's no tax impact to this conversion. You've effectively done in two steps what you would have done in one move if the IRS didn't think you made too much money. And of course the money now resides in your Roth account, where it can forever grow free of taxes.

You might think that the IRS frowns on this strategy. You are, after all, circumventing the income limits on Roth IRA contributions in order to make what is in effect a Roth IRA contribution. But in fact the IRS has come out and said that this strategy is okay, so if you want to contribute funds to your Roth account but are over the income limits for Roth IRA contributions, this could be an important strategy for you to incorporate.

There is one caveat. Remember that the key to this strategy is that you don't pay taxes when you convert those IRA contributions. This is because those dollars have already been taxed. However, this may not be the case if you already have existing traditional IRA accounts with *pretax dollars* in them.

If this is the case, the IRS will look at the value of your after-tax dollars in the context of all of your IRA dollars (pretax and after-tax). Only a pro rata portion of your conversion will then be free from taxation. In many instance this means that if you have IRAs with pretax dollars, it may not make sense for you to pursue the backdoor Roth strategy.

Fortunately, there are several other ways to get money into a Roth account.

Roth 401(k) Contributions: If you have a defined contribution retirement plan available at work, the plan may offer a Roth component. For the purposes of this discussion, I'll refer to the plan as a 401(k), but the option discussed here may apply equally if you have a 403(b), TSP, or other type of defined contribution plan.

If your 401(k) has a Roth component, you will have an option of contributing to either your traditional plan or the Roth plan. You can also choose to split your contributions between the two plans. The traditional plan would fall within the tax-deferred pool discussed earlier. You get an immediate tax deduction for your contributions, but in the future you'll face all of the challenges and drawbacks inherent in tax-deferred accounts.

With the Roth 401(k), you won't get an immediate tax deduction. In fact, if you've been contributing to your pretax 401(k) and you now switch to the Roth 401(k), the loss of the tax deduction will actually feel like you've been hit with a tax increase. However, once you get past that initial pain, you'll experience the tax-free growth and distributions inherent in a Roth account.

For 2020 you can contribute $19,500 to a Roth or traditional 401(k). If you're over age 50 you can also add a $6,500 catch-up contribution for a total of $26,000. There are no income limitations on eligibility for Roth 401(k) contributions.

It is important to note that even if you choose to participate in the Roth 401(k), any matching funds provided by your employer will always be deposited into the pretax 401(k) plan.

Interested in getting even more money into that tax-free pool? That's great, because you might have access to one additional method of making Roth contributions.

After-Tax 401(k) Contributions: Although the 2020 contribution limit for a 401(k) is $19,500 ($26,000 if over age 50), the total amount that can be deposited into a 401(k) is actually $63,500. This amount can be comprised of your pretax or Roth contributions, any employer matching contributions, and then any after-tax contributions you choose to make. For instance, if you are 55 years old, you could theoretically deposit:

- $19,500 employee contribution
- $6,500 over 50 catch-up contribution
- Your employer's match, say $10,000
- $27,500 "after-tax" contribution

These contributions would then total $63,500, which is the limit for total contributions to a 401(k) in 2020. Let's talk a little more about those after-tax contributions.

Remember, the benefit of putting your 401(k) contributions into the pretax option is that you get an immediate tax write-off. But the drawback of doing so is that all future growth is taxed as ordinary income when you take funds out.

Well, when you make an after-tax contribution, the dollars are deposited in the traditional 401(k), but you don't get a tax deduction (hence the name *after tax*). But because the dollars are in the traditional account, all future growth is still taxed as ordinary income, even though you didn't receive a tax deferral when you contributed. In that regard, making after-tax contributions is kind of a lose-lose proposition. So then, why am I talking about them?

Because, what you might do is make an after-tax contribution to your traditional 401(k) and then, if your plan allows it, immediately roll those dollars into the Roth component of your plan. Because you're using after-tax dollars, there are no tax consequences to your actions. And once the dollars are in the Roth part of the plan, all future growth is free from taxes.

This after-tax strategy is sometimes referred to as a "mega-backdoor Roth" because it allows you to funnel large amounts of money into your Roth accounts on a yearly basis. However, it is important to note that your ability to take advantage of after-tax contributions to your 401(k) will be dependent upon what your particular plan does and doesn't allow, so make sure to check with your benefits department prior to pursuing this strategy.

Accelerating the Flow of Funds to Your Tax-free Pool

Now let's shift our attention to Roth *conversions*, which can be a powerful tool for accelerating the flow of funds into your tax-free pool. Roth conversions occur whenever you take dollars from your tax-deferred account and move them into your Roth account. There are no income limits for doing a Roth conversion and you don't need to be working or have earned income to process a conversion. There are also no limits around how much you can convert in a given year.

The bad news is that dollars converted from your tax-deferred account are considered a distribution. This means that any funds converted are taxed as ordinary income in the year you process the conversion.

The good news is that the amount you convert, and any future gains, are free from taxes. You've bought back your share of the partnership you've been running with the IRS. Your account is now yours, and you have certainty around how much money you actually have for retirement. Life is grand.

So, the end result of a Roth conversion is tax-free Nirvana. But the process of getting there involves paying taxes. So how do you determine whether a Roth conversion makes sense for you? And if the strategy does make sense, how much should you convert?

Remember, you're going to pay taxes on the assets in your retirement accounts at some point; the goal here isn't tax avoidance. The goal is to minimize your tax bill across your lifetime, to shelter future portfolio gains from taxes, and to give you control over your finances in retirement.

With that in mind, the starting point is to prepare a tax projection. This tax projection should identify your current tax bracket while also forecasting your future taxes. This process will help you to identify what tax bracket you want to be in now and in the future.

Once you've drawn this line in the sand you can then calculate how much of a Roth conversion might make sense this year, next year, and beyond.

One thing to be aware of is that the deadline for completing Roth conversions is December 31 of each year, which means that you might not have a completely accurate picture of what your annual income looks like prior to facilitating the conversion. This situation is exacerbated because since the Tax Reform and Jobs Act of 2017, Roth conversions are irrevocable, which means that you need to be comfortable with the amount you convert, since you can't change your mind and undo a conversion.

It's also important to note that, in order to move as much money as possible at as low a tax rate as possible, you might want to convert each year, which means that you'll need new tax projections each year. So, you can see that although this strategy is a fantastic way to maximize the tax efficiency of your retirement income, it's also somewhat challenging to put into place.

Building Your Taxable Pool of Money

We've been focusing on how to get money into your tax-free pool, but let's shift now and talk about the taxable pool. Moving money into this pool is easy. Another name for the taxable pool is nonqualified. That means that there are no government rules or regulations around putting money into or taking money out of this pool. You are free to contribute when and how and in whatever increments you wish. You are also free to withdraw funds whenever you want. So, the question then becomes why might you put money into this pool?

Well, for starters that lack of rules and regulations is nice. The taxable pool has the most flexibility of any of the pools. So, if your income or cash-flow sources are such that you're ineligible to contribute to retirement accounts, this will be the receptacle for your future savings. Also, remember that retirement accounts (both tax-free and tax-deferred) have rules and restrictions around withdrawals prior to age 59½, and early withdrawals are generally subject to a 10% penalty. There are several potential workarounds to circumnavigate those rules, but for the most part if you're planning to retire prior to age 59½, you'll want to have some money in the taxable pool in order to avoid penalties.

The taxable pool also qualifies for special tax treatment. Depending on how the funds in this pool are invested, they could be subject to either ordinary income tax rates or long-term capital gains rates. As you may recall, long-term capital gains rates are significantly lower than ordinary income tax rates, which you can see in Figure 9.1.

As you can see, the rate you pay on capital gains is lower than the rate you would pay on ordinary income. That makes it important to be aware of what investments generate ordinary income and which qualify for long-term capital gains treatment.

- Interest is considered ordinary income so if you own bonds in your taxable pool, you'll pay taxes at ordinary income rates. The same holds true for most "cash," including money markets, CDs, and savings accounts.

If taxable income falls below the 22% tax bracket	0%
If taxable income falls at or above the 22% tax bracket but below the 37% rate	15%
If taxable income falls in the 37% tax bracket	20%

Figure 9.1 Federal Capital Gains Tax Brackets
SOURCE: Analysis by Brian Perry. Information from the Internal Revenue Service.

- Income from real estate investment trusts (REITs) is considered ordinary income. By law, REITs must distribute most of their earnings each year, and given that these earnings qualify as ordinary income, REITs are among the least tax-efficient investment vehicles around.
- Short-term capital gains are ordinary income. It is very important to note that there are two types of capital gains. Short-term capital gains occur when an asset is held for one year or less and then sold for a profit. Long-term capital gains occur when an asset is held for more than a year and then sold at a profit. Long-term capital gains receive the preferential capital gains rates, whereas short-term capital gains are considered ordinary income and taxed as such.
- Ordinary dividends are taxed at your ordinary income tax rate, whereas qualified dividends receive the preferential long-term capital gains rates. Qualified dividends are dividends received from a U.S. corporation or a qualified foreign corporation. The exact treatment of each foreign company can vary but in general the company is considered qualified if it resides in a country that has a tax agreement with the United States. Furthermore, in order for a dividend from a U.S. or foreign company to be qualified, and receive the lower tax rates, the stock must be held for more than 60 days during a 121-day period that begins 60 days before the ex-dividend date (the date by which an investor must own the stock in order to qualify to receive the dividend payment).

If all of that sounds complicated, that's because it is. Strategic tax planning isn't easy, but the rewards are significant. For instance, would you rather pay 24% in taxes on a dividend or 15%? That 9% tax savings is your reward for putting in the effort on tax planning or hiring someone to do it for you.

When it comes to finances, I really like the idea of paying taxes at lower rates. But do you know what I like even more than paying taxes at low rates? My absolute favorite thing is not paying taxes at all. So, with that in mind let's look at how you might avoid taxation on investments in the taxable pool.

Tax Loss Harvesting: There are two ways to avoid taxes on income from your taxable pool. The first is to keep yourself in a low ordinary income tax bracket, because if your ordinary income falls within the 10% or 12% tax brackets, your long-term capital gains rate is zero. Accomplishing this may be possible if you focus on some strategic forward tax planning with your CPA or financial advisor. For now, though, let's assume that your income falls above those levels, but you still don't want to pay taxes.

When you have funds located in a taxable account, you can utilize a technique called tax loss harvesting (TLH) in order to manage your future taxes. The concept of TLH begins with the basic premise that some financial markets, particularly stocks, tend to fluctuate up and down while also tending to trend higher over longer periods of time.

If you own stocks, you're going to ride that rollercoaster, and so you take advantage of the ride by selling securities when they fall in value and then immediately buying back into the market. Because you immediately buy back in, you continue to participate in the longer-term upward trend, but the sale causes you to realize a "loss." This loss can be used to offset future gains, allowing you to generate income more tax efficiently in the future.

This is just a basic overview of the technique. In practice, you need to carefully consider what securities you buy and sell. You want to keep your portfolio consistent, but IRS regulations prohibit claiming losses if you buy back the same security within a month of selling it. Therefore, you need to utilize similar but not identical securities.

Furthermore, while many people only harvest tax losses near year-end, you should ideally evaluate the opportunity on a daily basis.

Between preferential tax rates and tax loss harvesting, the taxable pool provides robust opportunities for tax efficient retirement distributions. And we've previously discussed the glorious future you'll face when living off the tax-free pool.

Now that you're convinced that having money in each of the three pools is going to be your key to a low tax future, let's examine how you can marry your investments with your taxes. This next section is important, because it represents an opportunity that is about as close to free money as anything you are ever going to find.

Do You Want to Keep More of What You Make?

When it comes to investing, the usual way to get higher returns is to take more risk. So when someone tells you they are going to help you earn more, the part they generally don't share is that they are also going to subject you to the possibility of greater losses. Remember, risk and reward are always related in the financial universe. Anyone who tells you otherwise is probably trying to sell you something.

With that being said, I'm now going to tell you how to make more money without taking more risk.

I know, I know. I just said that wasn't possible and that anyone who claimed otherwise was trying to sell you something.

But I promise I'm not trying to sell you something. I'm just going to help you marry your investment strategy with your tax planning in a way that improves your returns.

Here is the caveat. I don't have a wand I can wave to get you higher absolute returns with less risk. What I do have, though, is a magic bullet that can allow you to earn higher after-tax returns with the same amount of risk.

What's so magic about that? It's magic because if you do what I'm about to discuss, less of your returns will go to Uncle Sam in the form of taxes. And if less goes to Uncle Sam, more goes to you and your family. Which means that you are effectively earning higher returns for the same amount of risk, which is magical indeed. Here is how it works.

Because of their characteristics, some types of investments are more or less appropriate to hold in a particular type of account. Therefore, the idea is that you are going to be extremely selective about which investment you own in which account.

Think about it like this. What is the good thing about the tax-free pool of money?

The answer of course is that all future withdrawals are free from taxes. But exactly what is tax-free? Not just the money you put in, but all the future growth on that money, too. Therein lies the beauty of the tax-free pool.

So, if you have a pool of money that is going to grow free from taxes forever and then come out tax free, what kind of investments do you want there?

Well, if every single dollar of growth is tax-free now and forever, you want as much growth as possible. And some investments, such as stocks, have higher expected returns, which means that you expect them to grow more in the future. These investments should therefore go in your tax-free pool (Roth accounts). In fact, you should maximize this concept by owning not just stocks, but the kinds of stocks with the highest expected returns in your Roth accounts.

Continuing with this thought process, what is the downside of the tax-deferred pool? Well, the upside is the immediate tax reduction, but the negative is that the money you put in, plus every single dollar of future growth, is taxed at the highest possible rate. Since that is the case, you aren't as interested in generating growth in that pool, since many of your gains are going to go to your partners at the IRS. Instead, more conservative investments (such as bonds) should go in the tax-deferred pool.

To be clear, growth is always a good thing, and if you have more money but have to pay taxes, that is better than having less money and not paying taxes. Let's not lose the forest for the trees here. Its not like you don't want your tax-deferred pool to grow. But the idea is that in a diversified portfolio, you are going to hold some more aggressive assets and some more conservative assets. And so, relatively speaking, you want to concentrate your future growth where it is most tax advantaged.

What about your taxable accounts? What kinds of investments do you want to hold there? Remember, this is the pool of money where the taxation can vary the most, depending upon what type of assets you hold. Whenever possible in the taxable pool you want to hold assets that produce either long-term capital gains or qualified dividends. Doing this will allow you to take advantage of the special tax rates we discussed earlier.

Furthermore, any price appreciation isn't taxed until the asset is sold, so stocks and other growth assets often make sense for your taxable pool. Then, when the asset is sold, the gains are taxed at the special rate. And as an added bonus, you can also incorporate tax loss harvesting and utilize any capital losses you might accrue. These losses would be wasted in your IRA or other tax-deferred account.

Importantly, while each type of account will have different investments, your accounts will, in aggregate, ultimately reflect your target asset allocation. That allocation doesn't change, because your financial goals and required rate of return haven't changed. The only thing that changes is where you hold each investment.

The goal of everything I've been discussing is to minimize your tax bill and maximize your after-tax returns. Now, as I've already admitted, strategic tax planning and finding synergies between your investments and your taxes are not necessarily easy concepts. In order to take advantage of the opportunities available to you, you'll likely either need to substantially increase your knowledge base and time commitment to your finances, or find a qualified professional to help you incorporate these concepts.

But the bottom line is that by combining an effective investment strategy with savvy tax planning, you can end up keeping more of what you make.

And that, dear reader, is going to greatly enhance your future lifestyle.

Chapter 10
Sorry, But You're Probably Your Own Worst Enemy

Are you ready for some bad news? I hope so, because I'm here to tell you that when it comes to your finances, the sad reality is that you are likely to be own worst enemy. In fact, the most painful recession or bear market probably won't hurt you as much as you'll hurt yourself.

It's not really your fault; the problem is that your brain didn't evolve in a manner designed to facilitate optimal financial decision-making. How could it have?

Evolution teaches us that humans have been around for roughly 200,0000 years. Before that we evolved from apes, small mammals, lizards, and, long, long ago, tiny single-celled sea creatures. And I'm guessing that pretty much none of those long-forgotten predecessors spent a lick of time worrying about whether to buy U.S. or international stocks, or if Amazon's stock was overvalued, or whether they should go short the Yen versus the Euro.

Take a moment now and spread your arms as wide as you can. If that distance from your fingertips on the left to your fingertips on your right were a timeline that represented the history of the earth, then proportionally, the length of time humans have been around would be about as wide as your fingernail. That should give you a sense, on a cosmic scale, of how unimportant financial decision-making has been across the eons.

That's the nature. Now let's consider the nurture. Because even if we flash forward to the point where humanity was well established, and then flash forward further still to the time when recorded history began, we would still see little need for financial sophistication.

Money was only first used somewhere between 3,000 and 7,000 years ago, and the first official currency wasn't minted until 600 BC by the Lydian King Allyattes. His son Croesus used that platform to build a fortune that prompted the old saying that someone is "as rich as Croesus." Even though that marked the advent of official money, currency usage didn't become widespread for quite some time after that. In fact, even throughout the Middle Ages and Renaissance, many European economies rested on a foundation of barter, rather than currency usage. Actual coins were fairly scarce and were often reserved for the wealthy nobility.

And even if you'd had a bunch of coins back in the day, where would you have kept them? Would you have carried them in your pocket or buried them in the yard? Perhaps.

You certainly would not have kept your coins in the bank, because banking, too, is a relatively new concept. Although crude banks have been around for several millennia, they really only came about in the form we know them in the Italian City States during the late Middle Ages and into the Renaissance.

And what about the stock market? Well, as the famous story goes, the New York Stock Exchange was founded under a buttonwood tree back in 1792. But the world's first exchange was actually the Amsterdam Stock Exchange, established in 1602, although, to be fair, it didn't actually trade stocks at its inception, because *stock companies and therefore stocks themselves* have only been around since 1606, when King James I formed the Virginia Company for the settlement of Jamestown. And while stock companies and stock exchanges were around in the seventeenth and eighteenth centuries, anyone who's ever read a Dickens novel or *The Journals of Lewis and Clark* could probably surmise that well into the nineteenth century, the vast swell of humanity probably never even contemplated a stock purchase.

Many popular investment products are even more recent creations. Jack Bogle at Vanguard invented the first index mutual fund in 1975. The exchange-traded fund (ETF) is an even more recent phenomenon, with the first such vehicle listed on the American Stock Exchange in 1993.

I could continue this history lesson, but I think you get the point. Not only are humans not biologically designed for investment success, but the very concept of investing, and many of the aspects of investing we take for granted, are staggeringly new when measured against the scale of human development.

Tales Your Parents Told You

If you had a typical upbringing, your parents might have read you bedtime stories from Doctor Seuss or *Winnie the Pooh*. As you got older, dinner conversations might have revolved around upcoming vacation plans, your grades in school, or dad's favorite football team.

And speaking of school, your favorite subject might have been math, or history, or science.

Saturday nights out with your friends probably revolved around a few drinks, a few laughs, and maybe a few misadventures.

Then college came and went, and there were more drinks, more laughs, and maybe a few more misadventures. Maybe you studied art history, or chemical engineering, or French literature.

Finally, you entered the workforce, maybe you got married or had kids, and the cycle repeated itself.

Notice if you will, that at no point in the progression I just laid out did you ever talk about one of the most important aspects of modern life – an area that has the capacity to cause significant angst and unhappiness, an area that can literally cause health issues and even premature death, an area that, if done correctly, can provide opportunities for enrichment and enjoyment.

I'm talking of course about finances. And I'm willing to bet that the vast majority of the population never discussed this vital topic with their parents, their siblings, their classmates, their teachers, or their friends.

Maybe that's why the most frequent comment I hear from folks I meet with is:

"I wish I'd looked into this stuff sooner."

People in their 70s tell me they wish they had started this process in their 60s. Those in their 60s wish they'd done something at 50. A 50-year-old wishes he was 40, and a 40-year-old says she hopes her 25-year-old sister learns this stuff.

The bottom line is that, despite the vital role financial success plays in a well-rounded life, very few of us get exposed to the subject during our formative years. By the time we do start to learn about money, we are often scrambling to catch up, or even worse, to correct mistakes we've already made.

What does this mean for you, today's investor, and why should you care? Well, as I began this chapter by pointing out, the unfortunate conclusion is that a combination of nature, nurture, and neglect has conspired to make you your own worst enemy on the road to financial success.

So, there you have the bad news. But this book is focused on lessons you can learn as opposed to reasons you are screwed. And so here is the good news: as with any challenge, the key to success begins with awareness. And once you're aware of how your brain is hardwired to sabotage your finances, you'll be in a far better position to overcome those flaws and achieve the success you desire and deserve.

With that in mind, let's explore some of the more common behavioral biases you might face, as well as some strategies you can use to mitigate those shortcomings. As you can see from Figure 10.1, the list of challenges you face is a long one.

Anchoring	Confirmation Bias
Overconfidence	Herd Behavior
Framing	Hindsight Bias
Self-Attribution Bias	Myopic Loss Aversion

Figure 10.1 Common Behavioral Biases
SOURCE: Analysis by Brian Perry.

Anchoring

The Behavioral Trait: Anchoring refers to a bias wherein the first data point received is given greater weight than subsequent data points. Here is a simple example. Imagine you look up the price of a stock for the first time, and it's trading at twenty dollars a share. You research the stock but ultimately decide not to buy it. Time passes and you happen upon the stock again and notice that it is now trading at ten dollars a share. A common bias is that people feel like the stock is cheap at ten dollars. This phenomenon is known as anchoring.

The problem with anchoring is that the belief that the stock is cheap is not based on a rational analysis of the company's current fundamentals and valuation, but rather a simple measurement against the initial value the first time you looked at the stock. The truth is that the stock may or may not be cheap, but that determination should have nothing to do with its price when you first stumbled on it.

A common manner in which this bias manifests itself is that people think the stock market is "expensive" because it's trading at a certain level. For instance, as of the end of 2019 the Dow Jones Industrial Average traded somewhere slightly below the 30,000 level. A decade earlier, the Index traded around the 10,000 level.

Some investors might think that stocks are too expensive because the Dow used to be at 10,000 and now it's approaching 30,000. But the reality is that the value a decade ago has absolutely no bearing on whether or not the Index is currently at, below, or above its fair value. Corporate earnings, interest rates, and the future direction of the economy will all decide whether the market is fairly priced. But none of those factors are in any way related to the level the Index happened to trade at in the past.

The anchoring trait can be particularly damaging as time goes by and the markets gradually move higher. For instance, if the Dow were to average 8% annual returns for the remainder of the twenty-first century, the Index would trade somewhere north of the 13 million level. In other words, your grandchildren, and perhaps even your children, are likely to live in a world where **the Dow trades above 10 million**!

Whether or not those future levels represent attractive values will have absolutely nothing to do with the fact that you can remember a time when the Dow traded in the tens of thousands. Anchoring bias will argue otherwise, but you'll need to overcome this temptation.

The Rational Response: New data points should be given equal weight with older data points and both should be analyzed according to fundamentals and valuations. New information should be given full consideration and incorporated into the decision-making process.

Furthermore, if you follow the principles in this book, you'll hopefully avoid the temptation to manipulate your portfolio based upon your guesses of where markets might go in the future. Following a well-thought-out plan based upon empirical research should reduce the impact that anchoring can have on your portfolio and your finances.

Confirmation Bias

The Behavioral Trait: Confirmation bias occurs when an individual seeks out or lends greater credence to information that supports his or her existing hypothesis. For example, if you're bullish on the stock market and subsequently seek out information that supports the case that stocks will go higher, you are engaging in confirmation bias.

Here's a real-world example from outside the world of finance. If someone holds liberal political beliefs, they tend to consume media (TV news, radio talk shows, Internet stories) that support a liberal agenda and demonize the right wing and its politicians. Right-wing Republicans tend to do the same thing in the opposite direction. This information then corroborates their initial beliefs that policy "X" or politician "Y" is right or wrong, or good or bad.

In the world of finance, this might occur when someone is concerned about the future course of the economy. The individual might then seek out news stories highlighting weaker economic reports. Or maybe they read strategy notes from economists known for their gloomy views. These reports then reinforce and exacerbate the reader's preexisting fears.

The Rational Response: There is nothing inherently wrong with this practice, particularly in areas such as politics in which opinions vary and decisions need not be made based on a rational analysis of the data. However, in the investment arena, it's important to always remain open to the possibility that your hypothesis is incorrect. The best way to do this is to analyze information that disagrees with your position.

In fact, many of the best investors deliberately seek out the opinion of those who disagree with them. Reading a report that argues against your view can help you identify why the writer feels the way he or she does. You need not agree with their conclusions, but the process of seeing how and why they formulate those conclusions will help you make sure you haven't missed any important data in your prior analysis. The exercise will also help crystalize how events could unfold in a manner contrary to what you are expecting. Then, you can be on the lookout for this possibility, and react swiftly and decisively if it comes to pass.

A textbook example of this process in action would be if a bullish investor sought out and considered the opinions of bearish investors in order to see if the bearish arguments have merit. Again, that does not mean the investor needs to change their bullish view. The idea is simply to be open to a variety of possibilities, as well as to identify what events could come to pass outside of the investor's base case.

Overconfidence Bias

The Behavioral Trait: In the game of baseball, even the best hitters fail to reach base the majority of the time. In other words, failure is the expected outcome each time a batter comes to the plate, yet many of them are at the top of their field and make millions of dollars a year.

Investing is similar in the sense that even the greatest of investors sometimes "fail" by losing money. That has to be the case, since investing involves anticipating future expected outcomes, and the future is inherently uncertain.

Furthermore, the fact is that the shorter the time horizon and the more speculative the investment, the higher the degree of uncertainty, and with it, the potential possibility of loss. And yet, research shows that investors repeatedly display an overconfidence bias, in that they place too much faith in their forecasts.

The problem with overconfidence is that it results in a slew of investment errors such as:

- Position sizes that are too large relative to the size of the overall portfolio
- Holding on to losses too long, because "it has to come back"
- A failure to properly diversify
- A refusal to consider alternative possibilities

One subset of investors is particularly prone to overconfidence bias. That cohort consists of anyone with a Y chromosome. That's right, studies have shown that male investors are far more prone to overconfidence bias than female investors. Frankly, I'm not sure why that's the case, but I suspect it's linked to whatever it is that makes men less prone to ask for directions, even when they're hopelessly lost.

A typical way the overconfidence bias might manifest itself would be an investor who has too much of their money in aggressive assets relative to their goals, time frame, and appropriate risk tolerance. For example, maybe the "right" portfolio mix for them is 50/50 stocks and bonds. But this person has "done their research" and is highly confident in the outlook for stocks in general, and technology stocks in particular. And so they plough 80% of their holdings into stocks, with the majority of that in tech because they "know the industry."

Of course, what usually happens in that situation is that things go well for a period of time, which further enhances our investor's already healthy self-confidence. Then, inevitably, the tide turns. Stocks in general sell off, led by technology. Our investor loses far more than they can afford to lose, which sets them back on the road to retirement. Now, the individual faces the unpleasant task of choosing between working longer or reducing their lifestyle in order to make up for their ego-driven mistakes.

The Rational Response: As with many behavioral biases, the first step to overcoming overconfidence bias is to recognize its presence. Now that you are aware that you may be subject to overconfidence bias, the steps to mitigate it are relatively straightforward. Having a written plan of action in the form of an Investment Policy Statement (IPS) will lay out in black and white your approach to investing, your target asset allocation, and your position limits. Then, as long as you stick to your written parameters, *regardless of your current conviction level*, you should be able to manage the downside risk that overconfidence can produce.

Remember, it's not the presence of behavioral biases that causes you harm. The damage is only done when you act upon impulses driven by those biases. So you don't need to try to correct your nature or your nurture. You simply need to put guardrails in place to help you avoid succumbing to the temptation to give in to your baser instincts.

An additional tip for overcoming overconfidence bias is to remember the difference between strategic and tactical asset allocation. Your strategic asset allocation is the mix of investments most likely to help you meet your financial goals with the least amount of risk possible. This strategic allocation should seldom change unless your life circumstances change.

Your tactical allocation reflects small tweaks to your strategic allocation, based on your current perception of market conditions. These alterations are designed to be relatively modest so that they help you a bit when you're right but don't cause too much harm when you're wrong. This approach can help you implement your views in a manner designed to prevent you from going "all in" due to an inflated confidence level.

Herd Behavior

The Behavioral Trait: Remember back in high school when you really, really wanted to be part of the cool crowd? Back then, your parents probably urged you to chart your own course and avoid the temptation to blindly follow others. Hopefully that advice worked, but it turns out that in some ways we never really outgrow the desire to be part of the crowd.

Herd behavior refers to the tendency on the part of investors to all move in the same direction at the same time. If most investors are bullish, an investor is more likely to be bullish. And if the news is filled with stories of people making money in the market, an investor is prone to become more aggressive in order to replicate the gains he or she suspects others are making.

If you don't believe this is a real thing, think back to a party or dinner you've been to during a time when markets were up or down sharply. If the conversation turned to the market, most of the crowd was probably suitably bullish or bearish. Either way, I strongly suspect that no one stood up to take the opposite position, explaining to the crowd why they were wrong, and why he had sold stocks while the market surged higher.

There are a variety of reasons for this behavior. A desire to fit in and be part of the crowd is certainly one of them. But there is also the dreaded **FOMO**, otherwise known as **Fear Of Missing Out**. Fear of missing out is just another version of keeping up with the Joneses, but in this case it's manifested in the fact that investors generally can't stand to watch other investors make money while they themselves sit on the sidelines.

This phenomenon has been the impetus for every market bubble in history, and explains part of the reason so many people piled into technology stocks in the late 1990s or Sunbelt real estate in the mid-2000s. This fear of missing out isn't a new thing. Back in the 1600s, the Dutch went bananas for tulips, driving prices on prized flowers to absurd levels. That saga ended the same way all subsequent manias did; with those brave few souls who managed to keep a lid on their emotions exceptionally grateful to have done so, and with the rest of the masses financially devastated.

The Rational Response: Herd behavior can be quite difficult to avoid, but again having a plan and the discipline to stick to that plan can help. Another trick to keep from getting caught up with the masses is to *Ignore the Hype*.

The way to do this is to avoid, to the degree possible, hearing about what everyone else is doing. So, for example, during the real estate bubble, if someone had avoided reading sensationalist stories about overnight fortunes being made from Florida condos, they'd have had a better chance of staying on the sidelines and not getting drawn into the melee.

Bucketing, or segmenting your money can help, too. This means that you keep the vast majority of your portfolio invested in a prudent manner designed to meet your long-term goals. Then, if you feel compelled to get involved with the latest fad, you have a separate play account that you use. This way, if you just absolutely, positively can't bear the thought of missing the party, you at least join the fun in such a way that the inevitable hangover isn't too bad.

Before we move on, I'd like to point out one last thing about herd behavior. Although following the crowd can be detrimental to your financial health, moving in the opposite direction can provide potentially fantastic opportunities for wealth creation. People that fade the crowd are known as contrarians, and that's a label applied to some of the most successful investors in history.

Just look at some of these quotes by well-known investors:

> The best investment opportunities are often scary.
>
> **Rob Arnott**

> The way to make money is to buy when blood is running in the streets.
>
> **John D. Rockefeller**

> I will tell you how to become rich. Close the doors. Be fearful when others are greedy. Be greedy when others are fearful.
>
> **Warren Buffett**

I could list countless more quotes, but you get the point. The best time to buy is when prices are down sharply, which is when everyone else is selling. The best time to sell is when prices are soaring, which is when everyone else is buying. Following this approach is exceptionally difficult, but if you can get comfortable with standing out from the crowd, your odds of achieving financial independence will skyrocket.

Framing Bias

The Behavioral Trait: Consider the following two news headlines:

1. In the third quarter, the economy grew at 2.5%, which was below expectations of 3.0% growth.
2. In the third quarter, the economy grew at 2.5%, which was an increase from the 2.0% growth in the prior quarter.

Both of those headlines give you the same data point: the economy grew at 2.5% in the third quarter. But which of those headlines is going to make you feel better about the economy? The first headline makes it sound like economic growth was disappointing in the third quarter. The second headline makes it sound like economic growth is picking up. Clearly accelerating growth is going to make you feel better than disappointing growth.

But which of the headlines is accurate and factual? The answer is both of them.

Both of those headlines convey the same facts. And both are truthful. Yet one of them makes you feel more positive about where the economy is headed and the other makes you more concerned about the direction of the economy. And in turn, your view on the economy could influence your investment choices.

The situation just described is an example of *framing*, which is yet another behavioral finance trait you need to be on the lookout for. Framing refers to the tendency for people to make decisions based not upon the facts themselves, but rather upon how those facts are presented to them.

Imagine a scenario in which two people tell you the same thing. One of those people is your best friend. The other is your biggest rival. Chances are you'd be far more likely to believe your friend. That is framing in action.

Perhaps the biggest impediment to overcoming framing bias is the media. A great deal of media content is agenda driven, but even when coverage is truly impartial, its still difficult to write or record a story in such a way that the information isn't framed at all. In fact, pretty much the only way to avoid framing a story is to simply present the facts as stand-alone data points and then let the reader draw their own conclusions from the numbers. Unfortunately most people would find that approach horribly boring, which is why almost everyone who conveys any sort of news always fills in some sort of commentary around that news.

The Rational Response: You can start to protect against this bias by accepting that virtually any information you consume is going to be tilted in one direction or another. This tilting may not even be intentional, but it is usually there.

Knowing that, you should seek out multiple competing information sources. If you take in many different viewpoints, it's unlikely they are all going to have the same take on a story. This will allow you to ingest similar information, but presented in different ways. When you consider the same information presented in differing formats, you reduce the odds that your analysis of the info is heavily influenced by the agenda of the author or speaker.

Hindsight Bias

The Behavioral Trait: When stock markets reopened following the tragic attacks on September 11, 2001, airline stocks plummeted in value. They did so because market participants thought that the events of that day would significantly alter people's travel plans and decrease their propensity to fly. That was a logical conclusion based on what had happened, and it turned out to be correct.

Imagine an investor who had analyzed American Airlines stock in the summer of 2001. They looked into the airline's growth plans, their cost structure, the future of the economy, and competition in the industry. Based upon that analysis, they forecast that American would not do well, and based upon that forecast, they sold the stock short in the summer of 2001. (Selling a stock short is effectively a wager that the price will fall.)

Flash forward a couple of months, and the stock, which had been declining, plummets in value. Our investor pats himself on the back and takes a victory lap, congratulating himself on the quality of his analysis.

Our investor is engaging in hindsight bias. Although his analysis may or may not have been sound, that analysis was not why the stock plummeted following September 11. The stock plummeted due to the attacks, concerns about the future of air travel, and questions about the impact the attacks would have on economic growth.

None of these factors were part of the investor's initial research, since the terrorist attack that prompted them could not have been foreseen. In other words, the effect is what the investors forecasted, but the cause was something other than what he anticipated. If the investor accepts this and moves on, no harm is done. But if he ascribes the outcome to his own brilliant analysis, he is building false confidence in himself and the research he has conducted. That in turn can lead to errors in analysis or judgment down the road.

The Rational Response: Honest reflection on the thought process behind investment decision-making is necessary for avoiding hindsight bias. This can be aided if you keep a written record of investments you made and the rationale behind those investments. For example, if our investor had written down why he was betting against American Airlines stock, he could have then reviewed that thesis after he exited his position. Doing so would have revealed that while part of his thesis was indeed correct, a great deal of his success was a result of factors he had not predicted or even considered in his analysis.

Any written notes around an investment don't need to be Pulitzer Prize worthy. A simple spreadsheet will do. All you're really after are a couple reasons that you entered a position so that when you later evaluate it you can see whether your forecast was correct.

An alternative, and perhaps superior, method to overcoming hindsight bias is to avoid forecasting all together. Instead, a written Investment Policy Statement (IPS) will map out how you look at your investments and the circumstances under which you might choose to buy and sell securities. Then you simply execute your plan. Doing so means you'll buy and sell according to a structured and disciplined roadmap. For instance, maybe your IPS says that you buy more of a security when it reaches an attractive valuation level, or sell some of it when you achieve a certain level of profits or the position becomes overvalued according to some metric.

The bottom line is that you want to avoid giving yourself credit for something you didn't see coming, because the alternative is that you'll soon begin feeling omniscient, which will likely feed into your overconfidence bias. And overconfident investors who believe they have perfect foresight eventually blow themselves up.

Self-attribution Bias

The Behavioral Trait: We just finished discussing hindsight bias, which occurs when investors incorrectly link cause and effect between their analysis and the performance of an investment. Self-attribution bias continues this theme, but with a twist.

Some investors succumb to the temptation to give themselves credit for investments that turn out well while blaming bad luck for investments that go poorly. This is known as self-attribution bias.

When this occurs it becomes impossible to rationally analyze your decision-making process, which in turn makes it impossible to improve. Consider a golf example. Imagine a player who credits every good shot to their skill. It doesn't matter if it's a perfect shot or if the ball takes a fortunate bounce off a tree before rolling toward the cup. Either way a good result is the byproduct of skill. On the flip-side, every poor-approach shot is blamed on a gust of wind. Every missed putt is the fault of bumpy greens.

Clearly such a golfer is unlikely to rationally step back and analyze their true skill level and where there are gaps in their game. They are unlikely to go out and practice the way that they need to. And of course they are unlikely to ever reach their maximum potential.

The same would be true for an investor who blames bad investments on luck and moneymakers on their own skill. Such a mindset would make an honest self-assessment impossible. And since honest self-assessment is the key to improvement in any endeavor, an investor who succumbs to self-attribution bias is never going to reach their full potential.

The Rational Response: Let's be honest here. What are the odds that everything good in your life is happening because you're awesome and that everything you don't like in your life is due to bad luck?

Does bad luck exist? Sure. And are a lot of the good things that happen due to your skill, talent, and effort? Sure, but not 100%.

The same is true with your investments. Like all investors, you've undoubtedly made poor decisions in the past that were subsequently bailed out by unrelated market movements. And you've likely made some good investment decisions that were based upon a rational and disciplined thought process. And there were times that these investments did not turn out well due to unforeseeable circumstances beyond your control.

But you need to acknowledge that some of your poor investments came about as a result of faulty investment decision-making, just as some of your successful investments came about as a result of plain old-fashioned good luck.

If you can accept these truths, you'll be able to more honestly assess your investment acumen and decision-making process. This is important because that assessment will lead to better future outcomes.

Myopic Loss Aversion

The Behavioral Trait: In a perfect world, investors would receive a measure of satisfaction from their gains that is proportional to the pain they suffer from a similar loss. Unfortunately, this is not the case, and many studies have demonstrated that the pain investors feel from their losses outweighs the joy they get from their gains.

The result of this is that investors subconsciously avoid the pain of loss, which leads to a fixation on short-term results at the expense of potential longer-term gains. An example of this behavior would be investors who initiate a position in say, Microsoft stock. They have done so because, having done their research, they come to the conclusion that Microsoft has great long-term prospects, and that over the course of years or decades, the stock will multiply several-fold.

Unfortunately for our investor, in this example, Microsoft misses its next quarterly earnings target, and the stock falls 12%. The pain of this loss overwhelms our investor, despite the future hope of significantly larger gains. So our investor sells, becoming in effect a short-term trader, and an unsuccessful one to boot.

The myopic part of this refers to the frequency with which individuals look at their portfolios. Studies have shown that the more frequently people check their portfolios, the more they are likely to suffer from loss aversion. And the more likely they are to suffer from loss aversion, the less likely they are to own risky assets (because of the pain of potential losses). Unfortunately, it is those risky assets, such as stocks, that are most likely to produce the returns needed to meet financial goals.

Following that chain of logic, the more frequently someone looks at their portfolio, the less likely they are to meet their financial goals. You'll notice this is a recurring theme of this book. Maybe that is why the *Wall Street Journal* once published an article titled "*Keep Stock Market Apps Off Your Phone.*" The article discussed how the continuous feedback the phone provided increased the odds of poor investment decision making.

The Rational Response: If our Microsoft investors were perfectly rationale, they would have evaluated the fact that a temporary 12% loss is relatively insignificant in light of the hoped-for upside return of 100% or more. In doing so, our investors would have weighed the probabilistic expected return, and reached the conclusion that the best course of action was to do nothing and hold onto their position.

Now certainly whether that decision would ultimately prove to be right would depend on a multitude of factors, not least of them the quality and accuracy of our investors' initial research into Microsoft. But at least that research was conducted at a time of emotional tranquility, since our investors did not begin with a position in the stock, and were therefore better able to conduct a rational analysis of the company's prospects.

Remember, in the game of baseball even players who reach the Hall of Fame fail 7 out of 10 times they come up to bat, in the sense that even the best players only get a hit approximately 30% of the time. If a player experienced greater psychic pain from striking out than the pleasure he felt from hitting a home run, he probably wouldn't last very long in the league.

Investing is no different; even the best of investors "fail" and lose money on a regular basis. The key is to keep it in perspective, and to attempt to weigh positive and negative outcomes equally.

And of course, given the volumes of research that have shown that more frequent feedback on portfolio performance leads to inferior outcomes and a greater tendency toward myopic loss aversion, the rational conclusion would be to reduce the frequency with which you check your portfolio results.

This is easier said than done, given human nature and the world we live in. Nevertheless, the main goal of this book is to provide you with the tools necessary to avoid getting sucked into the mayhem. Your odds of success are far higher if you can do so, but the media exists to make this task more difficult.

So let's shift our attention now, and look into the financial media and its influence on your family's future.

Chapter 11
FYI, the Media Doesn't Care If You Make Money

And now we reach the crux of this book. Remember, your objective is to ignore all the mayhem that surrounds you so that you can focus on time-tested principles designed to pave the way to long-term financial freedom. This is difficult because even once you've identified your emotional biases you still need to accept that they will never be completely eliminated. You are human after all. The best you can hope for is to reduce the impact of emotions and set up systems and processes to allow the logical, rational part of your brain to win out.

As you've hopefully gathered by now, one of the most important things you can do when it comes to managing your emotions is to have a written plan in place. This plan should be constructed at a time when you are thinking clearly. This is the best environment to lay out reasonable steps to meet your financial goals. The written plan then becomes the template you refer back to when your emotions urge you to do something that may not be in your long-term best interests.

But Then There's the Media ...

Having a written plan in place becomes even more important when you consider the constant barrage of media headlines you're subjected to, as well as the fact that those media headlines are specifically designed to exacerbate your behavioral biases. You are more likely to be deeply engaged when your emotions, rather than your intellect, are stimulated. The media knows this and so, in addition to providing you with information, they also try to excite you, or frighten you, or motivate you, or sometimes even offend you.

Think about that last one for a moment. Polarizing media figures such as Glenn Beck, Rush Limbaugh, or even Howard Stern are well known for their controversial, and sometimes offensive, content. There is even a term for this, and media figures known for extreme views are often referred to as "shock jocks." But – and here is the important part – while some love them and others loathe them, these controversial figures have one characteristic on which all can agree: they are hard to ignore.

The reason they are hard to ignore is that people connect with them on an emotional level. Their supporters love them. Their detractors hate them. But almost no one who tunes in walks away not feeling *something*. And because of that, listeners, viewers, and readers come back for more.

They come back for more.

And that, my friends, is what the media wants. They want you to come back for more.

Here's a little hint for analyzing many things in this world: if you want to know how people are going to act, figure out how they get paid. Yes, that sounds cynical, and it certainly isn't always true. But I think it often is, especially in the corporate world.

With that in mind, ask yourself, how does the media get paid?

The answer is that the media gets paid for having a larger and/or more engaged audience. In other words, they get paid for attracting and keeping eyeballs. And the single best way to attract and keep eyeballs is by entertaining folks. Because entertainment engages people on an emotional level, which in turn leads to an audience that comes back for more.

The financial media is no different than any other media, so let me be very clear on this – the purpose of much of the financial media is to entertain and inform, *in that order*. That doesn't mean that the financial media isn't providing you information. It also doesn't mean that they are making up stories or lying to you. What it does mean is that when they are providing you information, they are going to strive to convey that information in a way that pulls you in and makes you want to know more. Sometimes that might also involve making you feel anxious or afraid. Sometimes that might also involve feeding your desire to keep up with the Joneses.

Oh, sure, the information is there, and if you were a robot you'd simply slice your way through the surrounding fluff, extract the nugget of information you need, coldly and rationally analyze that information, incorporate it into your decision matrix, and act accordingly. But you aren't a robot and so the way in which the information is presented is going to impact how you view that information and what you do with it. If that concept sounds familiar, it's because we discussed it in the previous chapter when we discussed the behavioral bias known as *framing*.

The financial media are masters of framing information so that you react to it more strongly than you probably should. For example, if you were to spend eight hours watching CNBC on a relatively slow news day, you'd still witness dozens of *breaking news alerts* and other assorted *big events*. These breaking news alerts might include:

- A news conference held by the president of one of the regional Federal Reserve banks (For the record, there are 12 such regional banks, each with a president holding periodic news conferences. This is in addition to the seven members of the board of governors, which includes the Federal Reserve Chairman.)
- The release of weekly natural gas inventories, which tend to fluctuate based on wintertime temperatures in the Northeast and Midwest

- An earnings release from companies such as Oracle, McDonalds, Caterpillar, or Walmart
- Economic data such as the producer price index (not to be confused with the consumer price index) or monthly housing starts (not to be confused with monthly housing permits)

Of course, in reality, the average investor probably doesn't care whether or not the president of one of the regional Federal Reserve banks just finished giving an interview or that the weekly natural gas inventories number was just released. Neither of these events is likely to impact the performance of an investment portfolio over time or make any difference about whether you achieve your financial goals.

But, on the other hand, no one is going to tune into CNBC to watch an anchor say something along the lines of:

> Well folks, nothing much is happening today that would impact your financial future. Natural gas inventories were released, but to be honest, they don't really matter. And the president of the Kansas City Fed gave a presentation, but his topic was really boring and had nothing to do with your retirement savings. So, to be honest we're looking at a lazy summer afternoon here, and all-around Wall Street trading will be slow, so I suggest you stop looking at your portfolio and head to the beach. Better still why don't you increase your 401(k) contributions by 2% and then not look at your portfolio for the next 18 months while you let the long-term upward momentum of markets work in your favor.

That approach wouldn't attract eyeballs and it wouldn't sell advertising. Instead, the anchor will try to make every story seem critically important in order to generate excitement, attract and retain viewers, and increase advertising sales.

And that's where framing comes in. Because the anchor's actual verbiage, based on the exact same information as earlier, will probably be something like this:

> *Well folks, we're entering the middle of the trading day and we've got a lot going on up and down Wall Street. Natural gas inventories spiked 1.2%, causing prices to drop sharply before recovering. Right*

now, prices are basically unchanged on the day. We also had the president of the Kansas City Fed talking about the long-term impact of supply chain bottlenecks on the railroad industry. Bond prices reacted, with 10-year interest rates spiking two one-hundredths of 1%. Volume is light on Wall Street with a lot of traders out on summer vacation, which is leading to thin trading and increased volatility. This could lead to a sharp move higher or lower in the next month.

Both those monologues relay the same basic information, but ask yourself which is more likely to have you put down the remote and stay tuned in?

I don't know about you, but that last line about how there could be "a sharp move higher or lower in the next month" has me a little bit excited and a whole lot nervous. In fact, I'd better stay tuned in to find out more, because I definitely want to know if a sharp drop is coming next month.

And bang! Now they have me. Now I'm sucked in because I sure as heck want to know about that sharp drop that might, or might not, be coming.

Never mind that the anchor didn't convey information that was any different than in the first monologue. And never mind that the anchor told me absolutely nothing about where the market might be headed.

This could lead to a sharp move higher or lower in the next month.

Well, no kidding. There is always the possibility of a sharp move up or down. Saying so on TV doesn't change that. It neither increases nor decreases the odds of a move higher or lower. It conveys no new information. It should in no way impact my portfolio or my future finances. It certainly doesn't change my future tax planning.

If it doesn't do any of those things, what does it do? You guessed it. It grabs me on an emotional level and pulls me in. Now I have to watch to see what might happen. After all, my future is at stake! And I'm afraid.

And fear sells. Greed and the urge to keep up with the Joneses sells, too, but not like fear. The more worried you are, the more you watch. Think of the last time a politician you disliked ran for office. The more worried you were about what they might do in office, the more you probably tuned in. It's like watching a train wreck that you can't take your eyes off of.

Your finances are no different. The more worried you are, the more you tune in. Don't believe me? Take a look at Figure 11.1.

The financial crisis was the greatest thing that ever happened to CNBC. People tuned in and then couldn't look away. They were worried their futures would be destroyed and they wanted to watch it happen live. Then, markets started to recover and a long bull market got underway. And folks stopped watching. Now that they weren't going to be destroyed, they didn't care anymore.

The bottom line is that fear sells. The media knows that and so they follow the number-one rule of business, which is simply that a business should give their customers what they want. People seem to want fear, so the media gives you fear.

There is nothing at all wrong with this; it's how media outlets stay in business and make money. But it's important for you to keep in mind that, for all the reasons discussed in the previous chapter,

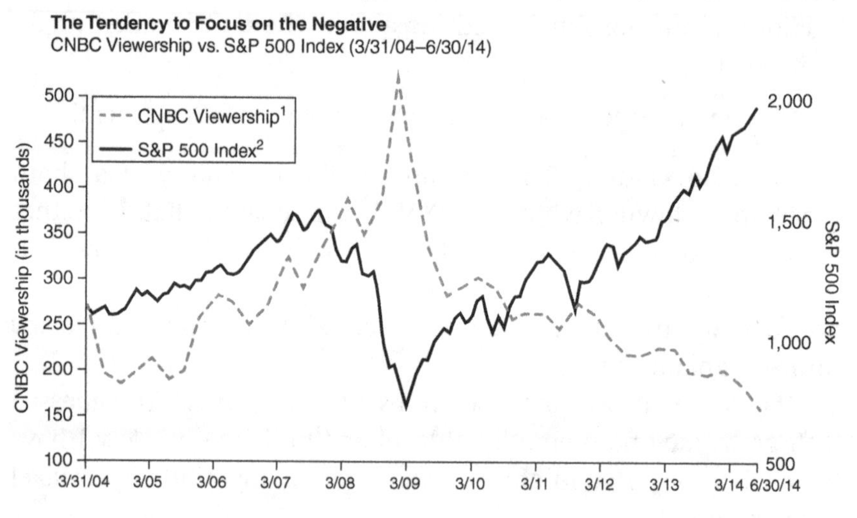

Figure 11.1 Stock Market Movements and CNBC Viewership
SOURCE: Analysis by Brian Perry. Information from Guardian Wealth Management.

you are susceptible to flawed decision-making based on irrational fears. It's also vital that you know that the media is going to flame those fears in an effort to drive viewership.

The key then is to use the media for information, but not get overly swayed by the framing. Because its not the way the information is conveyed that will harm you. Nor is it your emotions. What will destroy your finances is allowing your emotions to force you to act on the information you take in. Therein lies the greatest threat you face on the road to financial freedom.

Did Black Monday Spell Doom for Investors?

Despite how they are framed, the vast, vast majority of every financial news headline ever written will literally have zero impact on your future. Furthermore, even news events that really are important are unlikely to impact most long-term investors. Remember, there is a world of difference between the approach used by a **professional trader** and that used by the average **individual investor**. Neither is good nor bad; they're just different. Wall Street professionals are measured on quarterly or annual performance, so short- and intermediate-term market fluctuations matter. After all, a single news item can impact their careers.

But it's different for individuals. As an individual investor, you should only have money sitting in risky assets if you have a long time horizon. If you are likely to need the money within, say, the next five years, you shouldn't own risky assets. Funds needed in those shorter time frames should be in less volatile asset classes such as money market funds, savings accounts, CDs, or high-quality bonds.

If your investment time horizon stretches further, then you can begin to consider riskier asset classes such as stocks, real estate, natural resources, and lower quality bonds. Of course, if you have that long-time horizon, shorter-term fluctuations shouldn't have too much of an impact on your ultimate success. Think about it this way: a 50-year-old individual saving for retirement probably has a 30- or 40-year time horizon for some of their investments. And let's face it, if your time horizon is three or four decades, a single day's stock price movements are unlikely to have much of an impact on your success.

Don't believe me? Well, here's a pop quiz: on Black Monday, October 19, 1987, the Dow Jones Industrial Average fell more than 22%, a decline that as of this writing remains the largest single-day collapse in U.S. market history. And that drop occurred only 10 weeks before the end of the year.

To understand just how catastrophic Black Monday was, consider that during the Financial Crisis of 2007–2009, the largest single-day percentage decline in the Dow was less than 8%. In other words, the Black Monday market crash was nearly three times worse than any day you enjoyed during the more recent Financial Crisis. Black Monday wasn't a bad day. It was a disaster.

So, let me ask you, following the worst day in its history, do you think the Dow finished 1987 in the black or in the red? In other words, was the Index up on the year or did it finish with an annual decline?

SOURCE: Pixabay.com

The answer, somewhat counterintuitively, is that in 1987 the Dow actually finished up for the year. And while it never makes sense to draw too many conclusions from a single data point, I do think it's instructive that even in the face of a 22% collapse, the impact of a single day's movement didn't sink the market's annual performance. And if we extend the time frame further, the 1987 stock market crash barely registers as a blip on the radar.

Again, on Black Monday the Dow lost nearly a quarter of its value in a single day, but in Figure 11.2 the decline is barely even noticeable. Staying the course despite such a massive single-day loss would admittedly be difficult, but investors who did so remained on track to meet their financial goals. And remember, as an individual, you have the advantage of not having to report quarterly or annual returns.

Most important of all, and as discussed throughout this book, *you should be measuring your performance to plan*, not versus some arbitrary market benchmark. This allows you to focus less on daily market fluctuations and more on whether your portfolio is generating the kind of returns you need to meet your financial goals.

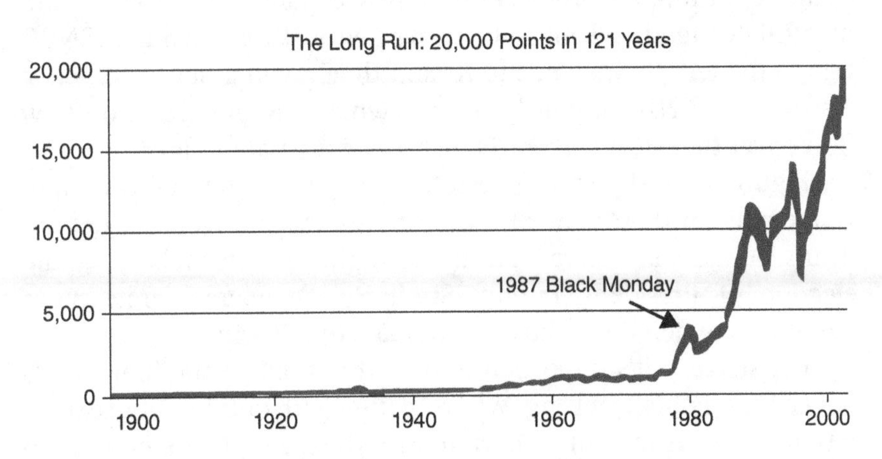

Figure 11.2 The Impact of a Single Day On Long-Term Returns
SOURCE: Based on data from Measuring Worth.com and Dow Jones.

What Side of the Aisle Are You On?

Hopefully by now you're convinced that breaking news alerts and short-term market movements are relatively meaningless in the scope of your financial planning. Accepting this fact should alleviate 99% or more of your need to consume financial news or track market events. And again, the news of the day does have an impact on financial professionals. In fact, part of my job involves staying on top of the latest headlines and market movements. But you, as an individual, have the significant advantage of being able to ignore the headlines and focus instead on tracking your longer-term progress toward your financial goals.

But let's assume for the moment that although you realize that you don't *need* to follow the news in order to manage your finances, you *want* to do so. Maybe you enjoy being on top of things. Maybe it's interesting to you. Maybe you find the daily news flow intellectually stimulating.

If you choose to track the news of the day and how it might impact your finances, it is imperative that you consider the source of that news and any biases or tendencies the source might have. For example, I think it's pretty commonly accepted that Fox News and its affiliates tend to lean toward the political right while MSNBC tilts to the left. So it stands to reason that, given a news story, Fox News and MSNBC might have somewhat different slants on how they cover that story. Figure 11.3 shows why that matters.

Figure 11.3 shows the results of a poll of Republicans and Democrats on their view of the economy. As you can see, Republicans became far more optimistic in the months following the election of President Trump. Similarly, Democrats grew more pessimistic when their chosen candidate didn't win.

For starters, it's important to note that none of the individuals polled were actually wrong. When dealing with opinions and expectations, there is of course no right or wrong. People are entitled to believe and think whatever they want.

However, and this is the important point, it does seem unlikely that economic prospects for half of Americans collapsed in a

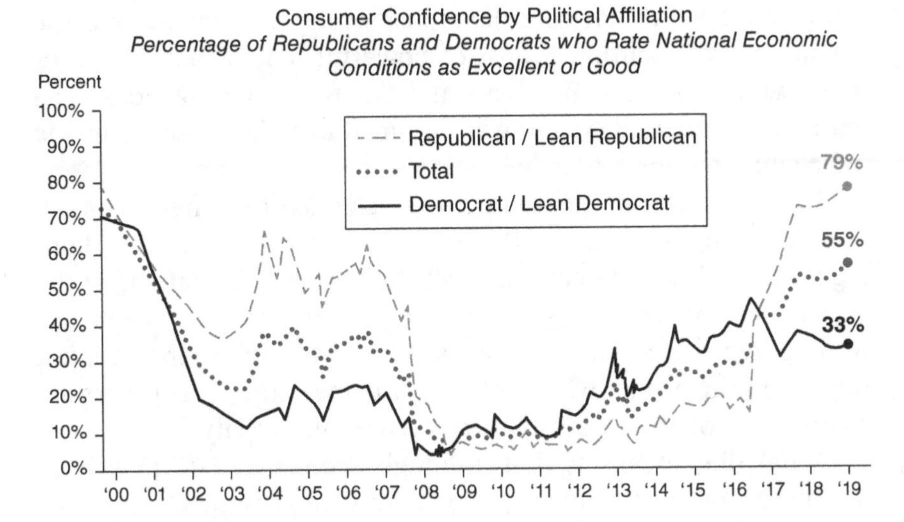

Figure 11.3 How Politics Impacts Economic Outlook
SOURCE: Based on data from Pew Research Center and JP Morgan Asset Management.

six-month window while those for the other half of Americans surged. After all, even though the political climate in the United States is incredibly fractured, we certainly aren't in an environment where a newly elected president sets out to destroy the economy for half of the country's citizens.

Taken to the absurd, Figure 11.3 might make sense if a new president forced businesses to fire all workers who voted for the other candidate. But we're a long way from that scenario.

I hope!

The more logical explanation is that Republicans were more likely to consume media from sources that lean right of center. These sources were more likely to paint an optimistic outlook for the country and the economy if the Republican candidate won and his economic policies were enacted. Democrats, on the other hand, were more likely to get their news from sources casting a downbeat assessment of the future, given a Republican victory.

Importantly, the truth was probably somewhere in the middle. Although presidents certainly have power, their ability to enact wholesale changes is intentionally limited. Even the most powerful presidents need to navigate the House of Representatives and the Senate, not to mention a host of powerful federal bureaucracies filled with lifelong staffers carrying out their own agendas. The entire governmental system was designed in order to avoid drastic policy fluctuations.

Furthermore, the government as a whole only has so much impact on the direction of the economy. Private businesses, both big and small, make decisions each and every day that shape the course of economic growth. And consumers, deciding each day what purchases to make or avoid, ultimately have the greatest impact on the economy. In fact, by some measures, consumers are responsible for 70% of the country's economic activity.

What that means is that although economic data may have improved slightly during the period following Trump's election, the economy as a whole probably didn't surge to the degree Republican opinion would indicate. Similarly, the data probably didn't collapse in a manner consistent with the plunging economic outlook prevalent among Democrats.

The reality, as in many things, was probably somewhere in the middle.

Okay, let's bring this conversation back to your finances and why you need to be careful about letting the media unduly impact your decision-making. The bottom line is that it's perfectly fine to hold political views and opinions on the direction the country or the world is headed in. *The important point is to avoid letting your opinions of the way things should be override the reality of the way things actually are or the way they are likely to be.* In other words, if a politician you don't like is in office, it's important to assess the likely direction of the economy and markets regardless of whether you personally agree or disagree with the politician's policies.

Furthermore, if you're ignoring the mayhem and following the concepts laid out in this book, you probably won't need to change your strategies regardless of who is in office. Now, to be fair, some of your tactics might shift slightly if a politician raises or lowers taxes, or a politician's policies cause the economy to grow or contract much more than usual. But your basic financial roadmap

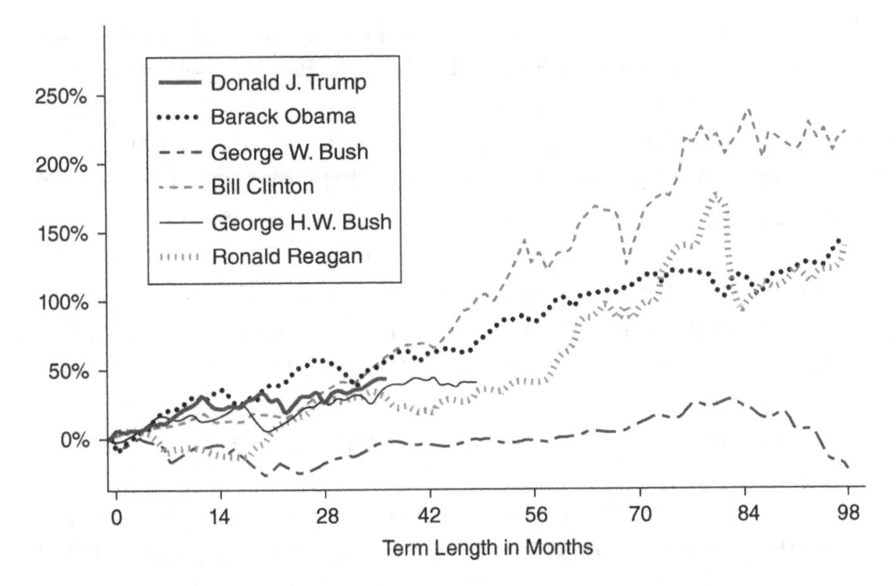

Figure 11.4 Stock Market Performance by President
SOURCE: https://www.macrotrends.net/2481/stock-market-performance-by-president.

and the strategies you utilize to follow that map shouldn't change, regardless of the mayhem going on in the current political circus.

This is particularly true because it turns out that stocks have mostly moved higher regardless of what party is in office. This makes sense given the upward momentum of markets over time. In fact, despite dire predictions, Figure 11.4 shows that no presidential regime in the past four decades has spelled doom for your portfolio, which is a valuable lesson to keep in mind next election cycle.

Unfortunately, though, you'll now see that politics isn't the only news arena that would make Barnum & Bailey proud.

Would You Hitch Your Family's Future to the Circus?

Maybe you're familiar with Jim Cramer, the host of *Mad Money* on CNBC. Mr. Cramer is quite knowledgeable about markets, having worked at Goldman Sachs and run his own hedge fund. He shares this knowledge with his audience, exhorting them to buy or sell stocks based upon his opinions of future market movements.

There's nothing wrong with this, and in fact Cramer's background actually makes him better suited for financial journalism than many media pundits who have little or no actual investment experience. But before you rush to act upon Cramer's recommendations, consider a couple of items.

First of all, much of what Cramer recommends is what I would classify as short-term trading. And as I've repeated throughout this book, I believe that the average individual should eschew short-term trading in favor of long-term investing, which is a completely different endeavor and one which I believe holds far better prospects for success.

Secondly, because of the nature of his position, you may not get both sides of the trade from Cramer. For example, pretend that Cramer recommends stock XYZ on his television show. Presumably he's done his research and has a sound basis for his recommendation. And let's say you act on his advice and go out the next morning and buy the stock he recommended.

Okay, fine. But let me ask you something. When will you sell the stock? After all, this is a trade, so you don't plan to hold it forever. In fact, the very definition of a trade is that it has an entry point and an exit point, both of which should be identified in advance. And Cramer himself may not like the stock forever. At some point the rationale for the trade might change, or the stock may appreciate to where it's no longer attractive, or a better opportunity may come along. The problem is that there isn't time on a TV show to review every single previous suggestion and tell viewers whether they should continue to hold the stock. And so even if the initial buy suggestions are valid, viewers are left to their own devices to figure out when to exit their position.

Additionally, all investors have a finite supply of dollars to put to work. This is important because it means that even if the stock you bought does well, your purchase may not have been a good thing. That is because in order to buy that stock you had to either (1) forgo buying a different stock or (2) sell a different stock and use the proceeds to purchase your new stock. Remember, you are trying to build a portfolio, not a collection of stocks. And whoever is giving you advice on TV doesn't know what other holdings make up your portfolio.

But you can't analyze your stock purchase in a vacuum. Instead, you need to analyze that purchase relative to how it complements your other holdings, as well as the opportunity cost of not owning the other choices available to you. Ultimately, you can only determine that purchasing the stock was a wise move if, and only if, your new stock purchase complements your existing holdings and is also better than the alternative choices you have forgone.

What all the above means is that there are two hurdles to surmount if you want to follow Mr. Cramer's (or any other TV journalist's) advice. The first hurdle is that the recommendation needs to be a good one, and the stock needs to act as expected. This is not an insurmountable obstacle, but as has been discussed throughout this book, forecasting stock movements with greater precision than all other market participants is an exceedingly difficult task. But again, this is not an impossible obstacle.

The problem is the second hurdle, which is insurmountable. The second hurdle is that Mr. Cramer needs to have known all the other positions in your portfolio, the alternative stocks available to you, and your financial goals and risk tolerance. If he knows all of that and still thinks the stock makes sense for you, then you have crossed hurdle number two.

But of course, no TV host or other media outlet could ever know all of that about you and your portfolio. And so, even if Mr. Cramer's recommendations pass hurdle number one and beat the market, they still cannot hope to pass hurdle number two.

That's why financial advice aimed at a general audience must, by its very nature, focus on broad concepts rather than specific recommendations. This book is no different. If I were meeting with you in a one-on-one setting, I might recommend a specific portfolio or a specific tax strategy to you. But of course I'm not meeting with you one-on-one. And just like a CNBC host or writer for the *Wall Street Journal,* I don't know the particulars of your financial situation. And so I avoid making specific recommendations that may or may not be appropriate for you. Instead, I focus on strategies and concepts that almost all individuals should consider and can benefit from. Then, you can take those concepts and, either on your own or with the help of your financial professionals, you can implement them in a manner that makes sense for you.

Far too many people lose sight of this important distinction and instead take recommendations made in a book or on TV and apply them to their own situation without first considering whether those recommendations fit their unique circumstances.

Before moving on, I want to make one final point regarding financial journalism in general and Mr. Cramer in particular. But first let me segue by asking if you've ever watched *The Jerry Springer Show*? You know Jerry Springer, the former mayor of Cincinnati turned daytime talk show host. The same Jerry Springer who brought us such thought-provoking and meaningful show segments as:

"A Man Marries a Horse"

and

"The Kung Fu Hillbilly"

You're no doubt wondering what Kung Fu hillbillies and men marrying horses have to do with investing, and the answer is: **ABSOLUTELY NOTHING**!

Which is why you might be interested to know that the producer of Jim Cramer's *Mad Money* used to have a different role prior to joining CNBC. That role, in case you haven't guessed, was as producer of *The Jerry Springer Show*.

And so, I'll repeat the question I asked as the header to this segment: Would you hitch your family's future to the circus? Because some people find circuses entertaining, just like some people find Jerry Springer entertaining. And just like some people find Jim Cramer entertaining.

If you're one of those folks, and you enjoy financial entertainment, then great.

But I strongly suggest that you think long and hard before committing your future to an industry that exists to entertain, attract eyeballs, and sell advertising.

You'd be far better off creating a financial roadmap and identifying time-tested strategies designed to meet your financial goals regardless of the mayhem that surrounds you. Then you can either implement those strategies yourself or find a trusted professional to help you tune out the mayhem, manage your emotions, and reach your financial goals.

Chapter 12

Avoid the Wolf in Sheep's Clothing

Your quest for financial independence will have far greater odds of success if you manage to avoid the wolves of Wall Street. This probably doesn't come as much of a surprise to you, and it's no secret that the financial industry doesn't always enjoy a sterling reputation. The problem is that it can frequently be difficult to differentiate between good and bad advice, particularly since highly compensated financial professionals are often motivated to put lipstick on a pig by making investment products and services sound far better than they actually are.

So how do you distinguish good from bad, and honest from corrupt, especially when all the advice you're hearing is delivered by well-groomed, well-educated, well-spoken financial professionals?

Well, there's no magic bullet to guarantee you're working with the right person, but read on for a few thoughts and suggestions on how to evaluate your financial advisor, as well as some pitfalls to avoid if you hope to find financial freedom.

Does It Pass the Sniff Test?

Before I go into details and specifics, let's start at the most basic level. After all, you're probably already aware of the role common sense plays in most areas of your life, so why should your finances be any different?

So, when it comes to your finances, please use common sense. If something sounds too good to be true, it probably is. If someone doesn't seem trustworthy, they probably aren't. If you feel a financial provider isn't sharing the whole truth with you, they probably aren't.

My grandmother used to call this the "sniff test." In other words, if something doesn't smell right, it probably isn't. She used this on milk and other perishables to avoid getting sick, but it makes just as much sense in the financial arena. After all, imagine how nauseous Bernie Madoff's victims felt!

It sounds simple but I'll say it again. Using your common sense can help you avoid a heck of a lot of financial mistakes.

Who's Got Your Back?

When managing your finances, you'll want to monitor and evaluate your investment providers. All sorts of people fall into this category, and you'll use at least one or two of them. Some people want to work with a financial advisor who guides them in all aspects of their finances. This advisor might provide investment guidance as well as tax planning, insurance reviews, and cash flow planning for retirement.

A less comprehensive, but perhaps more common type of financial advisor might only provide guidance around investments. Some of these individuals might also do some abbreviated cash flow or retirement planning, though these are often a secondary consideration to the investments.

Even if you don't have a financial advisor, you'll still have financial providers. If you have an IRA or a brokerage account, it has to be housed somewhere. Maybe it's at Schwab or Fidelity. That firm and the people there are your financial providers. Alternatively if you have a 401(k) or similar employer-sponsored retirement plan, that company and its employees are your financial providers even if you didn't have the freedom to choose them yourself.

Stepping beyond investments, if you purchase insurance, or file taxes, or utilize banking products, you are again employing financial providers.

Why am I emphasizing the financial providers you'll interact with in your life? Because when it comes to financial providers, there are two different standards. And importantly, those two standards are as different as night and day.

The vast majority of the financial industry follows what is known as a **suitability standard**. The brokerage industry is regulated by FINRA. Here is FINRA's definition of the suitability standard:

> (a) A member or an associated person must have a reasonable basis to believe that a recommended transaction or investment strategy involving a security or securities is suitable for the customer, based on the information obtained through the reasonable diligence of the member or associated person to ascertain the customer's investment profile.

There is nothing in the suitability standard that requires a financial advisor to act in your best interest. In other words, they can choose to sell you the product with the highest fees or commissions, as long as it is broadly appropriate for someone like you. Not surprisingly, the product deemed "most suitable" is often the one with the highest commission.

Please note that just because someone operates under the suitability standard it doesn't mean that they aren't an honest and ethical person or a competent financial advisor. Someone can be employed at a firm that operates under the suitability standard and still choose to act in your best interests. There are undoubtedly excellent and ethical advisors operating under this standard. However, the important points are that:

1. They don't have a legal obligation to do what is best for you
2. Even if they appear to be acting in your best interest you won't be able to have 100% confidence that they are.

3. Although your advisor might strive to act in your best interest, he or she is operating in an environment not designed for that. Even for exceptional individuals, it is hard to fight the machine.

There is an alternative to the suitability standard. The **fiduciary standard** is followed by a small subset of financial advisors. The fiduciary standard simply means that the financial advisor is legally obligated to act in your best interests. The advisor doesn't have to work for free, and, of course, they need to make a living. But they do so by disclosing exactly what fees you will pay, and those fees remain the same regardless of what products or strategies you employ. That means the advisor has no incentive to sell you one product over another, and instead is going to suggest whatever is most likely to help you meet your financial goals.

So, how do you know if your financial advisor is a fiduciary? Well, it depends in part on how they are regulated. If the firm you're working with is subject to the Investment Advisers Act of 1940, they are required to act as a fiduciary. Under this Act, larger investment advisor firms are regulated by the Securities and Exchange Commission (SEC). Smaller firms are regulated by the state where they are domiciled. Additionally, CERTIFIED FINANCIAL PLANNER (CFP®) professionals who are providing financial planning services must abide by the fiduciary standard.

CERTIFIED FINANCIAL PLANNER (CFP®): So what exactly is a CERTIFIED FINANCIAL PLANNER? Well, according to Investopedia:

> *CERTIFIED FINANCIAL PLANNER (CFP®) is a formal recognition of expertise in the areas of financial planning, taxes, insurance, estate planning, and retirement (such as with 401ks). Owned and awarded by the Certified Financial Planner Board of Standards, Inc., the designation*

is awarded to individuals who successfully complete the CFP Board's initial exams, then continue ongoing annual education programs to sustain their skills and certification.

In order to earn the CFP® certification, an individual must have a bachelor's degree and complete advanced coursework in the following subject matters:

- Professional conduct and regulation
- General principles of financial planning
- Education planning
- Risk management and insurance planning
- Investment planning
- Tax planning
- Retirement savings and income planning
- Estate planning
- Financial plan development (capstone) course

Individuals then need to pass a comprehensive exam that tests their knowledge on all the subject matter they have learned. Finally, if they pass the exam, the candidates need to submit to a background check prior to being awarded the CFP designation.

The goal is to create a reasonable standard of excellence and ethics in the financial advisory business. Importantly, once they hold the credentials and if they are providing financial planning services, a CFP® professional must act in a fiduciary capacity.

It's important to note that it isn't always clear whether a financial advisor is operating in a fiduciary capacity. Someone can say that they are "acting in your best interests" without having to hold themselves to a fiduciary standard. In that situation, you are simply taking them at their word.

Now that you understand the important distinction between a fiduciary standard and a suitability standard, I'll leave it to you to decide for yourself whether you want to trust your family's future to someone legally obligated to act in your best interests, or whether you'd rather trust someone operating under the suitability standard.

If you've decided it makes more sense to work with someone who has your best interests in mind, then I have some news for you. In 2016, the Obama administration passed a law requiring all financial advisors to act as fiduciaries. Under this law, the vast majority of the financial industry would no longer be able to operate under the suitability standard. Instead, all financial advisors, no matter where they worked, would be required to put their clients' interests ahead of their own.

So, the good news is that a law was passed requiring financial advisors to act in their clients' best interest.

Unfortunately, there's some bad news, too.

The bad news is that the industry spent billions of dollars fighting the law that would have required them to act in their clients' best interest, and in 2018 the law was overturned before it could be implemented.

That's right, the financial industry, tasked with helping you achieve your goals and dreams, **spent billions of dollars fighting a law that would have specifically required them to do what is best for you.**

No wonder that industry enjoys an approval rating in roughly the same neighborhood as Congress.

Making matters even worse, and as discussed earlier, it can often be difficult to determine exactly who is and is not a fiduciary. As a starting point, any one who charges a commission of any sort is not a fiduciary. Unfortunately, the ranks of these providers include the vast majority of brokers and advisors at the largest brokerage firms and banks, as well as insurance companies.

On the other hand, many registered investment advisors (RIAs), as well as some limited offerings within the larger brokerage firms, generally act in a fiduciary capacity.

If you decide you want an advisor who has to act in your best interests, ask prospective advisors if they are fiduciaries. If they answer with anything other than an unqualified "yes," you know that they are not legally obligated to put your family's best interest ahead of their own paycheck.

Focus on Minimizing Unnecessary Fees

In addition to considering whether your investment professional is truly on your side, you'll also want to take a look at what sort of fees you are paying for your investments. Remember, every dollar paid in fees is a dollar not invested, and when all these dollars are compounded over time the difference can be enormous.

In general, excessively priced investment options don't offer advantages over more reasonably priced ones and are not worth the money. For instance, the mutual fund industry has some funds that charge a front-end sales fee, often referred to as a "load." These sales fees don't indicate that the mutual fund is superior to its peers. In fact, the fees don't go to the mutual fund manager at all. Rather, the sales fee on these mutual funds goes to the financial advisor who sold you the fund.

As a general rule, the only person who benefits from the sale of a mutual fund with a load is the advisor who sold it. Not paying a sales fee means you'll have more dollars at work, more dollars growing and compounding over time, and ultimately more dollars to meet your financial goals.

Let's assume for the moment that you're investing $50,000 into a mutual fund, and that you plan to hold that fund for 25 years. You have a choice of two similar funds, both of which will earn 10% over the life of your investment. One fund doesn't have a sales fee while the other fund has a 5% sales charge.

Five percent of $50,000 is $2500, so that's how much it costs you to purchase the fund with the fee. Right?

Wrong.

Your Initial Investment	Actual Investment (after sales fee)	Annual Growth Rate	Years Invested	Amount You Have to Enjoy
$50,000.00	$50,000.00	10%	25	$608,917.00
$50,000.00	$47,500.00	10%	25	$578,471.00

Figure 12.1 The True Cost of Mutual Fund Fees
SOURCE: Analysis by Brian Perry.

That $2500 represents money not invested for the next 25 years, so you need to take into account the impact of compounding over that time frame. As you can see in Figure 12.1, the true cost of that sales charge, in the form of money you don't have to spend on yourself, your family, and your retirement, is ... $30,000 and change.

That's right, in this hypothetical example, purchasing the mutual fund with the sales fee cost you and your family more than $30,000.

Now, if that mutual fund were superior to all its peers, it might have been worth it. But the fund wasn't. It produced the same returns as the fund without any sales charge. Remember, the sales charge doesn't go to the mutual fund manager and isn't a sign that they are better at their job. The sales fee went to your financial advisor.

Hopefully you really like him or her, because you just gave up $30,000 of your family's wealth in order to provide your advisor with a $2500 bonus, just for selling you something that you could have bought for free.

Although it's important to minimize investment fees, it also isn't necessary to be obsessive about this. When given a choice between two comparable products, you should usually choose the less expensive one. However, this only applies to comparable products. Some categories of investment options are simply more expensive. For instance, emerging market stock funds generally have higher expenses than funds designed to track the S&P 500.

This doesn't mean that you should avoid emerging market stock funds. The potentially higher returns they offer as well as the diversification they provide often argue for including some emerging market funds in your portfolio, despite their relatively high cost. However, when choosing from among different emerging market funds, investors will generally do better if they limit their selection to those with reasonable costs relative to their peers. In other words, when it comes to analyzing fees, make sure you are comparing apples to apples and oranges to oranges.

Again, there is nothing wrong with paying fees for quality advice and guidance. After all, this is your financial future we're talking about, and that's not really an area in which you want to automatically seek out the cheapest provider. Think about it this way. If you were about to head into surgery, would you try to find the least expensive surgeon? Of course not. You'd do your research to narrow down a list of the best surgeons, and then if those on the list were all equally competent, you'd choose the least expensive option from that list.

You should approach your financial providers in the same manner. Start by doing your research to identify the best, since these individuals and firms are the most likely to get you to your financial goals. Then, if you have several quality options, you might consider cost in making your selection.

When considering financial alternatives, ask yourself if your life and your finances are going to be better off for paying those fees. Do you have the **ability** to do what your advisor is going to do as well as they are going to do it? If you have the ability, do you also have the **time**? And finally, if you have the ability and the time, do you have the **desire** to do it or would you rather pay someone in order to free yourself up to do other things? After all, it's time, not money, that is the most valuable commodity you have. That is why, despite the fact that almost all of us have the ability to mow our own lawns, some of us choose to pay someone to do it for us so that we can spend our time doing something else.

The bottom line to remember with fees is simply this: it's not about cost; it's about value. There is nothing wrong with paying fees if you are receiving a value such that your overall financial picture improves because of the fees you paid. What you want to avoid, though, are unnecessary fees and fees where the value added isn't commensurate with what you are paying.

Is What You're Buying Even an Investment?

There are some "investment" products you might come across that are not really investments at all. It's important you are aware of this, because these are often the products most aggressively marketed, and you want to be prepared to evaluate their pros and cons free from hyperbole.

For starters, understand that the basic definition of an investment is that you take some of your current resources and invest them in something that will produce cash flows for you in the future. Then the way that you value that investment is by forecasting those future cash flows and the likelihood that you'll actually receive them. The more certain you are of receiving the cash flows, the less return you require from that investment and vice versa. But you are always going to require some return, because you're forgoing current consumption today and need to be compensated for that.

The key part of the earlier discussion is that you're valuing expected future cash flows. It's those cash flows that make something an investment. If something isn't expected to generate cash flows, either now or in the future, it's not an investment.

That doesn't mean that assets without present or future cash flows can't have value. They can. But that value comes about in a different manner. If you buy an asset in the hopes of making a profit, but it does not and never will generate cash flows, then in order to make a profit you have to hope that other people's perception of that asset's value changes. In other words you are now relying on psychology rather than math.

And that to me is one of the main distinctions between investing and trading. Investing is a math exercise wherein you forecast future expected cash flows and discount them back to net present value. Trading is a psychological exercise wherein you are trying to guess what people will think at some future date and what value they will assign to an asset.

Neither is inherently good nor bad, although, as you can tell, I believe most people should eschew trading and focus their efforts on investing. But the most important thing is that if someone is engaging in trading, they need to realize that they are doing so and not delude themselves into thinking they are investing when they are actually trading.

And that brings us to those types of "investments" that are commonly hyped as such but don't fit the basic definition of an investment. Included in this category are assets such as:

- Precious metals (gold, silver, platinum)
- Cryptocurrencies (Bitcoin and its peers)
- Collectibles (art, baseball cards, fine wine)

The reason I'm singling these assets out is twofold. The first is that they do not, by my standard, fit the definition of an investment. Gold has been around for millennia but has never produced a single dollar of cash flow. A bottle of wine or a baseball card will never send you a dividend check. Therefore, none of these are an investment. Again, that doesn't mean they don't have any value or that their value can't increase. It simply means that the present and future value is determined by how those assets are perceived by others rather than the value of their future expected cash flows.

The second reason I'm singling these assets out is that they don't fall under the same sort of regulatory framework as stocks, bonds, mutual funds, bank products, and even real estate. As such, these assets can be subject to hyperbolic sales practices and even outright fraud.

You want to be aware of this, so that the next time you see an advertisement or newsletter touting these assets, or hear a radio or TV commercial doing the same, you approach the subject with an appropriate degree of skepticism. You should also realize that the salesperson might not be giving you both sides of the story. As such, prior to purchasing any of these assets, you'll likely benefit from seeking out differing opinions in order to make sure you are taking all sides of the argument into account.

I want to make two final points on these assets. The first is that they are often sold on fear. As discussed elsewhere in this book, fear can be an incredibly powerful driver of behavior. Salespeople know this and are more than happy to feed upon it. For instance, precious metals and cryptocurrencies are often sold based on a thesis that something bad will happen: There will be a recession or higher inflation or a devaluation of government-issued currencies. Any of those things may or may not happen, but it's important to attempt to calmly and rationally evaluate the likelihood of those scenarios coming to pass, as opposed to irrationally giving in to the fear of something bad happening.

The second point to consider is that fees matter. And for the most part, fees and commissions on things like precious metals and collectibles tend to be very high, both when getting into the asset and again when getting out of the asset. These fees mean that your actual return from these assets needs to be quite robust in order to compensate for any commissions you might pay.

Drowning in a Sea of Complexity

Any fool can make things more complex. It takes a touch of genius to move in the opposite direction.

– Albert Einstein

I don't know about you, but any time I read a quote from a guy whose very name is synonymous with brilliance, I tend to sit up and pay attention. And it would behoove you to remember this quote the next time some salesperson tries to hit you up with some overly complex, opaque, fee-ridden pile of you know what.

History has repeatedly demonstrated that Wall Street has many failings, but there is one area in which they truly excel. Wall Street specializes in creating extremely complex investment products. Sometimes these products meet the needs of clients by allowing them to better express their market opinions or hedge against certain risks. But more often these products are just smoke and mirrors. In those instances, either the products are touted as filling a need you don't actually have, or if they do fill a need that you have, they do so in a manner that is unnecessarily complicated and difficult to understand.

You might ask why Wall Street would want to create things that people don't understand? Well, they do this because these are the products on which they can make the most money.

The commission a Wall Street salesman earns selling the common stock of a blue-chip company pales in comparison to what they can make by selling a complex derivative. In fact, as the years have passed and technology has led to greater efficiency and transparency in some corners of Wall Street, ultra-complex products are almost the only things a salesman can make any money on.

Of course, as history has demonstrated, some of these products have become so complex that not only can't the clients understand them but neither can the banks that build them. It was an inability to properly control the Frankenstein they created that ultimately led to the demise of many of the largest banks on Wall Street during the financial crisis of 2008.

If the very Wall Street banks that are creating these products can't understand them, it would stand to reason that the average investor is unlikely to fare any better. Not only are many of these products highly specialized, but they also require an in-depth understanding of advanced mathematics. Furthermore, properly analyzing these securities would take an inordinate amount of time. For instance, Warren Buffett estimated that in order to analyze a single CDO (CDO stands for collateralized debt obligation, which is among the most complicated fixed income instruments in existence and played a large role in the financial crisis) an investor would need to read 72,000 pages' worth of prospectuses.

72,000 pages!

For a single investment!

Which means that in order to build a portfolio of these things, literally millions of pages of reading would be required just to complete the most basic of research. Obviously, no investor, professional or otherwise, is going to read 72,000 pages of a dry legal document prior to deciding whether or not to make an investment. Few humans would have that kind of stamina and discipline, and no one has that kind of time. But even setting those considerations aside, if something is so difficult to analyze, it seems legitimate to question whether it belongs in an investment portfolio.

Do You Even Know What You're Buying?

Here's another example of the "benefits" of complexity. Some years ago a gentleman approached me following a seminar I gave in order to solicit my opinion on an investment opportunity he had been offered by one of the brokerage firms he dealt with. The product in question was a bond issued by a bank with a variable rate of interest and 30 years until final maturity. The rate of interest depended upon the slope of the yield curve (the difference in yield between 2-year Treasury securities and 10-year Treasury securities) and would vary over time – the steeper the yield curve, the higher the rate of interest. The initial rate of interest sounded quite compelling to this investor but he wasn't sure he understood how the security actually worked.

I began by asking this gentleman whether he was aware that the yield curve was, at that time, among the steepest it had ever been. He responded that he did not. I then asked him if he had run through the calculations with the broker over what the yield on the bond would be if the yield curve reverted to its long-run average. The broker had not explained this to the prospective customer, and the gentleman was quite surprised to discover that, if the yield curve reverted to its historical average, the return on his investment would be exceptionally low. Finally, the broker had also left the client with the impression that the security was free from credit risk since it was dependent on movements in U.S. Treasuries. Unfortunately, this was not the case; the ultimate guarantor of the bond was the bank issuing it, thereby exposing its purchaser to credit risk he was not fully aware of.

As we talked, it became very clear that this surefire investment was anything but. The gentleman in question walked away with a better understanding of why it is often best to avoid investment products one doesn't understand, and ultimately wound up investing his money in high-quality, short-term bonds, which in his case were precisely the type of investment he needed to meet his financial goals.

But alas, the commission his broker earned was tiny compared to what it could have been!

But My "Regular" Bonds Are Free from Commissions, Right?

When investing the bond portion of your portfolio, I generally recommend using some sort of professionally managed vehicle such as a mutual fund, exchange-traded fund (ETF), or separately managed account. However, some people, like the gentleman in the earlier story, prefer to own individuals bonds. As that story relayed, complicated bonds can have high fees buried in them, but surely "regular" bonds are cheap to trade, right? After all, your broker might have told you that there is no commission to trade bonds. And your broker would never lie to you, right?

Let me pause here and apologize to those of you who have been buying bonds from old-school brokerage firms because they are "commission free." The reason I'm apologizing is that I feel like I'm about to tell you there is no such thing as Santa Claus. It's true that a jolly old elf doesn't drop down the chimney every 25th of December to leave you presents and candy canes, but that doesn't make learning that fact any less disappointing when you're a kid.

Similarly, it's a fact that you've likely been paying to buy and sell bonds at your brokerage firm, but that doesn't make hearing about it any less disappointing.

The good news, though, is that, strictly speaking, your broker (who, remember, is legally *not obligated* to act in your best interest) didn't lie to you. Technically, you generally do not pay a commission to buy or sell a bond. Congratulations on that. Unfortunately, though, that isn't the whole story, and the average cost to buy or sell individual bonds is often 1.5% or more. Here's how your "commission-free" trade might wind up costing you.

When an investor buys or sells a security, there are always two different prices. There is the "ask" price, which is the price at which you can buy a security. This price is always higher than the "bid" price, which is the price at which you can sell a security. The difference between these two prices, which is known as the bid-ask spread, reflects a profit margin for the Wall Street traders who make a market in securities. These market makers essentially grease the wheels of the financial markets and make sure that when you want to buy or sell a security, it is possible to do so. Helping to maintain market liquidity is a valuable function, and since there is some risk involved in doing this, the traders need to be compensated. Hence, the bid-ask spread.

Now, with stocks, the bid-ask spread is pretty narrow. With a well-known stock like Apple, the difference between what you pay to buy and sell might only be a penny. However, the bond market is different than the stock market. Whereas stocks trade on an exchange and their prices are constantly posted online, bonds trade over-the-counter and their prices may rarely be posted. This isn't an exact analogy, but think of the way bonds trade as being a little bit more like real estate. When you buy or sell a house, you do so at a price you think is fair, but you never really know for sure. After all, it's not as if your house sold three times the day before you bought it, in order to give you a good price comparison. Instead, you're relying on comparable prices from websites like Zillow, as well as guidance from your real estate broker.

Similarly, with bonds you are often relying on your broker and the price he or she tells you that you can buy or sell at. And remember the price to buy is always going to be higher than the price to sell. That's how Wall Street traders make a living and get compensated for greasing the wheels of commerce. However, and this is the important point, that bid-ask spread is not fixed. It can vary from customer to customer.

And if it can vary from customer to customer, ask yourself this: Who is going to get better pricing, a large important client, or a smaller, less important client? Then, ask yourself which of those categories you fall into. And remember, we aren't talking about whether you're an important client to your broker. Instead, we're talking about how important you are, in the grand scheme of things, to the bank as a whole. Are you as important to that bank as a large hedge fund or insurance company? Probably not.

So then here is the bottom line. The Federal Reserve did a study on municipal bond pricing and found that bond markups vary widely. For larger customers, or those purchasing more than two million dollars' worth of bonds, the markup was around 10 basis points (0.10%) on average. However, for smaller customers, or those purchasing $10,000 worth of bonds, the markup was around 170 basis points (1.70%) on average. In other words, smaller customers were paying approximately 17 times more than larger customers. That, my friends, is the Costco effect translated to the bond market. Buying in bulk pays off. And on the flipside, buying in small quantities hurts.

There really isn't anything wrong with that per se. Larger clients get a bulk discount in a lot of industries. But let's flash back to the start of this section, and the conversation around how your bond purchases are "commission free." Well, yes, those purchases are technically "commission free." But they are hardly "free."

It's admittedly a small omission on the part of your broker. Only one word, after all. "Commission free" versus "free." But if your bond yield is 2%, and the markup you pay is 2%, then the trade you thought was "free" is actually costing you a full year's worth of your returns. In other words, if you bought a five-year bond and paid what the Federal Reserve said was an average markup, you really only get four years' worth of interest. The fifth year went to your broker to pay for your "commission free" trade.

Those average markups I cited are based on a Federal Reserve study into the municipal bond market. But in case you think the data might be cherry picked or that large markups are endemic to the municipal market, I'm here to tell you that very much isn't the case. Back in the late 1990s and early 2000s I worked as a bond trader and I can tell you that our average markup was well in excess of a couple of percent. Things may have changed in the ensuing years, but back then 3% or 4% was not at all uncommon.

More recently, I analyzed a portfolio where the individual had purchased $300,000 worth of bonds from a large bank. I calculated his markups, relative to what other purchasers had paid that day, at approximately $7,000. No wonder he had previously told me his broker was his "friend"!

As you've gathered by now, the bond market can be perilous to navigate, especially for smaller investors. If you still want to buy individual bonds for yourself, doing so through some of the larger online brokerage firms (Schwab, Fidelity) will give you more straightforward pricing and some protections against excessive markups. If you go that route, though, you'll still face the other difficulties of navigating a market geared toward large institutional investors.

If you want to completely avoid the problems discussed earlier, you can do so by using mutual funds and exchange-traded funds for your bond investing. Alternatively, you can utilize a professional manager experienced in navigating the bond market. As mentioned previously, it's my belief that these approaches generally make more sense than trying to buy individual bonds on your own.

There is a larger lesson to be found in this analysis of the bond market. The mere fact that your broker might be able to tell you that your bond purchase is "commission free" speaks to the industry's liberal relationship with the truth. And this in turn gets back to the discussion of the fiduciary standard versus the suitability standard.

If you're dealing with a broker operating under the suitability standard, you'll never quite know whether you're getting the full truth. And you'll never quite know whether you're paying undisclosed fees or markups. If instead you utilize an advisor operating under the fiduciary standard, you'll always know in advance exactly what you're paying. The advisor doesn't have the ability to charge any further commissions, markups, or fees. And of course, they are always legally obligated to act in your best interest, which would, in the case of the bond market, force them to fight for the best pricing and lowest markups for the bonds you are going to own.

What Are You Using Derivatives For?

First, let me state that there is nothing inherently wrong with derivatives such as futures and options (or, for that matter, any of the other securities discussed in this chapter). Much like a brick, which can be used to build an orphanage or break a window, futures and options have practical applications when used correctly, but can be extremely dangerous when used improperly by uninformed investors.

It's possible that some individuals understand futures and options, the risks associated with them, and how best to incorporate them into their portfolios. However, the vast majority of individuals are best served by avoiding vehicles that have been called "financial weapons of mass destruction."

As a quick reminder of exactly why most investors should simply say "no thanks" if someone offers to sell them futures and options, consider some of the characteristics of these instruments:

- Under the wrong circumstances, futures and options can expose their users to potentially unlimited losses. In other words, with some futures and options strategies, your potential losses are not limited to your initial investment. Instead, you can, in some circumstances, suffer losses well in excess of the amount you invested. This is known as a margin call and is not a situation you ever want to face.
- By some estimates, 90% of participants in the futures and options markets lose money. Most of the money in these markets is made by a small handful of professional speculators and hedge funds. Futures and options are a zero-sum game; for every winner there needs to be a loser and vice versa. Unless

you can make a strong case for why you are going to beat a hedge fund at its own game, you probably shouldn't be playing that game.

- Pricing models for these instruments are extraordinarily complex and difficult to understand. Myron Scholes is considered the father of options pricing models. He is the co-creator of the Black-Scholes pricing model, which is the foundation for all options pricing today. For his work, he was awarded the Nobel Prize in Economics, which generally isn't handed out for stuff you can do on the back of a napkin.
- Although extraordinarily complex, pricing models for these products are also famous for often being wrong. Want proof? Myron Scholes, our Nobel Prize winner, later joined a hedge fund known as Long-Term Capital Management (LTCM). LTCM was one of the world's most successful hedge funds, until its pricing models stopped working.
- Yes, you read that correctly. Even the guy who won a Nobel Prize for creating the models couldn't get them to do what they were supposed to do. The result was that LTCM blew up in 1998, and caused enough of a crisis that the Federal Reserve was afraid the financial system would collapse. Eventually a consortium of Wall Street banks rescued LTCM and orchestrated a managed liquidation of the fund.
- The use of futures and options brings a timing component into the investment process – in other words, not only do you need to be correct about the direction of the market movement but the movement also needs to happen within the time frame of the futures or options contract. It does you no good to see the market move in your direction after your futures or options contract has expired.

The too-cool-for-school crowd of market pundits often tout the virtues of these financial products, usually highlighting a great trade that makes money under virtually any scenario with minimal downside. This may be true, but it's important to remember that these are sophisticated techniques that are not appropriate for many people. The average individual, less concerned with being profiled in the *Wall Street Journal* than with being able to fund the life of their dreams, can meet their financial goals without ever using these products.

> **Note:** I want to emphasize again that options can be appropriate when used to hedge risks in a portfolio. In fact, that is what they were originally designed for. For example, earlier in this book, I discussed how options could be used to mitigate the risk of a concentrated stock position. However, even when used appropriately, options remain complicated.
>
> Therefore, the design and implementation of an options strategy should be left to more experienced investors. Individuals lacking expertise in this area should almost always seek guidance from a professional prior to utilizing futures or options.
>
> It is important that this professional should not be someone trying to sell you futures or options!

Market Voodoo (AKA Technical Analysis)

Another sexy area of the financial markets is technical analysis. Technical analysis refers to the act of analyzing charts of past market movements in order to forecast future results. These techniques are particularly popular among some short-term traders and market timers. Debate has raged for years over whether technical analysis has any merit at all. Some argue that charts can predict the future. Others say technical analysis is a fallacy and has no merit whatsoever.

Arguments about the validity of technical analysis as a means of forecasting future market movements are beyond the scope of this book. For the sake of our purposes here, I'll simply say that like most investment approaches technical analysis works for some users and not for others.

However, for average people seeking to meet their financial goals, technical analysis introduces a level of complexity into the investment program that is not necessary. Furthermore, technical analysis is primarily a short-term tool used by traders rather than by investors. As I have stated repeatedly throughout this book, ordinary folks looking to meet their financial goals should ignore the mayhem inherent with trading and focus instead upon time-tested principles designed to facilitate investment success. With that in mind, technical analysis is unnecessary for the individual trying to meet their financial goals.

Finally, as with any investment approach, technical analysis must be rigorously followed across market cycles. You either use technical analysis or you don't. Seeing a pundit on TV talking about a technical analysis chart and then deciding to follow their advice is no better than taking random stock tips from your cab driver. Remember, even the best market prognosticators are often wrong; they profit over long periods of time by being right slightly more often than they are wrong. That means that if you selectively follow only some of a particular pundit's advice, you are just as likely to lose money as make money, even if that person is a superstar.

Let Me "Sell" You an Annuity ...

All right, here comes my pitch. Brace yourself. And be honest, at the end of it, if you think this sounds like something that might help you meet your financial goals.

- Give me $500,000 to invest.
- I'll guarantee you double your money over the next 10 years, which works out to about a 7.25% annual return.
- In other words, at the end of a decade *I guarantee you'll have a million bucks and you don't have to worry about market fluctuations in the meantime.*
- Then, I guarantee you can withdraw $50,000 annually, which is equal to 10% of your initial investment.
- And better yet, I'll guarantee you that rate of withdrawal each and every year *for the rest of your life.*
- You'll get guaranteed income for the rest of your life. It will be like you've created a personal pension plan for your retirement.

So, to summarize, I guarantee you double your money in the next decade, and then I give you a guaranteed income stream each and every year for the rest of your life.

Be honest with me now.

What do you think? Does this product sound like something that you might be interested in?

Do you want to sign up right now?

If I'm being honest with you, that product sounds pretty good to me, too. In fact, I'm about to reach for the phone to place an order right now.

Except that ...

Now, Let Me "Explain" an Annuity ...

Except that what I just did was I "sold" you an annuity. And like any salesman I'm pretty good at putting lipstick on a pig, especially when I have the proper "motivation" – and we'll get to that motivation in just a bit.

Okay, here goes, I'm going to "explain" the same annuity I just "sold" you. Remember, the two products in question are *identical*, and both of these descriptions are *factually correct*, but framed very differently (there we go again with **framing**, which is an important and recurring theme of this book).

For starters, let's just assume you're 55 years old right now, and have $500,000 to invest. So,

- Today, at age 55, I want you to give me $500,000 to invest.
- Then, for the next 10 years, you do not receive any income, and your money is locked up and inaccessible. So, until you're 65, your money might as well be locked in a vault somewhere.
- Now that you're 65, a decade has passed and you've received no cash flows from your investment to date, but the "contract value" has grown to $1,000,000.
- Here is some good news, though, because for the next 10 years, I'll guarantee you $50,000 a year on that $1,000,000 contract value which is a 5% withdrawal rate.

- At age 75, 20 years have passed since you bought this product, and you've received $500,000 in total distributions ($50,000 a year for 10 years). In other words, you invested your money two decades ago, and now you've finally received your principal back.
- For the next 10 years, I'll continue to guarantee you $50,000 annually on that $1,000,000 "contract value," which is a 5% withdrawal rate.
- At age 85, three decades have passed, and you've received $1,000,000 in total distributions on that $500,000 initial investment.

So, you've doubled your money. Which doesn't sound that bad until you consider that it took you 30 years to do so. By the way, if investors double their money over three decades, that works out to around a 2.2% internal rate of return, which is absolutely terrible.

For comparison sake, and as of this writing, you can get probably 2.2% on a one-year CD, which:

- Is guaranteed by the U.S. government
- Imparts fewer penalties if you wish to access your money early
- Is **commission free**

Hmmm, I wonder why that salesperson didn't just sell you a CD. Oh, wait. I know. I'll bet it has something to do with that "motivation" we discussed.

The commission – the glorious commission. Although products vary widely, the commission on that annuity trade could easily be anywhere from 5% to 10% or possibly even more.

That's right, the annuity salesperson might have made $50,000 or more selling you that wonderful "opportunity" to lock your money up for decades while earning the same rate of return you could have gotten on a one-year CD. No wonder he was motivated to work on that sales pitch!

By the way, about that locking your money up for decades. Because the company that issues the annuity pays a large upfront commission to the salesperson, they need you to stay invested long enough to earn their money back. They do this in two ways. The first is by charging high fees on the money invested within the annuity, which is why your money doesn't grow very quickly.

The annuity company then needs to earn these fees for a long enough period of time to make up for the commission they paid and still generate a healthy profit. They do this by locking you into the product. These surrender periods vary, but a decade is not unusual. If you decide that you want to get out of your annuity prior to the end of the surrender period, you may be able to do so, but you'll usually pay a hefty penalty.

Here's the truth about annuities. Some of them (i.e., fixed immediate annuities) might have a place for some investors, though even there you can often recreate a similar strategy in a more efficient manner. But many annuities, especially the more **complicated** (there's that word again) ones, are simply excuses to take advantage of underinformed consumers who get sold a bill of goods by an unscrupulous, highly motivated salesperson.

Now that you've read this, please don't be one of those consumers.

And if you happen to come across a complicated annuity that sounds too good to pass up, give me a call before buying it. I'll talk you into a more appropriate solution, and my advice won't cost you the sticker price on a new BMW.

The Bottom Line

Thus, we conclude our brief tour of some of the more dangerous corners of Wall Street. As a reminder, many of the tools and techniques discussed earlier do have legitimate uses. However, you have to make certain that you have a genuine understanding of why products are being used, as well as any potential downsides that might arise from their use.

More importantly, consider the motivation of your financial providers in positioning any products and solutions. Remember, the financial industry has a bad reputation for a reason. The single best way to avoid conflicts of interest when it comes to meeting your financial goals is to work with a fiduciary that is legally obligated to act in your best interest.

If you instead choose to partner with a broker operating under the suitability standard, you need to understand that conflicts may exist, and that even if they say all the right things, they may work for an organization with different motivations.

The bottom line is that if you choose not to work with a fiduciary, you do so at your peril. Therefore, my best advice is to remain skeptical and submit any recommendations to the sniff test. Remember, as in most areas of your life, if something sounds too good to be true, it probably is, and if you can't understand something, ask for it to be explained again or just walk away.

Chapter 13 How to Survive a Bear Attack

If you want your money to grow, you'll have to invest in a way that exposes you to periodic market sell-offs. Avoiding bear markets is almost impossible; your goal should be to prepare yourself to withstand the inevitable fluctuations markets are subject to so that you can survive bear markets and then thrive when times are good.

Bear Markets: You've probably heard the term before, but do you know what actually constitutes a "bear market"? Traditionally, the term means that the market in question has declined at least 20% from a recent peak. When people refer to a bear market in stocks, they usually mean that a major index such as the Dow Jones Industrial Average (DJIA) or S&P 500 (S&P) has declined by at least 20%. When smaller subsets of the financial markets such as small company stocks or oil or technology stocks have declined by at least 20%, market participants generally

(*continued*)

(*continued*)

declare a bear market in that specific sector, but not in the markets at large.

Although a bear market is characterized by a 20% decline, there are many instances when markets sell off, but don't hit that 20% threshold. When markets fall at least 10% but less than 20%, the decline is referred to as a "correction." Corrections, though not quite as deep as bear markets, are far more common, and can still be painful.

According to Ned Davis Research the S&P 500 has experienced 95 corrections of 10% or more since 1928. There have been 25 bear markets during that time frame. On average, those bear markets saw a decline of approximately 30%, though the worst bear market (1929–1932) featured a cataclysmic drop of 86%!

For the purposes of this chapter, when I use the term *bear market* I am referring to any significant decline in the financial markets.

Prepare for the Bear

If you've ever taken a trip to Yellowstone National Park or other areas where grizzly bears are common, you've probably been exposed to some of the preventive measures you can take to avoid being attacked. For instance, signs at the ranger station will warn you never to hike alone, or to make noise when on the trail. Local sporting goods stores also sell bear spray, which is a high-powered pepper spray you are supposed to aim at a charging grizzly.

In the event none of this works, the standard advice is that you should play dead while the bear mauls you. Now, I've yet to be mauled by a grizzly, but I have to assume that it's not a lot of fun. Furthermore, it must take an incredible degree of willpower to play dead during a mauling while every instinct screams out that you should fight back and defend yourself. The bottom line is that the best course of action is to prepare ahead of time in order to avoid a truly unpleasant experience.

Surviving the bear in the financial markets is no different.

The best way to navigate a significant market correction is to position yourself appropriately ahead of time so that you don't feel compelled to react when markets are falling.

When I talk about positioning yourself appropriately, I don't mean that you use your clairvoyance to select the perfect time to sell all your stocks and move to cash. Hopefully by this stage in the book you're convinced of the impracticality of repeatedly accomplishing this.

Instead, I'm referring to the idea that you need to set your initial asset allocation in such a manner that you can still fall asleep at night, even during turbulent market environments.

Asset allocation refers to how your portfolio is broken down into different types of investments. These broad categories of investments, such as stocks, bonds, commodities, real estate, international securities, and cash, are generally referred to as asset classes, and the mix of these asset classes you choose to hold will go a long way toward determining the performance of your investment portfolio. Fortunately, the decision about which mix of investments to hold is completely within your control. This is great news, because asset allocation is arguably the most important tool an investor has.

Figure 13.1 summarizes returns on various asset classes over the 20-year period from 1999 to 2018.

Large Stocks	Small Stocks	International Stocks	Emerging Markets	Cash	Bonds	Real Estate	Commodities
S&P 500	Russell 2000	MSCI ACWI	MSCI EM Index	30-Day T-Bills	Barclays Aggregate	Dow Jones REIT Index	Bloomberg Commodity Index
5.6%	7.4%	4.6%	8.8%	1.2%	4.5%	9.8%	1.8%

Figure 13.1 Asset Class Performance (1999–2018)
SOURCE: Analysis by Brian Perry. Data from S&P, Russell, MSCI, Barclays, and Dow Jones.

The appropriate allocation among these asset classes depends heavily on an investor's required rate of return. The more return you require, the more aggressive your asset allocation needs to be. In other words, if you need your portfolio to earn more, you need to own more of the assets with higher expected returns. Of course, the flipside of this is that asset classes that have higher expected returns also tend to have greater volatility.

Risk Capacity versus Risk Tolerance

Therefore, the second consideration in building your initial asset allocation is how much risk to take on. How much risk you take is determined by both your risk capacity and your risk tolerance. Risk capacity refers to your *ability* to take on risk. In other words, how much risk can you take on without endangering your likelihood of meeting your financial goal. Risk tolerance measures your *willingness* to take on risk, that is, how much risk are you comfortable taking on.

Risk capacity depends on a number of factors, but one aspect commonly looked at is your time horizon. In general, long-term financial goals might allow for a somewhat more aggressive investment mix. Conversely, the shorter the time horizon, the more conservative the asset mix should be. Put differently, your capacity to take risk increases as your investment time horizon lengthens. Please note though that this is a general rule of thumb and there are a number of factors beyond your time horizon that could impact your risk capacity.

You may also recall that there are risks that come from investing both too aggressively and too conservatively. For instance, if investors are too conservative, they run the risk of not generating sufficient returns to meet their financial goals. On the other hand, investing too aggressively can result in higher than expected investment losses. Both of these considerations will go into formulating your risk capacity.

Once you've identified your capacity to take on risk, the next step is to determine your tolerance for taking on risk. Risk tolerance is a personal thing; some people can watch their portfolio plummet without blinking an eye, whereas others become nauseous at the thought of losing a dime of their hard-earned money. That being said, a very common mistake is that people overestimate their risk tolerance and think they can stomach more risk than they actually can. This generally happens for one of two reasons.

The first is that they might confuse risk capacity with risk tolerance. In other words, you might say to yourself, "I have 20 years until retirement, so I can invest most of my portfolio in stocks." From a risk-capacity standpoint, this might be true. If you have a couple of decades as a time horizon, from a numbers perspective you may be able to take on the risk that comes from owning a lot of stocks. The problem is that then the market falls sharply, and even though you have the time to wait out the decline, you panic and sell. In this instance your risk capacity allowed you to hold the majority of your portfolio in stocks, but your risk tolerance did not.

The second reason people overestimate their risk tolerance is simply that they forget what it feels like to lose money. Following a sharp market decline, the pain is real, and many people don't want to experience that again. But in life, most pains grow duller with age, and the same is true with financial loss. There is a very strong tendency for people's perception of just how painful a loss was to diminish over time.

The challenge here is that when it has been a while since a nasty bear market, you begin to forget how it actually felt. When that happens, you start to think your risk tolerance is greater than it actually is. Of course, if it has been a while since a bear market, that usually means you are enjoying a bull market, which further exacerbates the tendency to get a bit more aggressive than you should. And, of course, eventually the trend reverses and markets fall, right when you find yourself with a portfolio that's too aggressive for your true risk tolerance. So, you panic and sell.

As a general rule, when there is a gap between your risk capacity and your risk tolerance, you want to defer to your risk tolerance. In the end, what matters isn't how much risk you *can take*, but rather how much risk you *should take*.

I'll repeat myself one more time by emphasizing that many people are actually more conservative than they believe themselves to be. When people assess their risk tolerance, they tend to think that they can be aggressive, but when markets become volatile these individuals find that they are unable to tolerate the losses they are seeing. For that reason, it is *exceptionally important* to be as honest as possible with yourself when assessing your risk tolerance, prior to determining your asset allocation and investment approach.

Remember, the time to prepare for a bear market is before it occurs, and the way to do this is by making sure your portfolio mix is based on your required rate of return, your capacity to take risk, and your tolerance for taking risk. Whatever allocation you decide on, you need to analyze how it might perform in a down market, and then think long and hard about whether you'd be able to stay the course in a worst-case scenario.

Rebalance to Stay on Course

If a ship set sail from Los Angeles to Tokyo, it would likely be off course within the first couple miles as waves or wind nudged it to the left or right. If these course deviations are minimal, the ship's captain may not correct course right away, since small fluctuations on a long journey aren't that important. But, if the ship gets blown far enough off course that it's headed toward Australia, the captain had better do something if he wants to arrive at his intended destination.

The same concept holds true once you've set your initial investment allocation. As different asset classes move up and down at different rates, your portfolio will almost instantly be off course. Therefore, once you've set an asset allocation you can stick with through a severe market downturn, the next step is to make sure that you maintain a consistent exposure to that mix.

Consistent doesn't mean constant. Just like the boat captain was willing to let his ship slide slightly off course, you, too, should allow your portfolio mix to fluctuate a bit. Trying to keep your initial allocation exactly inline would likely involve an unreasonable amount of transactions, which would generate unnecessary costs while also driving you crazy. And there wouldn't be a whole lot of benefit to the exercise. But, just like the boat captain doesn't want to wind up in Australia, you don't want your portfolio to deviate too greatly from your intended risk-and-return targets. Therefore, some sort of disciplined rebalancing approach is vital to meeting your financial goals.

For starters, imagine the following scenario. Let's say that you've determined that your optimal asset allocation represents a mix of 60% in stocks and 40% in bonds. So, you structure your portfolio accordingly and you're on your way. If you started with a $500,000 portfolio, you'd have purchased $300,000 worth of stocks and $200,000 worth of bonds.

Subsequently, the stock market declines by 30% while the value of your bonds increases by 5%. You now own $210,000 worth of stocks and $210,000 worth of bonds, which is the same as saying you now have a 50/50 mix of stocks and bonds.

Of course, this 50/50 mix isn't your intended allocation, and it's not the allocation you previously determined was most likely to meet your financial goals. Rather, the appropriate mix for you was a 60/40 split of stocks and bonds. So, if you do nothing, you've allowed your portfolio to deviate meaningfully from your optimal mix. Even worse, you've done so at just the time when you'd most like to own stocks – namely, following a significant decline in value, which, all else being equal, means they are relatively less expensive than they'd previously been.

This is where rebalancing comes into play. Rebalancing involves a disciplined approach to maintaining your desired asset allocation. If an asset class increases as a percentage of your portfolio, you sell some of it to bring it back to your target. If an asset class declines as a percentage of your portfolio, you buy some more in order to bring it back to your target. Doing this accomplishes two objectives:

1. Rebalancing keeps your portfolio closely aligned with your initial, target allocation. Since that allocation represents the portfolio most likely to help you meet your financial goals, **this is a very good thing**.
2. All else being equal, rebalancing generally results in buying low and selling high, **which is also a very good thing**.

As mentioned earlier, rebalancing forces you to buy low and sell high. This practice of buying low and selling high can be emotionally challenging, but a rebalancing discipline can help overcome the natural human inclination to add to your winners while scaling back your losers.

Do you remember the bursting of the technology stock bubble in the early 2000s? Rebalancing would have been the single best tool available to protect yourself from that. The sharp bear market of the early 2000s damaged well-diversified investors who maintained their strategic allocation. But by focusing on what was within their control, they survived to fight another day.

Undisciplined investors, lulled into rapture by the glorious tech stock returns of the late 1990s and not willing or able to control what they could (i.e., rebalancing), were largely wiped out by the tech meltdown. Depending on their age and status in life, some of those investors may never have recovered.

Ultimately, buying low and selling high while maintaining a portfolio mix that closely approximates your strategic allocation is likely to prove a winning combination over time.

Note: Nearly all successful investors subscribe to the discipline of periodic portfolio rebalancing. However, the actual implementation of said rebalancing can vary. For example, should you rebalance your portfolio every day? After all, assets are unlikely to move in lockstep, which means that on a daily basis your asset mix is likely to be somewhat different from your target allocation. But on the flipside, these incremental differences are unlikely to produce large performance deviations, and the costs of trading, as well as the headaches associated with constant portfolio turnover, would argue against setting out to correct extremely small allocation drifts.

Others will argue that rebalancing should be done once a quarter, or perhaps on an annual basis. This may make sense in some market environments, but what if intrayear portfolio fluctuations lead to significant allocation deviations well in advance of your targeted rebalancing date?

Another, and my preferred approach, is to place comfort levels around your target allocations, and then to rebalance when or if allocations drift beyond those bands.

For instance, let's say that your target allocation is 50% stocks and 50% bonds. You might place bands of plus or minus 20% of your desired allocation. In other words, if either stocks or bonds increase (decrease) as a percentage of the portfolio by more than 10% (10% represents a 20% movement on a 50% allocation), you sell (or buy) accordingly. A practice such as this can help you avoid deviating too significantly from your target mix while also minimizing the amount of trading that you need to do.

Buy-and-Hold Investing

Having a buy-and-hold mentality means that you invest for the long term, and at times even intend to hold an investment forever. However, if circumstances meaningfully change (for instance, valuations become excessive), a buy-and-hold investor will sell their securities and reinvest the proceeds elsewhere.

This can be a difficult approach to take. For one thing, valuations are often at their most excessive at precisely the time when the crowd is most exuberant. So, just when everyone is excited about the limitless potential of a particular investment, a buy-and-hold investor should be thinking about selling. Not only does this mean that the investor must act contrary to popular opinion, but bull markets can last much longer than expected. Therefore, an investor who has sold may have to sit by and watch as prices continue to move higher for several more years.

A disciplined rebalancing process can help you avoid market extremes. Rebalancing doesn't mean that you abandon stocks (or any other asset class) if they reach historically high levels. But what rebalancing does provide is a means to gradually sell off securities as their values increase and their share of the portfolio does likewise. This systematic approach allows you to take some chips off the table and avoid being overexposed to an asset class just before the bubble bursts.

It also helps to remember what you're really trying to do. For most, the goal of an investment portfolio is not to achieve the highest return possible. Instead, the goal is to protect your hard-earned capital and produce returns sufficient to meet your financial goals. Accomplishing these goals doesn't require you to call every market top or bottom. If you're simply able to buy securities when valuations are reasonable, hold them for the long-term, and rebalance your portfolio to take some chips off the table as valuations become extreme, you're likely to meet your financial goals.

Buy-and-Forget Investing

I think it's important to differentiate between traditional buy-and-hold investing and buy-and-forget investing. Buy-and-hold investing means taking a long-term approach, selecting good investments, and holding those investments indefinitely unless something fundamental changes in either your personal circumstances or the characteristics of the investment. On the other hand, buy-and-forget investing misses a crucial component of the buy-and-hold philosophy – namely, the part where you only hold the investment **as long as the characteristics of the investment have not changed**.

This may seem like a small distinction, but it is crucially important. When buy-and-hold investors get in trouble and lose money over long periods of time, it's generally because the characteristics of their investment have changed but they haven't reacted to these evolving circumstances. These buy-and-forget investors instead hold on regardless of changes in the marketplace.

The most important change to be aware of and the one that causes the most damage to buy-and-forget investors is valuation. Typically, a buy-and-forget investor will purchase an investment and hold onto it as its value goes up and up and up. At some point, the price no longer reflects the true value of the investment but has instead entered a bubble phase. Bubbles always end in a crash and buy-and-forget investors often suffer as the once-inflated value of their securities spirals downward. This is exactly what happened to long-term investors in Japan who didn't consider the extreme valuations of Japanese stocks in the late 1980s. This is also what happened to technology stock investors in the United States during the stock market crash that followed the tech stock run-up of the late 1990s.

So, What Do You Do When Market Valuations Are Extreme?

Of course, it's difficult to know when you should sell, because valuations are extreme. There are no precise rules for identifying these times, but there are several symptoms that you can look for. Sophisticated investors might look for valuation metrics such as the price–earnings ratio. Other investors might want to keep abreast of the popular media; when the Internet or TV crowd is spouting off about the limitless potential of an investment that has already been going up for a long period of time, the end of the party may be near.

Finally, one of the best ways to make sure that you don't get caught up in a market bubble is to make sure that you can pass the sleep test. This means that if you're losing sleep at the end of the day because you're up late worrying about your investments, it might be time to reduce your exposure.

This lack of precision in identifying market tops or bottoms is one of the reasons why a disciplined rebalancing

approach makes sense. When investors utilize a rules-based approach to portfolio rebalancing, they remove guessing from the equation and instead force themselves to systematically buy low and sell high in their portfolio.

It's important to remember that reducing your exposure to an investment does not need to be an all-or-nothing proposition. You don't have to try to time the top of the market by selling all your stocks. Instead, if stocks have become somewhat pricey, sell a little bit. If prices continue to go higher, at least you still have some exposure. If on the other hand prices decline, you've reduced your potential losses. Again, this is what rebalancing can accomplish.

Does What Gets Measured Get Improved?

The short answer to the question above is yes, but you need to make sure you're measuring correctly, because performance measurement is an area where a great deal of confusion exists. For instance, if I were to ask one hundred people how their portfolio is doing, 95% of them would give me an answer somewhere along the lines of "I'm beating/lagging/keeping pace with the market." "The market" in this instance is represented by some vague sense of how stocks, or more explicitly the stocks of large U.S. companies, are doing.

As a starting point, these investors should be more specific about which market they are measuring themselves against, as well as how their performance ranks relative to that market.

But the problem goes much deeper, because the average person shouldn't measure himself or herself against some arbitrary market benchmark. After all, the S&P 500 is simply a collection of large U.S. corporations that fit certain criteria for index inclusion.

This might be well and good for an institutional investor whose sole job is to beat their benchmark, but it doesn't make sense for most individuals.

Why not, you may be asking? Well, simply because your future goals, dreams, and aspirations cannot be neatly encapsulated by an arbitrary collection of 30 or 100 or 1,000 securities. Therefore, any comparison of your performance to such a benchmark is inherently flawed.

A better approach is to *figure out what rate of return you require in order to meet your financial goals.* This rate of return will vary by individual, depending on circumstances, time frame, aspirations, and so forth. Indeed, one of the main goals of the planning process is to generate a required rate of return. *This required rate of return then becomes the basis for the decision of what type of portfolio to invest in.*

And once the required rate of return has been identified, portfolio performance should be measured relative to that rate. Performance will fluctuate widely, and may seldom match (or even be close to) the target return. But the key is not annual performance, but rather performance over time. In the long run, performance of the portfolio should align reasonably well with target return. When this occurs, the odds of achieving financial success increase significantly.

Furthermore, measuring performance to your target return, rather than some arbitrary market benchmark, will help you avoid the trap of falling prey to the ebbs and flows of market sentiment, with the corresponding ecstasy and depression that can prompt. And in case you haven't figured it out yet, when it comes to your finances, ecstasy and depression aren't appropriate emotional states for quality decision-making!

Yes, I realize that there is a certain sense of comfort that comes from knowing that your portfolio is performing in line with "the market." I also recognize that ego comes into play for some folks, either consciously or unconsciously. After all, many people want to keep up with the Joneses, so why should it be any different with your investment portfolio?

That last point deserves further clarification. For many people, happiness is not so much a matter of what they have in an absolute sense, but rather of what they have relative to their peers. In fact, studies have shown that people would rather have $100 if their neighbor has $100, than $150 if it meant that their neighbor has $200.

This carries over into the financial markets, too. In order to analyze the performance of a portfolio, it's important to have a relative measure to determine whether you've done "good" or "bad." And depending on circumstances, a 5% return might be good or it might be bad. The problem isn't with the act of comparing, but rather what people compare their portfolios to.

So again, I know it's tempting to compare your portfolio returns to "the market." But one of the **keys to financial success is to measure your performance to plan**.

Ready for Some Good News?

By the way, there's always a lot of talk about how the little guy can't compete in today's markets, but this is a good place to point out one major advantage the individual investor has over the pros. Unlike professionals, you don't need to report quarterly returns, which means you can focus on long-term results. This means that you can ignore the hype and focus on strategies designed to meet your financial goals, rather than succumbing to the mayhem all around you.

One of the worst inventions in the history of professional investing is quarterly reporting. Virtually every mutual fund, hedge fund, or professional investment manager reports its performance on this basis, comparing its returns to that of a benchmark index. In theory, this isn't a bad thing because it allows investors to track how the money managers are doing relative to the overall market. The problem is that three months isn't a sufficiently long period of time on which to judge performance.

What this means is that most professional investors are hyperfocused on performance in the next three to six months rather than over the next three to six years. As discussed throughout this book, investing is a long-term activity, whereas shorter-term trading is a completely different endeavor and one that involves a greater degree of speculation to boot. The need to report quarterly returns forces many professionals to move further into the speculation realm than they might otherwise prefer.

Warren Buffett has a talent for allocating capital that few investors can ever hope to duplicate. But think about it like this. You're probably never going to play golf like Tiger Woods, but there might be a few things he does on the course that can help improve your game. By the same token, there is at least one tremendous advantage Buffett utilizes that those of you reading this can easily incorporate.

Buffett's record of success has generated a great deal of goodwill among his investors, which means that they tend to be patient and don't overly focus on last quarter's results. That allows Buffett to focus more on long-term success than short-term market fluctuations. Over the course of four or five decades, this faith has paid great dividends to investors who have seen Buffett produce spectacular returns for them.

You may not have Buffett's track record, and you almost certainly will never possess his genius for investing. But you do have the ability to maintain the same long-term focus that Buffett is famous for *because you don't have to report quarterly returns to any clients or investors*. In other words, because you don't have an audience, you can ignore the hype and take a long-term perspective without worrying about what your portfolio returns look like from week to week, month to month, or even year to year.

A Better Life

This is important because ultimately there are only two ways to significantly improve your future standard of living. The first is to win the lottery. The likelihood of this occurring is slim, and even if it does happen statistics indicate that many lottery winners eventually wind up declaring bankruptcy.

The second, and more reasonable way to improve your standard of living is to invest for the future. By saving and investing over the

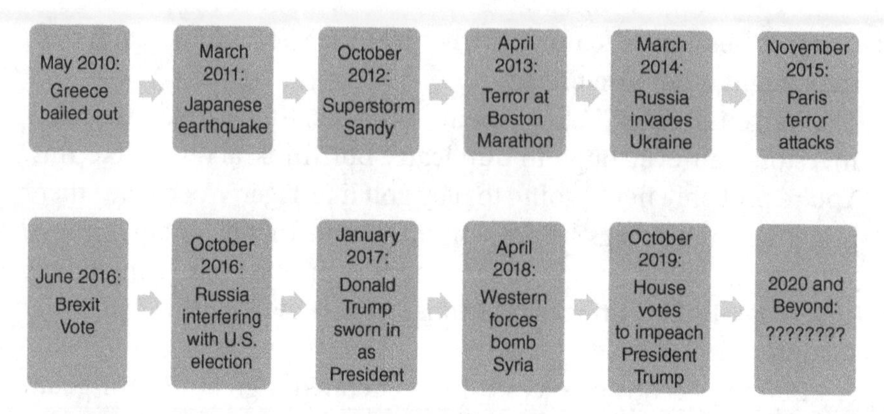

Figure 13.2 Representative "Bad News"
SOURCE: Analysis by Brian Perry.

course of years and decades, you may be able to build a portfolio that allows you to enhance your lifestyle.

Building a large portfolio can take time, but time is the ally of the patient investor. That is because of the power of compound interest, Albert Einstein's "most powerful force in the universe."

So, as we near the end of this book, let me leave you with two more visuals.

A decade ago we were just coming out of the worst financial collapse since the Great Depression, and it was fair to say that the bear had probably given you a pretty good mauling. Hopefully, you managed to stay the course through those dark days and if you did, consider for a moment Figure 13.2's major events, terrorist attacks, elections, and natural disasters that investors "enjoyed" over the 10 years that followed. And of course "2020 and Beyond" already features COVID-19 and its associated economic and financial turmoil.

Against such a backdrop, it would seem implausible that you could have prospered. Surely, at some point investors must have fled en masse from the turmoil all around them.

And at times they did. For example, following the British vote to leave the European Union, the London stock market fell more than 12%. Worldwide, nearly two trillion dollars in value was erased as global markets plunged following the Brexit vote. The response to

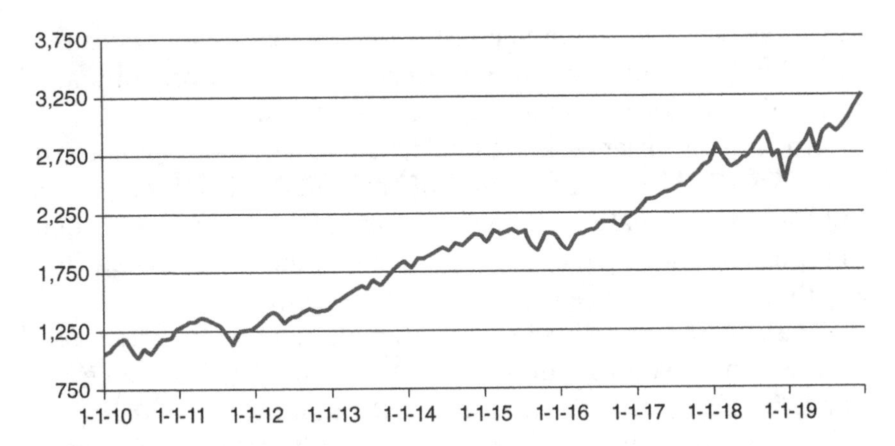

Figure 13.3 S&P 500 (2010–2019)
SOURCE: Adapted from MacroTrends and S&P.

Trump's election in 2016 was similar, with futures on the Dow Jones Index plunging 800 points overnight.

But markets recovered from both those votes, just as they did from all the other assorted disasters, plagues, and breaking news headlines we've seen. In fact, the market has done better than recover. Even in the face of an onslaught of breaking news and volatility, the stock market has moved higher, rewarding disciplined investors who braved the bear and stayed the course.

Just look at Figure 13.3, which shows the S&P 500 over the decade ending in 2019. I bet you'd be hard pressed to identify where those elections, natural disasters, and breaking news headlines even show up. Oh, sure, in the moment they all moved the markets, and short-term traders needed to be nimble to navigate the volatility that came their way.

But answer this question for yourself: Despite all that's happened in the past decade, is there a single event that really, truly impacted you as a long-term investor? Is there anything that in retrospect you can look back on and say, "I should have changed my approach because of that"?

And if nothing the past 10 years threw at you should have caused you to abandon ship or change your course, why would the next decade be any different? And yes, I'm including COVID-19 and its associated economic and financial impacts here. Because, while the pandemic caused unprecedented market volatility and economic shutdowns, in the long run these too will subside.

And that, my friends, is the final lesson to take from this book. If you believe in the upward progress of humanity and that companies will continue to create goods and services to fuel that progress, then you must be optimistic about the markets. And so ultimately, the way that you beat the bear isn't by running away.

The way that you beat the bear is by making sure you can survive an occasional mauling, confident that once the bear has done his worst, financial markets will resume their upward progress.

And it is that upward progress that will ultimately guide you to financial freedom.

Conclusion

Stop for a moment and consider how much life has changed in the past hundred years. Heck, consider the pace of change in just the past couple of decades. For a bit of perspective, I graduated college in 1996, and throughout the course of my undergraduate studies, I never owned a computer. I also never logged onto the Internet. And of course, no one I knew had a cell phone. Globalization wasn't even really a thing yet, and computerized trading was only in its infancy.

Flash forward 20 years and the thought of a college student without computer, cell phone, and Internet access is literally unfathomable (at least in the developed world). And in the financial markets, the concept of human beings shouting at each other to execute trades seems archaic. In fact, humans are largely superfluous to institutional trading, having been replaced by computers. Increasingly, humans aren't even programming those computers, relying instead on artificial intelligence.

SOURCE: Wikipedia.

Many of the innovations we now take for granted have enhanced the world of the individual investor. Lower commissions, greater transparency, and more equal access to information have all served to empower you. Yet, buried deep within these developments are the seeds of trouble, because a byproduct of the world we live in is that it is harder than ever to resist the Siren's call of easy profits and overnight riches. And as always, humankind's primordial brain conspires against you while the constant flow of information makes it ever harder to, as Jack Bogle said, "*Don't do something, just stand there!*"

Of course, the media is there, too, hungry for eyeballs and willing to feed your behavioral biases in their ongoing quest to build a bigger audience.

Hopefully this book has convinced you that the surest path to financial success lies in ignoring the noise, resisting the urge to do something, and following a patient and disciplined investment approach. Remember, the game of investing is like the NBA; there are very few All Stars, and only one Michael Jordan. If you're five foot eight and can't jump, what are the odds you're going to be a star? And, to be honest, do you really even belong in the game?

But the good news, as you've learned, is that financial success doesn't require you to play the game, or to compete with the pros, because success can be achieved by systematically following a long-term financial plan.

Here are the principles you must accept, if you want to know financial freedom:

One: The world of investing has changed, both for better and for worse.
Two: When confronted with a game you can't win, finding a new game to play makes a lot more sense than trying to beat the pros at a game they've rigged.
Three: Pundits, analysts, and so-called experts almost all have very spotty records when it comes to successfully predicting the future.
Four: Examine what history teaches you about the risk-and-return characteristics of various types of securities.
Five: Commit to planning for your future by getting specific about what your goals are and what steps are necessary to achieve those goals.
Six: Determine the required rate of return to meet your goals and build a portfolio to get you there with the least possible risk.
Seven: Allocating among countries, asset classes, sectors, and securities can increase your potential returns while reducing your risk.
Eight: Taxes will likely be your largest future expense, and knowledge is the first step in reducing that expense.
Nine: While you can't dictate the direction of markets, you can control how much of your returns you keep rather than share with your partners at the IRS.
Ten: Understanding your behavioral biases can help you take steps to control them.
Eleven: The media's job is to play to your weaknesses in an effort to attract viewers while your job is to secure your financial future.

Twelve: Financial success is possible, but only if you avoid risky or high-commission products sold by those without your best interests in mind.

Thirteen: Bear markets will happen, but you can survive by setting a portfolio mix you can stick with and then adjusting as needed to stay on course toward financial freedom.

So, there you have it: a set of simple principles designed to help you achieve financial freedom.

Remember, though, that simple doesn't always equate to easy. Your emotions, fueled by volatile markets and fanned by media headlines and public sentiment, will regularly challenge your ability to stay the course. When you are tempted to abandon time-tested principles in favor of the urge to *do something*, refer back to your written financial plan or reread the lessons found in this book. Or better yet, go to the park, or walk the dog, or spend time with friends, or do any one of a thousand more productive activities than staring at the day-to-day gyrations of your portfolio.

And when all else fails, focus on the most important lesson of all – namely, that the principles in this book are not theoretical. For many decades they have worked for countless investors across a range of market and economic environments.

You aren't charting a new course when you walk down this path. All you're doing is following the precise steps taken by generations of people just like you who found financial freedom through a straightforward plan that ignored the mayhem around them and stayed true to a set of time-tested principles.

And with a willingness to learn from the past, as well as a bit of intestinal fortitude, you, too, can join the ranks of those who've found financial freedom.

Good luck!

Index

24-hour news cycle, impact, 24–9
401(k) account
  after-tax 401(k) contributions, 175–6
  balances, increase, 140
  business partnership, 160
  contributions, increase, 208
  creation, 20
  investment willingness, 69
  management, 22
  possession, 159
  Roth 401(k) contributions, 174–5
  tax deferral, 162
403(b) account
  possession, 159
  usage, 21
457 account, possession, 159

A
Active mutual funds, index underperformance, 73
Advice. *See* Financial advice
  fees, 231
Aesop's Fables, tortoise/hare tale, 5
After-tax 401(k) contributions, 175–6
Allocation deviations, 257
American Stock Exchange, ETF listing, 187
Amsterdam Stock Exchange, establishment, 186
Anchoring, 189f
  behavioral trait, 189–90
  bias, manifestation, 189
  response, 190
Annual returns, impact, 42f
Annuities
  CDs, contrast, 246–7
  explanation, 245–7
  investment, assumptions, 245–6
  purchase, example, 244–5
AQR Capital Management, 77
Arnott, Rob, 196

Ask price, 238
Asset classes
  data, irrefutability, 72
  movement, rate variation, 254
  performance, 38, 39f, 149, 251f
  returns, 38–9
  risk, consideration, 211–12
  sectors, performance, 40–1
  selection, 39
Assets
  allocation
    building, risk assumption (consideration), 252
    example, 255
  examination, 233
  locations, 41
  safety, 132
  skepticism, 233–234
  tax-deferred assets, 159
Average investor, performance, 40f

B
Baby Boomers, retirement savings amount, 101
Bad news, representation, 264f
Balanced portfolio, example, 131–2
Bankruptcy, 87, 133
Bears
  attack, survival, 249
  markets, 270
    defining, 249–50
    preparation, 250–2
  money, making, 130
Behavioral biases, 189f, 269
Benchmarks
  beating, 260
  index, 262
Bid-ask spread, narrowness, 238
Bid price, 238
Black Monday
  cash, movement, 60
  catastrophe, 212
  crash (1987), 61
  impact, 211–3
  S&P500 single-day gain, 49
Black-Scholes pricing model, 242
Bogle, Jack, 67, 187, 268
Bonds
  bond market factors, 87–93
  corporate bond option-adjusted spread (OAS), 93f
  investment, commissions (examination), 237–41
  junk bonds, 92
  markets, problems, 129, 240
  municipal bond pricing, Federal Reserve study, 239
  over-the-counter trading, 238
  purchase, return (potential), 91–2
  purchase/sale, cost, 238
  role, 92
  S&P rating scale, 91f
  stocks, contrast, 90
  yield, markup payment, 239
Breaking news alerts, 265
  meaningless, 214
  types, 207–8
Bridgeway Capital Management, 77
Brokerage firms, commissions (absence), 18
Brokers
  partnering, 248
  suitability standard, 240–1
Bucketing, 195
Buffett, Warren, 84–5, 196, 235, 263
Bulls
  bull market, bonds (abandonment), 62
  money, making, 130
Butterfly Effect, 59–60
Buy-and-forget investing, 258–9

Buy-and-forget investors (damage), valuation (impact), 259
Buy-and-hold investing, 257–8

C
Cable news channels, rise (impact), 25–6
Call options, sale, 144–5
Capital allocation, 263
Capital gains
  long-term capital gains, preferential capital gains rates (usage), 179
  rate, payment, 178–9
  reduction, 171–2
  short-term capital gains, ordinary income (consideration), 179
Capitalism, power, 82
Casinos
  cards, counting (difficulty), 70
  evolution, 71
  games, odds, 44
  lucrativeness, 69–70
Certificates of deposit (CDs)
  annuities, trading, 246–7
  investment, example, 246
Certified Financial Planner (CFP), defining, 226–7
Charity, donation, 152
Charles Schwab
  commissions, absence, 18
  rules-based vehicles, 77
Citigroup, demise, 60–1
CNBC
  commentary, audience attention (example), 208
  Mad Money (Cramer), 217–21
  popularity, increase, 210
  viewership, stock market movements (relationship), 210f
Coin tosses, randomness, 55
Collar, 145
Collateralized debt obligation (CDO), prospectus examination, 235–6
Collectibles, asset classification, 233
Commissions, 237–41, 246
Companies
  long-term profits, 81
  market value, list, 141
  prospects, change (list), 140
Compound interest
  defining, 41
  power, 3, 11, 12, 264
    impact, 36–7
Concentrated positions, usage, 143–5
Confirmation bias, 189f
  behavioral trait, 190–191
  response, 191–2
Consumer confidence, political affiliation (contrast), 215f
Consumer loans, example, 91
Contributions. *See* Roth 401(k) contributions; Roth IRA
Conviction
  importance, 10
  levels, 193
Core lifestyle, income level, 162
Corporate bond option-adjusted spread (OAS), 93f
Corporate corporations, list, 138
Corporate earnings, impact, 82
Cramer, Jim, 217–21
Credit crisis, 147
Credit premium factor, 91–2
Credit risk, exposure, 236
Crisis, opportunity (comparison), 48–50
Crypto currencies
  asset classification, 233
  sale, basis, 234

Currency
hedges, usae, 90
volatility, impact, 90

D
Dealer, beating, 69–70
Defined benefit plans (pensions)
operation, 20
pension boards, oversight, 21
Defined contribution plans, 20
increase, 20–1
Derivatives, usage (reasons), 241–2
Dimensional Fund Advisors, 77
Discipline, importance, 5
Distribution rate, determination, 104–5
Diversification. *See* Smart diversification
benefits, reduction, 92
logic, 149
tax diversification, 158–9
Diversified portfolio, wealth (growth), 150f
Dividends, taxation (ordinary income tax rate), 179
Dow Jones Industrial Average (DJIA)
decline, 249–50
losses (Black Monday), 213
return, 116
trading level (2019), 189
Drawdown measures, maximum, 119
Dutch East India Company, inflation-adjusted market value, 141–2, 142f

E
Earnings release (breaking news alert example), 208
Economic data
breaking news alert example, 208
improvement, 216
Economic outlook, politics (impact), 215f
Economy
awareness, 28
changes, 16, 17f
direction, government (impact), 216
future, uncertainty, 4
growth, 82
variables, 59
Emerging market stock funds, avoidance/investment, 230–1
Employees
defined benefit plan coverage, 22
defined contribution plans, impact, 20–1
Employers
defined benefit plans, impact, 20
employer-sponsored plan, possession, 159
Energy companies, investor overweighting, 136–7
Enhanced indexing, 76
Entitlement programs, funding, 157
European Union, Britain (exit), 264
Exchange-traded funds (ETFs)
American Stock Exchange listing, 187
focus, 72
usage, recommendation, 237
Expected return, increase, 80, 124

F
Factor-based approach, 76
Factor premiums, 93
Factors (investing), 78–9
Family, money (giving), 152
Fear
irrational fear, 59

reduction, 13
selling, 209–10, 234
susceptibility, 28–9
Fear of Missing Out (FOMO), 195
Federal capital gains tax brackets, 157f, 178f
Federal income tax brackets, 155f
Federal Reserve (Fed)
estimates/forecasts, 58
rate increases, impact, 129
Fees, reduction, 229–32
Fidelity Investments, 67
commissions, absence, 18
dead clients, returns, 19
Fiduciary standard, 226, 240–1
suitability standard, contrast, 226–8
Finances
education, 188
news, impact, 214
Financial advice, 35
advisor, personal financial situation (understanding), 10
aim/focus, 219–20
problems, 9–10
Financial advisers
fiduciary actions, law (overturning), 228
fiduciary classification, determination, 226
impact, 224–5
Financial analysts, predictions (study), 56
Financial companies, investor overweighting, 136–7
Financial crisis (2009), 142
CNBC popularity, increase, 210
Financial Crisis (2007-2009), consideration, 212
Financial decision making, media (impact), 216
Financial freedom, 270
navigation, 2
principles, 269–70
Financial goals, 95
identification, 12
investment, requirement, 113
meeting, 50, 61, 121, 213
failure, 15
Financial independence, achievement, 99, 223
Financial life
accumulation phase, 49
distribution phase, 49
taxes, navigation, 152–3
Financial markets
awareness, 28
bear survival, 251
changes, 16, 17f, 267
evolution, 14, 70–1
fluctuations (volatility), 120
navigation, approaches, 5
Financial media
entertainment/information purpose, 28
information, framing, 207–8
purpose, 207
Financial news
channels, impact, 25–6
dissemination, 14
Financial plan, information (relationship), 10
Financial providers
approach, 231
impact, 224–5
standards, 225
Financial success, 2–3, 111, 270
hype/noise, ignoring, 9
key, 15
performance measurement, 262
roadblocks, avoidance, 5
role, importance, 188

Financial success (*continued*)
time/discipline, 5
Financial weapons of mass destruction, avoidance, 241
First Index Investment Trust, launch, 67
Fixed income sources, 103
Forecasts
fun, 52–3
guesses, comparison, 51
problems, 59–60
usage, 62–3
worthlessness, 57
Fox News, political leaning, 214
Framing bias, 196–8, 245
behavioral trait, 196–7
overcoming, media (impact), 197
response, 197–8
Funds, flow, 73f
acceleration, 176–7
Future
forecasting, attempt, 75–6
investment, 263–4
planning, commitment, 269
Future income streams, taxation (control), 154
Futures
avoidance, 241–2
investment process, timing, 242
pricing models, complexity, 242
unlimited losses, 241

G
Galbraith, John Kenneth, 54
Gambling, long-term investing (contrast), 43–5
Garzarelli, Elaine, 61
Global bonds, investment, 90–1
Global diversification, 90
benefits, 29
Global investing, information flow (increase), 29–30
Globalization, 29–31
Global stock market results, information, 30
Go-Go years, 101
Great Depression, 82, 264
S&P500 single-day gain, 48f
Greater fool theory, 11
Great Recession, 147
Greed, reduction, 13
Gross, Bill, 69
Growth
tax-free status, 182
value, outperformance (contrast), 85f
Growth stocks, 80–1

H
Headlines, accuracy, 197
Health Savings Account (HSA), tax-free income distribution, 159
Hedge fund managers
risk/reward scenarios, problems, 11
upside incentive, comparison, 11
Hedge funds
closure rates, 31–2, 32f
initiation, 61
resources, availability, 32
Hedging, methods, 144–5
Herd behavior, 194–6
behavioral trait, 194–5
response, 195–6
High-frequency traders, impact, 24
High-frequency trading, 23–4
appearance, 14
Hindsight bias, 198–9
behavioral trait, 198–9
response, 199
Holdings

concentration, problem, 133
period returns, investor control, 24
Housing
collapse, 60
expense, 151
Human condition, exacerbation, 53
Hype
barrage, 9–10
ignoring, difficulty, 12–14

I
Income. *See* Retirement income
future income streams, taxation, 154
Roth IRA contributions income limits, 173
tax-free distribution, 159
Income in Respect of a Decedent (IRD), 165–6
Income taxes, 154–7
calculation, example, 156f
federal income tax brackets, 155f
marginal rates, 155
personal income taxes, reductions (forecast), 157
Indexed products, 72–5
investment, movement, 67
portfolio component, 73–4
Indexes
construction, 74
gaming, 74–5
index funds tracking, 74–5
market weighting basis, 74
reconstitution process, 75
style drift, 75
Index mutual funds, focus, 72
Individual investors, professional traders (contrast), 211
Individual Retirement Account (IRA)
business partnership, 160
creation, 20
investment, willingness, 69
losses, waste, 183
possession, 159
stretch IRA, 165–6
tax deferral, 162
Industrial companies, investor overweighting, 136–7
Industry downturn, impact, 133
Inflation
impact, 4, 87, 100, 163
pace, keeping, 125
Information
availability, problems, 27–8
dispersion, impact, 27
financial plan, relationship, 10
Innovations, impact, 268
Institutional investors
rise, 31–3
sophistication/competitiveness, increase, 14
Interest, ordinary income consideration, 178
Interest rates
economists, prediction (polls), 54
timing, components, 54–5
Internal Revenue Service (IRS)
investment partner, 160
loan, 163
penalties, 166–7
International economics, background (requirement), 30
International securities, investor allocation, 29
Internet
adoption, 25
development, impact, 18
impact, 26–7
Inventories, release (breaking news alert example), 207

Investing, 5
approach, implementation/identification, 2
buy-and-forget investing, 258–9
buy-and-hold investing, 257–8
certainties, absence, 6
competition/game, avoidance, 14–15
factors, 78–9
focus, 233
fortitude, 1
global investing, information flow (increase), 29–30
long-term activity, 262–3
long-term approach, usage, 11
process, components, 12
self-directed investing, 20–3
speculation, contrast, 10–12
success, 92
odds, 5
trading, contrast, 16, 232–3
Investment
allocation, considerations, 254–5
characteristics, stability, 258–9
decisions, impact, 201
definition, examination, 232
errors, overconfidence (impact), 192
exposure, reduction, 260
familiarity, advantages/disadvantages, 132–7
fees, reduction, 229–32
growth (S&P500), 47f
growth (example), annual returns (impact), 42f
growth rate, example, 105–6
options, 68, 121
partnership, 159–161
IRS, impact, 160
performance, 142–3
portfolio, performance (impact), 208
products, complexity, 234–6
professionals, fees (reduction), 229–32
providers, monitoring/evaluation, 224
purchase, identification, 232–4
requirement, 113
returns, factors, 67
risk, types, 46
rules-based approach, usage, 72
solution, 71–2
time horizon, length, 211–12
types, 233
understanding, importance, 236–7
usage, determination, 103–4
value, decrease, 144–5
volatility, reduction, 90
Investment Advisers Act (1940), 226
Investment Policy Statement (IPS)
action plan, 193
usage, 199
Investors
all-star team, 60–2
average investor, performance, 40f
balanced portfolio, example, 131
Black Monday, impact, 211–13
financial news channels, impact, 26
international securities allocation, 29
ownership propensity, 136f
psychological challenge, 132
self-impact, 185–7
time horizons, increase, 24
IRD. *See* Income in Respect of a Decedent
Irrational fear, 59

J

Jerry Springer Show, The, 220
Johnson, Edward, 67
Junk bonds, 92

L

Large companies
  large-company stocks, performance, 38
  risk, decrease, 86
  small companies, performance (contrast), 85, 86f
Large-value companies, index (investment), 83
Las Vegas casinos, niceness, 43–5
Life
  certainty, 163–7
  expectancy, increase, 96
  fulfillment, 6
  shortness, 127–8
  speed, 15–16
Lifestyle
  core lifestyle, income level, 162
  cost, 100
  determination/questions, 97
Living expenses, accumulation, 126
Living standard, increase, 100
Load, 229
Longer-term bonds
  interest, payment, 89
  risk, 88
Longer-term gains, expense, 201
Long-term capital gains, preferential capital gains rates (usage), 179
Long-Term Capital Management (LTCM), crash/rescue, 242
Long-term investing, gambling (contrast), 43–5
Long-term investors, tools/techniques, 5
Long-term returns, impact, 213f
Lost Decade, 147–150
  headlines, 148f
  wealth, growth, 148f
Lynch, Peter, 132

M

Macro trading, 30–1
Mad Money (Cramer), 217–21
Markets
  avoidance, 147, 149
  benchmark, 213
  capitalization, 77
  constitution, 149
  crash, warnings, 60
  direction, information, 209
  events, 116f
  market-tracking products, focus, 72
  mistiming, 46
  recovery, 265
  selloffs, impact, 117
  time/timing, contrast, 41–2
  timing, difficulty, 45–6
  tops/bottoms, identification precision (absence), 259–60
  valuations, problems, 259–60
  volatility, 4, 120
    increase, 23
Markets, beating
  difficulty, 32, 75
  impossibility, 71–2
  possibility, 69–70
Markup, payment, 239–40
Married couple, income tax calculation (example), 156f
Maturities, risk (equivalence), 90
May Day, 18
Media. *See* Financial media
  barrage, continuation, 206
  figures, polarization, 206
  impact, 197, 205–11, 216, 269

Media. *See* Financial media (*continued*)
money, making (consideration), 206–7
Media pundits, impact, 57–8
Mega backdoor Roth, 176
Money
accumulation, plan (determination), 105–7, 110
doubling, consideration, 246
history, 186
increase, 125–7
legacy goal, 119
lending, 88
making, amount, 114–15
determination, 115
making/keeping, 181–3
placement, 152
requirements, determination, 105, 110
taxable pool, building, 177–81
tax-free pool, building, 172
usage, continuation, 172
Monthly mortgage principal and interest (P&I) payments, impact, 108
Mortgage payment, calculation, 100
Motivation, 245–6
MSNBC, political leaning, 214
Municipal bond pricing, Federal Reserve study, 239
Mutual funds
active mutual funds, index underperformance, 73
fees, cost, 230f
managers, index performance (problems), 71
resources, 32
usage, 90–1, 240
recommendation, 237
Myopic loss aversion, 201–3
behavioral trait, 201–2
response, 202–3

N
News
conferences (breaking news alert example), 207
media, acceptance, 28–9
New York Stock Exchange
commission
deregulation (May Day), 17–18
levels, 17
founding, 186
turnover, increase, 23
No-Go years, 102
Noise, barrage, 9–10
Nonmortgage spending, factor, 109
Nonstop news coverage, Internet (impact), 26–7

O
One Up on Wall Street (Lynch), 132
Online trading, impact, 18
Opportunity, crisis (comparison), 48–50
Options
appropriateness, 243
avoidance, 241–2
investment process, timing, 242
pricing models, complexity, 242
risk, 145
unlimited losses, 241
Ordinary income, considerations, 178–9
Other people's money, impact, 21–2
Out-of-consensus call, 62
Overconfidence bias, 192–4
behavioral trait, 192–3
manifestation, 193
response, 193–4

Overconfidence, investment problem, 192
Ownership share, increase, 160

P
Pension. *See* Defined benefit plans
Pension fund
  resources, 32
  target mix, example, 62
Performance, focus, 262–3
Performance, measurement, 213
  improvement, 260–2
Periodic portfolio rebalancing, 256–7
Perma-bears, 61
Personal income taxes, reductions (forecast), 157
Political uncertainty, 3–4
Portfolio
  alignment, 255
  analysis, example, 240
  balanced portfolio, example, 131–2
  building, 113–14, 235–6
  decline, example, 133
  distributions, determination, 109–10
  diversified portfolio, wealth (growth), 150f
  holdings, turnover (rapidity), 19
  identification, 117
  investments, examples, 123–4
  leverage, 140
  mixes, determination, 12
  monitoring/adjustment, 12
  performance, 38, 39f
    feedback, 203
    improvement, 22–3
  periodic portfolio rebalancing, 256–7
  rebalancing, 49–50
  return generation, assumption (absence), 122
  risk/return, 118f
  selection, 124–5
    risk reduction, 117–19
  standard deviation
    example, 119
    usage, 120
  tilt, 79
  tracking, 31
  values
    decline, 22
    fluctuation, 38
Portfolio bonds
  ownership, 90
  role, 92
Precious metals
  asset classification, 233
  sale, basis, 234
Presidents, term length (impact), 217f
Pretax dollars, usage, 174
Price appreciation, taxation (absence), 183
Principal and interest (P&I) payments, impact, 108
Professional traders, individual investors (contrast), 211
Public behavior, guiding/shaping, 58
Put options, purchase, 144–5

Q
Quarterly reporting, problems, 262

R
Real estate investment trusts (REITs), 132
  income, ordinary income (consideration), 179
  wealth, growth, 39
Rebalancing, 254–6
  periodic portfolio rebalancing, 256–7

Rebalancing (*continued*)
provision, 258
Registered investment advisors (RIAs), offerings, 228
Required minimum distribution (RMD), 163–5
table, 164f
Retirement, 96
accounts
assets, tax payments, 177
types, 159
Baby Boomer savings amount, 101
distribution rate, determination, 104–5, 110
enjoyment, 125, 127–8
investments, usage (determination), 103–4
lifestyle, determination/questions, 97
mindset shift, requirement, 117
money
accumulation, plan (determination), 105–7, 110
requirements, determination, 105
planning
difficulty, 161
steps, summary, 106f
portfolio distributions, determination, 109–10
rules, 125
savings, usage (determination), 103–4
spending, 101–2
determination, 107–9
status, 98–9
step-by-step example, 107–11
sustainable distribution rate, determination, 110
timing, determination, 99, 108
vision, determination, 96–8, 107
withdrawal rate, determination, 104
Retirement income
determination, 99–100
sources, determination, 103, 109
sources, taxation process, 158
Retirement taxes
bill, deferral (hype), 153
bracket, reduction (hype), 153
payments, reduction (hype), 153
truth, 154
Return
expected return, increase, 80, 124
generation, 147
absence, 121–2
improvement, 146
increase, stocks (impact), 122
keeping, control, 269
maximization, 92
potential, increase, 124
rate
calculation, 12
requirement, determination, 261, 269
required rate, 123, 128
achievement, 118, 122
increase, 118
meeting, 132
usage, 115, 116
Risk, 181. *See also* Shortfall risk
bond risk, 88
capacity
factors, 252
tolerance, contrast/confusion, 252–4
company decrease/increase, 86
compensation, 89
increase, maturities (equivalence), 90
investment-by-investment basis measurement, 125

reduction, 12, 132, 144
taking, amount, 116–20
tolerance
determination, 252–3
honesty, 254
overestimation, 253
types, 46
RMD. *See* Required minimum distribution
Rockefeller, John D., 196
Roth 401(k) contributions, 174–5
Roth account
mega backdoor Roth, 176
tax-free income distribution, 159
Roth IRA
backdoor Roth IRA contributions, 173–4
contributions, 172–3
income limits, 173
conversions, 172–4
Rules-based approach
defining, 76–7
usage, 72, 75–8
Rumor, attention, 13
Russell 3000, U.S. stock market proxy, 74

S
Sale, tax implications, 144
Santayana, George, 1
Savings
market selloffs, impact, 117
usage, determination, 103–4
Scholes, Myron, 242
Securities, investor purchase/sale, 238
Self-attribution bias, 200–1
behavioral trait, 200
response, 200–1
Self-directed investing, 20–3
Shorter-term bonds
interest, payment, 89
risk, 88
Shorter-term trading, speculation requirement, 262–3
Shortfall risk, 46, 115
impact, 120
Short-term capital gains, ordinary income (consideration), 179
Short-term market movements, meaninglessness, 214
Short-term trading
Cramer recommendations, relationship, 218
long-term investing, contrast, 5
speculation, equivalence, 11
Slow-Go years, 102
Small companies
large companies, performance (contrast), 85, 86f
risk, increase, 86
small-company factor, 83–5
small-company stocks, performance, 38
small-company universe, 87
investment, 83–4
Small stocks, risk (increase), 86
Small value stocks, purchase, 84
Smart beta, 76
Smart diversification, 129
behavior, avoidance, 131
defining, 130
impact, 145–7
practice, 129
Smart phones, usage, 15–16
Sniff test, 224
Social media
impact, 14
opinions/news stories, bombardment, 27
Sovereign wealth fund, resources, 32
Soviet Union, collapse, 52

Speculation
 definition, 12
 investing, contrast, 10–12
 short-term trading,
  equivalence, 11
Spending
 calculation, 99
 complication, 99
 estimate, 98
 nonmortgage spending, factor, 109
 status, determination, 98–9
Springer, Jerry, 220
Sputnik 1 (Soviet Union launch), 51
Standard deviation, usage, 119–20
Standard of living
 enjoyment, 172
 improvement, 263–4
Standard & Poor's (S&P)
 bond rating scale, 91f
 performance, 265f
 sector performance, differences,
  134f
Standard & Poor's 500 (S&P500),
 249, 260
 bear markets, impact, 22
 corrections, 250
 increase, 133
 investment, growth, 47f
 level, increase, 37f
 negative returns, 147
 performance, tracking, 67
 portfolio
  allocation, 47
  ownership, 149
 single-day percentage gains, 48f
 tracking, 230
 wealth, growth, 148f, 150f
Stock market
 best performing stock markets,
  139f
 crash (1929), 82
 crashes, predictability, 131
 decline (1987), 4
 decline, example, 255
 factors, 79–87
 movements, 92
  CNBC viewership, relationship,
   210f
 performance, president term
  lengths (impact), 217f
 sell-off/rebound, 23
 worries, 126–7
Stocks
 addition, 121–3
 bonds, contrast, 90
 concentration, example, 131–2
 finding, 84–5
 growth stocks, 80–1
 identification, 84
 impact, 122
 movements, prediction
  (difficulty), 219
 performance differential, 56
 prices, research, 25
 proportion, 126
 purchase
  analysis, 219
  choices, 122
  mechanisms, 218–19
 selection, 83
 U.S. stock fund flows, 73f
 volatility, 124
Stretch IRA, 165–6
Style drift, 75
Success. *See* Financial success
 demonstration, 79
 factors, 78–9
 guarantee, absence, 76
 odds
  reduction, 68
  smart diversification, impact,
   145–7

planning, impact, 95
rate, 55
repetition, 61
trap, 140–3
Suitability standard, 225–6
fiduciary standard, contrast, 226–8
FINRA definition, 225

T
Tactical allocation, 194
Target allocation
establishment, 62
example, 257
portfolio alignment, 255
Target return, performance measurement, 261
Taxable pool, flexibility, 178
Tax Cut and Jobs Act (2018), 157
Taxes. *See* Income taxes; Retirement taxes
avoidance, 171
control, 154
deferral, 161
diversification, 158–9
expense, 269
federal capital gains tax brackets, 157f
federal income tax brackets, 155f
hype, 153
increase, question, 157–8
inevitability (hype), 153
inimization, examination, 144
navigation, 152–3
optimization, 161
payment, reduction, 152
tax-deferred account
losses, waste, 183
money (conversion), distribution (consideration), 176
money, movement, 171
tax-deferred assets, 159
tax-deferred pool, advantages/disadvantages, 182–3
tax-free pool, funds flow (acceleration), 176–7
understanding, 151
U.S. individual tax return form 1040, example, 156f
Tax loss harvesting (TLH), 180–1
Tax Reform and Jobs Act (2017), impact, 177
TD Ameritrade, commissions (absence), 18
Technical analysis, 243–4
complexity, 243
rigor, 244
Technology companies
bankruptcy, 133
investor overweighting, 136–7
survival, 134–5, 135f
Technology stocks
decimation, 134–5
returns, impact, 256
Term premium factor, 87
Thrift Savings Plan (TSP), possession, 159
Time
horizon, length, 211–12
usefulness, 42
Trading, 5
activity, high-frequency trader (domination), 23
avoidance, 233
investing, contrast, 16, 232–3
Transaction costs, reduction, 17–19, 27
Treasury bonds, maturities, 88
Tweak, definition, 2

U
Uncertainty, source, 87
United States, companies/economy, 137–9
Upside incentive, hedge fund manager (comparison), 11
U.S. individual tax return form 1040, example, 156f
U.S. one-month T-bills, wealth (growth), 148f
USSR, collapse, 51–2
U.S. stock fund flows, 73f
U.S. Treasury yield curves, 89f

V
Valuation
  impact, 259
  market valuations, problems, 259–60
Value
  factor, 79–83
  growth, performance (contrast), 85f
Value companies, returns, 80
Value stocks, 81
  risk, increase, 86
Virginia Company, formation, 186–7
Volatility, 46, 119–20
  market volatility, 120
  measurement, standard volatility (usage), 120
  navigation, 265
  reduction, 90
  stock volatility, 124

W
Wall Street
  analysts, impact, 55–7
  investment products, creation, 234–6
War, threat, 3
Weapons of mass destruction, risk, 3
Whitney, Meredith (trouble, prediction), 60–1
Work, continuation (intention), 99
World, changes, 16, 17f
World Wide Web, ubiquity, 26
Wynn Casino, losses, 44

Y
Y chromosome, impact, 192
Yield curve, 88–9
  focus, 89
  shape, variation, 89
  slope, 236
  steepness, emphasis, 90